The Sunny Slopes of Long Ago

Edited by

Wilson M. Hudson
Allen Maxwell, Associate Editor

Publications of The Texas Folklore Society Number
XXXIII

University of North Texas Press
Denton, Texas

Copyright © 2000 by The Texas Folklore Society

All rights Reserved

Copyright © 1966 by The Texas Folklore Society
Southern Methodist University Press, Dallas

Printed in the United States of America
All rights reserved

Permissions:
University of North Texas Press
P. O. Box 311336
Denton, Texas 76203
(940) 565-2142 FAX (940) 565-4590

ISBN 1-57441-106-3

Preface

J. FRANK DOBIE left an article on his old friend John A. Lomax which Mrs. Dobie has kindly permitted us to publish. What could more fittingly begin this book than one of Dobie's last pieces of writing, and that on the cofounder of the Texas Folklore Society? Our title comes from Lomax's favorite toast, which he liked to give when he relaxed with Dobie or others at the end of a working day, "Here's to the sunny slopes of long ago!"

A copy of Lomax's "Cowboy Lingo" was found among Dobie's papers. Since only the latter half of it had been published, we are printing all of it here. We thank the Lomaxes—Shirley, Bess, John, and Alan—for permission to do so.

There follow articles by Rhodes and Adams on the cowboy, both of which appeared in out-of-the-way periodicals. These articles should be made readily accessible, we felt. W. H. Hutchinson and Andy T. Adams agreed with us and generously allowed us to reprint them.

A kind of sequence on the cowboy and the West continues in the articles by Paul Patterson, Mody C. Boatright, John O. West, and Everett A. Gillis. These men are all active members of the Society, as are the rest of the contributors.

William D. Wittliff's assemblage of Dobie's pronouncements on folklore provides a kind of review of Dobie's opinions on the subject. Dobie's attitude toward folklore has influenced the Society and its publications and no doubt will continue to be influential for some time.

The second half of the book is made up of articles most of

which were read at one of the Society's annual meetings. They deal with a wide variety of subjects, as a glance at the table of contents will show.

For pictorial material thanks are due Jon Richard Tinkle of Dallas and Albuquerque; Mrs. Pat Maguire and the *Alcalde,* alumni magazine of the University of Texas; and the *Dallas Morning News* and its staff photographers, especially Joe Laird and Clint Grant.

With two exceptions, this is the first annual publication since 1937 not to bear Mody C. Boatright's name as either editor or associate editor. Having worked with him for a number of years, we wish to thank him for his guidance and friendship in the past and to warn him that we expect his help with our knottier problems in the future.

WILSON M. HUDSON
ALLEN MAXWELL

Austin and Dallas
June 6, 1966

Contents

John A. Lomax	3
J. FRANK DOBIE	
Cowboy Lingo	12
JOHN A. LOMAX	
The Cowboy: His Cause and Cure	26
EUGENE MANLOVE RHODES	
The American Cowboy	33
ANDY ADAMS	
The Cowboy's Code	39
PAUL PATTERSON	
The Cowboy Enters the Movies	51
MODY C. BOATRIGHT	
Billy the Kid, Hired Gun or Hero	70
JOHN O. WEST	
Laureates of the Western Range	81
EVERETT A. GILLIS	
J. Frank Dobie on Folklore	89
PASSAGES COLLECTED BY WILLIAM D. WITTLIFF	
The Hat-in-Mud Tale	100
JAN H. BRUNVAND	
The Baby-Switching Story	110
JAMES T. BRATCHER	
Saved from a Bullet: Miraculous Escapes from Death	118
JOHN Q. ANDERSON	
Tobacco and Longevity	128
J. T. MCCULLEN, JR.	

The Sanctified Sisters	136
A. L. BENNETT	
Running the Fox	146
FRANCIS E. ABERNETHY	
The Charcoal Burner	151
E. J. RISSMANN	
Creeping Ignorance on Poke Sallet	157
JAMES W. BYRD	
The Penny Dreadful as a Folksong	164
JAMES WARD LEE	
The Ballad of Bob Williams	171
JACK SOLOMON	
Buckwheat Cakes, 1898 Variety	176
ROGER P. MCCUTCHEON	
Jung on Myth and the Mythic	181
WILSON M. HUDSON	
Contributors	198
Index	201

Illustrations

J. FRANK DOBIE AT PAISANO RANCH, 1959 — *Frontispiece*

THE GENIALITY OF J. FRANK DOBIE — *Preceding page 3*
    Studio portrait of Dobie, 1955
    Dobie, William Goyen, Roy Bedichek, 1950
    Bertha McKee Dobie, Paul Horgan, Dobie, 1954
    Dobie and Bedichek, 1957
    Bertha and Frank Dobie at Paisano, 1959: three views
    Dobie and portrait of John A. Lomax, 1964

The Sunny Slopes of Long Ago

The Geniality of J. Frank Dobie

Dallas News Staff Photo by Joe Laird

In a rather more formal pose than was his wont, Dobie takes pen in hand to autograph a copy of *Tales of Old-Time Texas*, newly published at the time of the photograph (November 2, 1955).

Dallas News Staff Photo

Dobie shares good spirits with fellow writers at the Texas Institute of Letters annual awards dinner in Dallas November 17, 1950, where he and Katherine Anne Porter shared the A. Harris prize for achievement in the arts. William Goyen, center, was recipient on the same occasion of the McMurray best Texas first novel award for *The House of Breath,* while Dobie's close friend Roy Bedichek, right, took the Carr P. Collins prize for the best Texas book of the year with *Karánkaway Country.*

Dallas News Staff Photo by Clint Grant

Bertha and Frank Dobie join Paul Horgan at a launching party in Dallas October 19, 1954 for Horgan's *Great River: The Rio Grande in North American History,* which won both the Texas Institute of Letters Collins award and the Pulitzer Prize.

Dallas News Staff Photo by Joe Laird

As president of the Texas Institute of Letters Dobie finds particular pleasure in congratulating Roy Bedichek, winner of the Institute's Collins award for the second time February 1, 1957, in Dallas. The prizewinning volume was *Educational Competition: The Story of the Interscholastic League of Texas.*

Jon Richard Tinkle

Alcalde

"I stand here looking at the portrait"—Dobie and J. Anthony Wills's painting of John A. Lomax, at its presentation to the University of Texas April 18, 1964. Dobie's remarks on this occasion proved to be his final public address.

Jon Richard Tinkle

Bertha and Frank Dobie, above and on the two pages following, savor the quality of a quiet August afternoon in 1959 at Paisano, in company with visitors from Dallas, the Lon Tinkle family. Young Jon Richard Tinkle, eldest of the *Dallas News* Book Critic's three sons, had not only brought his camera along for the outing, but had dressed the part of a rancher—with an addition which brought this comment from Dobie:

"Jon, I like your Lucchese boots. And that belt with your name on it in back is a good one. But no real rancher wears those sun glasses. A real rancher wants to see as far as he can and with all the light in the sky. He wants to look at everything. . . . The important thing in life is to see clearly. See all you can. And above all, live by what you, yourself, see."

Jon Richard Tinkle

John A. Lomax

J. FRANK DOBIE

MR. CHANCELLOR, Mr. President of the Board of Regents, Dick Fleming, members of the Lomax family, the artist, and others. I stand here looking at the portrait. I want to take out my pipe and talk to Lomax as we used to talk. I am afraid that if I start reading something that is composed I can't quit reading. It's fatal to have a piece written and then try to be extemporaneous.

I shall not undertake to sketch the life of Lomax. It has been pretty well done. Part of it is in this program. The *Handbook of Texas*, that remarkable two-volume compendium of life, geography, and history of Texas that Walter Prescott Webb engineered and edited, has a very good sketch of John A. Lomax. I would rather consider him as a human being and as a landmark in preserving and popularizing the folksongs of the United States.

When he came to Texas at the age of two with his family from Mississippi in 1869, he settled or was settled on a farm in Bosque County about two miles from Meridian. This farm was located on the Chisholm Trail, or a branch of it, and here Lomax as a boy heard cowboys keeping their cattle quiet at night by singing quiet songs to them. His people, who were very poor, were not cow people. He was never a cowboy, but before he was twenty years old he had written down numerous cowboy songs.

In 1940, the Texas Folklore Society brought out a volume of widely assembled personal narratives of facts and imaginings called *Mustangs and Cow Horses*. Harry H. Ransom, who graduated into something else, and Mody C. Boatright, who has left the Texas Folklore Society editorship to another, were co-editors of that volume. In it there is a piece by Lomax on Peepy-Jenny, a mare that brought a colt every year on the Bosque County farm while working, and seemingly none of these colts were sold. She came to have quite a progeny.

Lomax tells of driving wagonloads of wood to Meridian with if not Peepy-Jenny then Peepy-Jenny's descendants pulling. He always left the gate open so that all the family could accompany the wagon. They made a fine show in Meridian. His favorite horse was a son of Peepy-Jenny named Selim. When time came for him to go off to college—and the colleges he went to were hardly of the rank of the present-day high school—he rode Selim to Dallas. It took him two days to get there. He sold Selim for money to help pay for an education. As he walked away, Selim kept nickering to him, and Lomax would almost shed tears when he remembered that parting with Selim, the son of Peepy-Jenny.

About the time *Mustangs and Cow Horses* came out, the Texas Folklore Society was publishing a few books on rangemen. One of them was the memoirs of a man named McCauley, whom Lomax had found and who trusted Lomax and gave Lomax his own reminiscences. I don't think any more realistic cowboy has appeared between book covers than McCauley, and certainly none more humorous. I mention this because it illustrates the early familiarity of Lomax with the type, with the people, the cow people whose songs he would collect and make popular.

John Avery Lomax enrolled at the University of Texas in 1895 and graduated two years later. The university had been in existence only twelve years when Lomax entered it. After graduating, he remained as secretary to the president, as registrar, and as steward or manager of B Hall, the only men's dormitory ever to be located on the main campus. The combined jobs paid $75.00 a month.

In 1903 he went to A & M College to teach English at $1,200 a year. Here he gathered more cowboy songs. The A & M men were then predominantly rural. Long afterwards Lomax told me that he thought he'd made a mistake in giving low grades to interesting themes that were incorrectly written so far as grammar, sentence structure, and punctuation go.

In 1904 he married Bess Brown. By the time he got a scholarship in Harvard in 1906, Shirley Lomax, the first of four children, had been born. At Harvard Lomax took a course in American literature under Professor Barrett Wendell. Barrett Wendell, to quote Lomax's *Adventures of a Ballad Hunter,* a remarkable autobiography in many ways, announced to the class that he was utterly weary of reading dissertations on Hawthorne, Emerson, Thoreau, Holmes, Poe, and other standard American writers. He said, "You fellows who have something back home, I want you to write a piece on what you know scattered over the country." When Lomax proposed writing a term theme on cowboy songs, Barrett Wendell was exhilarated. He introduced Lomax to Professor George Lyman Kittredge, perhaps the greatest scholar who has ever taught English in an American university. And Kittredge had Lomax for dinner.

The Harvard attitude toward cowboy songs was in marked contrast to the attitude Lomax had found in Texas. In his *Adventures of a Ballad Hunter* he tells of showing his roll of cowboy songs to Dr. Leslie Waggener, under whom Lomax was taking a course on Shakespeare and who also was *ad interim* president of the University of Texas. I shall quote two paragraphs.

Dr. Waggener referred me to Dr. Morgan Callaway, Jr., a Johns Hopkins Doctor of Philosophy whose scholarship is reflected in three studies, *The Absolute Participle in Anglo-Saxon, The Appositive Participle in Anglo-Saxon,* and *The Infinitive in Anglo-Saxon.* Timidly I handed Dr. Callaway my roll of dingy manuscript written out in lead pencil and tied together with a cotton string. Courteous and kindly gentleman that he was, he thanked me and promised to report the next day. Alas, the following morning Dr. Callaway told me that my samples of frontier literature were tawdry, cheap, and unworthy. I had better give my attention to the great movements of writing that had come sounding down the ages. There was no possible connection, he said, between the tall tales of Texas and the tall tales of Beowulf. His decision, exquisitely considerate, was final—absolute. No single crumb of comfort was left for me.

I was unwilling to have anyone else see the examples of my folly. So that night in the dark, out behind Brackenridge Hall, the men's dormitory where I lodged, I made a small bonfire of every scrap of my cowboy songs. Years afterwards, an associate of Dr. Callaway in the English faculty, Dr. R. H. Griffith, asked to examine a first copy of *Cowboy Songs and Other Frontier Ballads,* published in 1910. The following morning he brought the book to my desk, thanked me for the loan, turned on his heel, and went away with no word of comment. The disfavor of my cowboy song project still survived.

After Lomax returned to Texas A & M College from Harvard with an M.A. degree in 1907, Harvard offered him a thousand dollars a year to go on with the cowboy song project, provided Texas A & M gave him a leave of absence from teaching. The A & M executives appeared to have no more interest in cowboy songs than the professors of English at the University of Texas had. They refused to grant a leave of absence. Harvard gave him three successive Sheldon Fellowships, however, and on this money, $500 a year, I believe, he went out to collect songs. His account of some individuals from whom he got songs and of circumstances under which he got them is as interesting as the narrative of any gold rush adventurer.

When his book, *Cowboy Songs and Other Frontier Ballads*, was published it was dedicated to Theodore Roosevelt, "who while President was not too busy to turn aside—cheerfully and effectively—and aid workers in the field of American balladry." Also, the book reproduced a handwritten letter to Lomax from Theodore Roosevelt. And it included an introduction by Barrett Wendell. Sometime after the book was published, Professor Kittredge came to Austin and Lomax took him to a Negro church, where there was a grand welcome and where Kittredge made known his great sympathy for Negro folklore of all kinds, spirituals included.

It is not correct to say, as is sometimes said, that *Cowboy Songs and Other Frontier Ballads* was the first collection of such songs to be printed. N. Howard (Jack) Thorp, of New Mexico, was a genuine cowpuncher, also a fine gentleman of generous nature with cultivation of mind that gave him perspective. In 1908 he had printed at Estancia, New Mexico, a little paperbound book of about fifty pages entitled *Songs of the Cowboys*. He carried it around in saddle pockets to sell to cowboys or anybody else with four bits to spend for it. He had some copies left a long time afterwards. I saw one advertised the other day for $150, and am positive that the book dealer sold it. Lomax took generously from this collection without any tedious explanation.

In 1920 the Thorp book, very much extended, was brought out by that highly respectable publisher, Houghton Mifflin of Boston, Massachusetts. I saw Lomax a few days after I procured my copy and spoke of it. He had procured a copy too. I said, "I see some things in Thorp's new book that are in *Cowboy Songs*."

"Yes," he said, "and no mention made of the source. I don't know whether to tell my publishers to bring suit or not."

He didn't, of course, and when in 1938, with the help of Alan Lomax, a very much enlarged collection of *Cowboy Songs and Other Frontier Ballads* came out, due indebtedness to Howard Thorp was acknowledged.

Lomax gave generous credit to many people. He gave generous help to many people. When I came to the University of Texas in 1914 at a salary of $1,200 a year—the salary that took Lomax to A & M College—Lomax was back in Austin as secretary of the Ex-Students Association. He was publishing the first literary magazine of consequence, the only literary magazine at the time, in Texas, the *Alcalde*. He published essays and poems. Leonard Doughty, whom Roy Bedichek could quote a long distance, wrote poetry for the *Alcalde*. At least one sketch by John W. Thomason of the *Jeb Stuart* and *Lone Star Preacher* books appeared in the *Alcalde*. Lomax offered me $100 a year to contribute monthly a feature on faculty news. Sometimes I managed to get a truth in the feature that wasn't exactly news. He would pay me twice or maybe four times a year. Anyhow, I was getting $100 for eight issues, and that was more than 8 per cent of my salary. It meant more then to me than several thousand dollars might have meant later. Lomax never censored what I wrote. One day he handed me, with a smile, a letter from Bishop Kerwin of the Catholic church, residing in Galveston, protesting what I had written on Roger Casement's "sophistry." The bishop characterized my style as that of a freshman lacking "intellectual grasp." So far as I know he received no response to his letter.

As time went on Lomax and I became, I won't say close friends, but very, very together friends. I doubt if I've heard any man the superior of Lomax in telling anecdotes of characters. Many of these anecdotes are in *Adventures of a Ballad Hunter*. Perhaps his skill in that kind of telling reached a climax in the sketch he wrote on "Will Hogg, Texan," published in the *Atlantic Monthly* in 1940, and in 1956 published by the University of Texas Press for the Hogg Foundation. Dick Fleming has told you considerable about the influence of Will Hogg on the University of Texas and how Lomax worked with him raising money to give University of Texas students who needed help and were worth helping—both necessary attributes. I take one instance from his essay on Will Hogg:

> One Christmas morning I visited Will Hogg in a New York hotel and found him unwrapping packages. "Here's something from home," Will Hogg said. He unrolled six or seven silk neckties. Inside were nearly a hundred penciled signatures on a long strip of paper whose margins were splotched with smutty fingerprints. "Christmas Greetings to Mr. Will Hogg from his friends, the newsboys of Houston, Texas."
> Will Hogg held the ties aloft, fingered them, and then walked over toward the window and looked down on Broadway far below. He stood with his back to me for a long time. When he turned around, as if angry at his tears he blurted out, "The damned little rascals! They ought to be horsewhipped for spending their nickels on me." He choked again and turned back to the window.

Never forget the humanity of this man Lomax.

In 1931, Bess Brown Lomax died. In 1933, Lomax entered into a long career of collecting not only the words but the tunes of Negro and other folksongs. Alan was with him a great deal of the time. At times after he married Miss Ruby Terrill in 1934, she accompanied him on his song-hunting expeditions. He always referred to her both in writing and in speech as Miss Terrill. I don't know if he had any other name for her to her face or not, although I've been with them together various times.

I wish I could convey the sympathy and the understanding Lomax had for the Negroes who sang for him into his recording machine. He and Alan took about ten thousand songs to the folksong archives in the Library of Congress. There was Iron Head. There was Lead Belly, about whom the two wrote books. There was Red Dobie, perhaps a distant relation of mine, who was expert at singing sinful songs as well as spirituals. To read the last half of *Adventures of a Ballad Hunter* is to enter into a character gallery of Negroes. The Lomaxes went to all the penitentiaries of the southern states. One passage expresses John Lomax's pervading feelings towards these people: "These songs and others I heard that day I shall carry in my heart forever. And those earnest black-faced boys, dressed in grizzly gray stripes, who sang them I shall never forget. The reaction from a high pitch of emotional excitement gave me a sleepless night."

Lomax was fond of whiskey. Many a congenial time I've seen him lift his glass and, quoting an ancient professor of the University of Texas, say, "Here's to the sunny slopes of long ago!" It was his favorite toast.

I remember one time when he didn't drink to the sunny slopes of long ago. He and Alan had a room up the hill from our house on Waller Creek in Austin. One evening Lomax came along about drink time. He had a very cheerful expression on his face. I said, "Lomax, you're just in time. We both need a drink."

He said, "No, not this evening."

I looked him straight in the eyes. I said, "You've got to explain."

With a glad gleam in his eye, he said, "I'm on my way to take Miss Terrill to dinner. She does not approve of whiskey."

Several years passed, and Lomax called on me here in Austin. He and "Miss Terrill" were back from the Brush Country around Cotulla, where he had recorded various vaquero songs and got my brother Elrich to sing for him. Elrich can sing Mexican songs better than he can sings songs in English. Now Lomax wanted me to quaver, or sing, or somehow sound out what is called "The Texas Lullaby." I can remember hearing it long, long ago on our ranch. "Who-o-o, who-e-e, ho-ho-ho, ha, ha, ha," it went, no printed syllables possibly suggesting the vocal sounds. They had a wonderfully soothing effect on wild cattle hemmed up in the brush.

Well, the Lomaxes had a room in the Alamo Hotel on West 6th Street. I went down there and did the best I could. Somebody else, I forget who, was being recorded, and Lomax seemed to get tired. I saw him go over to the corner of the room and take a dark-looking bottle—wasn't more than a pint— from under a bed and, standing there facing the corner, refresh himself with what Charles

Lamb called the better adjuncts of water. It was his idea that Miss Terrill wasn't looking. I was looking and I didn't know why she couldn't see. Lomax had come back to whiskey. I am glad he could afford it till the end, because the older you get the more you need it sometimes.

While I was at Cambridge University during World War II, Lomax in Austin got word to Bertha McKee Dobie that he wanted a certain book. She had influenza and couldn't receive him or anybody else, but he came to the house and the book was delivered by a maid. Then he stood out on the walk in front of the house and talked to Bertha Dobie as she stood at a window in something like these words: "As long as this old heart beats, I'll remember how good you've been to me and mine." In telling me this incident, she remarked, "I have done more for people who remembered it less."

During later years I sometimes felt a kind of chasm come between me and John Lomax. I don't think either ceased to respect and have a deep feeling for the other. The chasm can be illustrated by a story told numerous times by Roy Bedichek. He and Lomax had been friends, even comrades, since their B Hall days together at the University of Texas back in the 1890's. For years before his first book, *Adventures with a Texas Naturalist*, which appeared in 1947, Bedi (as his friends called him) had restricted the major part of his literary production to personal letters. In 1942, Lomax wrote me: "In his letters at least Roy Bedichek has more genuine originality and downright power of expression that any other man ever connected with the University—in my opinion."

One year Bedichek was going to Denton or some other place north of Dallas on business as director of the Interscholastic League of Texas. Lomax wanted him to come and stay out at his home near White Rock Lake. "No," Bedichek wrote, "I'm not going to stay with you. You'll whip yourself into a frenzy and go off on a tirade against Roosevelt. I won't listen to it." Lomax replied by letter that he would not mention the name of Franklin D. Roosevelt so long as Bedichek was in his house.

Dr. W. J. Battle, who had a sympathy for antagonism against Roosevelt, wanted to pay his old friend Lomax a visit. So it was arranged that Bedichek would deliver Battle and then go on and stop on his way back long enough to eat lunch and then drive to Austin. Bedichek delivered Battle and went on north. Two days later he came back. Had a fine lunch. Had a fine visit. Dr. Battle got his suitcase in the car, got himself in the car. He had already told Lomax goodbye. Bedichek told Lomax goodbye, had the car engine started. And there Lomax was standing right by him in the drive. The minute Bedichek started the car moving, Lomax began cursing out, his face purple. He had kept his word, you understand, not mentioning the name of Roosevelt so long as Bedichek was his guest. Now, in rising accents, it was, "God damn Roosevelt! God damn Roosevelt!" After Bedichek drove past him he could still hear the combination of God and Roosevelt.

Well, we go back to the sunny slopes of long ago. We go back to a man who more than any other made the cowboy songs and Negro songs a part of the inheritance and folklore of the world. We go back to a mighty and deep understanding of people, to a man who loved and also hated. Anybody who knew him knew where he stood—on anybody—and I am glad to see him standing here today.

Dobie delivered the principal address at the presentation of a portrait of John Avery Lomax, painted by J. Anthony Wills, to the University of Texas on April 18, 1964. He had a manuscript, but he did not confine himself to reading it. A tape recording was made as he spoke, and a transcript was sent to him. He used some of the material for two articles in Sunday newspapers. It was his intention to write an article for publication in a magazine, but he did not live to do so. Mrs. Dobie has blended together his manuscript and the tape recording.

"B Hall" is the way everyone on the campus referred to Brackenridge Hall, named for George W. Brackenridge.

George Lyman Kittredge attended the third meeting of the Texas Folklore Society in Austin on April 4 and 5, 1913, and gave two formal addresses. He wrote a preface for the Society's first book-length publication, which was edited by Stith Thompson in 1916.

Cowboy Lingo

JOHN A. LOMAX

ABOUT THREE MONTHS AGO, just at sunset, Frank Hastings,[1] Bill Hyatt, and I rode up to the S M S headquarters on West Fork Ranch, thirty miles west of Spur, Texas, where the railroad ends. Ten miles beyond we could see a line of hills four hundred feet high, running north and south—the cap rock of the plains, until recently labeled in geography the Llano Estacado, or Staked Plains, now rapidly filling up with immigrants. For it has been found that cotton as well as cattle can flourish there. Out among the mesquites were the chuck wagon, the campfire, the ranch house and garden nearby, the horse corral a little farther away, and the cowboys, twelve or fifteen of them, including the cooky, the horse wrangler, the straw boss, and the boss, just finishing a late dinner. These bronze-faced men, quiet in manner, sparing and direct of speech, strangers to fear, about whom something lingers of the romance and mystery that tends to dwell with one who lives in the open and sleeps facing the stars—these men, the American cowboys, are to me the most interesting breed this nation has produced. To see them work and hear them talk I had traveled more than three hundred miles.

The Big Boss, Mr. Hastings, was my host. I may illustrate his quality by saying that within fifteen minutes after our arrival a white-faced yearling, weighing perhaps six hundred pounds, was slaughtered for my gustatory delectation. On the following night a cowboy dance was held in my honor, the spirit of which I shall let Larry Chittenden suggest:

The leader was a fellow that came from Swenson's ranch,
They called him "Windy Billy" from "little Deadman's Branch."
His rig was "kinder keerless," big spurs and high-heeled boots;
He had the reputation that comes when "fellers shoots."
His voice was like the bugle upon the mountain's height;
His feet were animated, an' a *mighty movin' sight,*
When he commenced to holler, "Neow fellers, stake yer pen!
Lock horns to all them heifers, an' russle 'em like men.
Saloot yer lovely critters; neow swing an' let 'em go,
Climb the grapevine round 'em—all hands do-ce-do!
You Mavericks, jine the round-up—Jest skip her waterfall,"
Huh! hit wuz gittin' happy, "The Swenson Ranch's Ball!"

During the one full day I spent with the S M S outfit I ate at the chuck wagon, watched the men rope out their horses from the remuda, rode with them in two small roundups, saw them branding, dehorning, castrating, and cutting out. I slept in the open, rolled out of my blankets at four o'clock in the morning, and then danced that night so that the girls didn't start home until the morning. I thought this company would enjoy knowing that the words I present come fresh from the mouths of real cowboys on a modern Texas ranch of 400,000 acres, 40,000 cattle, 1,000 saddle horses, and more than 100 cowpunchers. Practically all the words I give I heard spoken on this trip, many of them, of course, not for the first time. Having had no opportunity or leisure to check the list with others already printed, I give all that may possibly be included within the limits of my title, "Cowboy Lingo."

The cowboy's best friend is his saddle horse, which he changes daily—many times twice a day. His mount consists of as many as twelve horses, and no one—not even the big boss himself to whom all the horses belong—dares to ride one of these horses without the special permission of the cowboy to whom they are temporarily attached. He has many vivid names for them, in most cases picturing some attribute of the animal. For instance, a high-pitching horse is called "Aermotor";[2] one given to sudden and violent movements, "Dynamite"; another, somewhat stupid, is called "Absentminded"; a small, efficient horse, "Big Enough"; a swift runner, "Cannon Ball"; one given to sinuous movements or untrustworthy in disposition, "Snake"; another, for obvious reasons, "Pole Cat";

a white-faced horse, "Towel Face"; and an albino, "Beadeye." "Red Hell," "Tar Baby," "Sail Away Brown," "Straight Edge," "Scissors," "Louse Cage," "Tater Slip," "Puddin' Foot" are other names of horses I found on Swenson's Ranch.

When a horse begins to pitch suddenly, he is said to "throw a fit" or "fall to pieces." In many instances, the cowboy uses the word "throw" for "put" or "place"; as, for example, "he threw a diamond hitch on the pack horse," meaning that the cowboy tied the pack on in a particularly effective way, leaving the rope in the form of a diamond. A stubborn horse is called "bull neck," while a bad one is an "outlaw" or a "man eater." A wild horse is a "broncho" or "bronc," and the horse breaker—meaning the man who reduces him to gentleness—is called a "bronc buster" or "bronc twister." If a man is a good rider, he is a "clean cutter." If the horse succeeds in throwing him, he is said to "get him a man," or "spill a man," or "shed a rider." At such time someone in the audience will say, "Let me to him," or "I'll take him a round," or "I'll give him a fall." If the horse pitches very hard, he is said to be "gettin' in a weavin' way"; if he pitches high, it is called "chinning the moon." A universal custom of the cowboy is to talk in a braggadocio way to the horse while he is pitching. Some of these expressions have grown into cowboy proverbs, as: "The higher you pitch, the sweeter my Navy[3] tastes"; "I'm double dew-clawed, knock-kneed, and bandy-shanked"; "I'm nine rows of teats and holes punched for more."

> I'm a gold bad man;
> I'm a desperado;
> All the way from Cripple Creek, Colorado.
> When I get back there'll be a tornado.
> Everywhere I go I give a warwhoop.

In such a speech the line of poetry is repeated as the horse goes up and down, while the contact of the horse with the earth constitutes the punctuation marks. There is a still longer one, more widely popular:

> Born on the Colorado;
> Sired by an alligator;

Raised on the Rio Grande;
Et prickly pear with grizzly bear;
Wish I had my pony back;
I'd make white folks hold their breath
And throw niggers through the crack.
Git higher; rough your hair;
Git high like the tree tops.
The higher you git's too low for me.
I'll show you how to ride;
Got my forty-five to my side;
I'm telling you, Big Little.

A man rides his horse "clean" or "slick" if during the pitching contest he does not put his hands on the saddle or "touch leather." It is almost downright disgrace for a rider to touch his saddle while the horse plunges; if he does, he is "pulling leather," "clawing leather," "gettin' the saddle strings." If he puts his hand on the horn during this struggle, he is said to be "hugging the nub," or "grabbing the peg," or "laggering." Ordinarily, the reckless cowboy not only spurs his horse as he pitches but hits him on the right and left flanks and over the head with his heavy white hat; in other words, he "fans him." And when the pitching is over and the rider has conquered, he is said to have "mopped up his bronc." Such expressions as "tuck them gently under him" and "hang them in him" refer to spurring the animal.

A pacing horse is called by the cowboy a "side-winder" or a "stern-wheeler." A "Sunday hoss" is one with an easy saddle gait. A pot-bellied or big-bellied horse is "whey-bellied"; a saddle mare is a "Dilsey," while range mares are "broom tails" or "willow tails," so named from their long straw-colored hair. The bunch of saddle horses under herd is a "cavvyard" or "remuda." The man who brings up the horses in the morning is the "horse rustler," "rustler" in this instance having no connection with another meaning of the same word implying a horse thief. A horse may be "burnt out" on a diet of grain, as a cowboy may be "burnt out" on camp fare. A man is said to "juice" a horse when he gives him water; in "juicing" a cow, the process is somewhat different.

When a man gets on his horse suddenly, it is said that he "took to him like a fellow sickening."

A saddle is called a "kack," a "mantura," or an "elm tree," the latter referring to the wood out of which the saddle frame was originally made. A "center fire" saddle has only one rigging on the saddle and one cinch or girth, the principal portions of the rigging being near the middle; a "rim fire" saddle has front and back rigging (which also makes it double-rigged, as opposed to single-rigged); a McClellan or army saddle is called a "muley" because it has no horn. The horn itself is often called the "nub" or "peg." The rolled cantle folded and placed between the horn and the rider of an outlaw horse is called a "life preserver," since it probably sometimes saves the life of a man when the horse suddenly plunges; the cantle breaks the collision that would otherwise be serious between the man and saddle horn. A saddle that fits and does not crawl (that is, go forward or backward) "stays put." A saddle that hurts a man is a "man eater," and the sore that it makes is a "setfast."

The cowboy calls his saddle, bed, and other paraphernalia his outfit. These he furnishes; the ranch owner provides horses, ropes, and food for the men and animals. The bed itself is usually termed in good-natured ridicule "a virtuous couch." A "tarp" or "tarpoleon" is the waterproof duck bag in which the cowboy keeps his blanket and "suggans," or heavy comforts bought from the store. The "tarp" is about six feet by sixteen feet in size, and is really waterproof, a common expression on a rainy morning being "Roll up your 'tarp' before the ducks light in it." The cowboy's pillow is a "nukin" and the entire bed furnishings is referred to as a "hot roll." The "war bag" contains the cowboy's change of clothing, tobacco "makins," and miscellaneous luggage. His spurs are "gal leg," "goose neck," or "straight shank" according to their shape, and they have "star" or "saw" teeth. A suitcase is a "go-away bag"; a white shirt, a "bald-faced shirt" or a "boiled shirt"; a knife a "messer"; a shotgun a "field piece." A pistol is called indiscriminately a "forty-five," a "six gun," a "billy," a "prop," a "cutter," a "gun," or a "hog leg." The pistol, so they say, got the name "hog leg" when a Negro from the East, after watching the cowboys strapping on their pistols, asked, "Whut dem men got all dem hog legs strapped on dey sides for?"

A rope is called a "tie rope" if used to "hog tie" animals by binding three legs together. A "catch rope" is used to lasso an animal. A "stake rope" is used to tie the "night horse." The Spanish words also used, "mecate" or "riata," refer to the material out of which the ropes are made. A "hackamore" is a special halter for wild horses.

Bridles are said sometimes to have "open reins," that is, reins not tied together, particularly if the horse is wild. Spurs are called "pet makers" when the rowels are dull, their constant pricking making the horse sluggish and indifferent to pain. They are also called "jobbers," "jiggers," "scrappers," "steels," "hackers."

The cowboy has many graphic terms for his food: "mountain oysters"; "dry land oysters"; "heifers' delight," a meat stew; eggs, "shanghai berries"; molasses, "lick"; rice, "moonshine"; butter, "cow salve"; cake frosting, "calf slobber"; biscuit, "terrapin" or "sinkers"; bakers' bread, "gun waddin' "; coffee, "alkali water." Bacon is called "Ned" (according to one cowboy explanation it got its name from a picture in McGuffey's First Reader, where the pig was named "Ned"); prunes are "nigger toes"; "dog bread" is the name applied to bread made of water and baking powder without shortening except tallow, wrapped around a stick and then baked over the coals; whiskey is called "road shortenin'," and a bottle of whiskey is a "bottle of barbed wire." On a long ride the crowd would stop to "wood up" or take a drink.

The cattle themselves are almost universally called "stuff." Cows are "she stuff"; cows without calves are "dry stuff"; poor cattle are "thin stuff"; aged cattle are "old stuff"; blooded cattle are "big stuff"; common-bred cattle, in contrast to blooded cattle, are "brindle stuff"; and then there are "young stuff" and "fat stuff." Cattle hard to control are called "wringy." The crippled or sick animals are called the "hospital bunch." Cattle not selected by the buyers under their contract are "culls." "Locos" are cattle suffering from loco poisoning. "Trash," "plunder," or "tailings" are cattle either left over when a herd is classed, or cattle unknown. The "drags" are the laggards in the herd going up the trail, as are also the "dogies." The "dogie" is ordinarily a motherless calf, being "pot-bellied" or "grass bellied." (A cattleman once gave me this story of the origin of the word "dogie": as these weak, laggard calves got most of the attention of the cowboys going up the trail, the epithet of "doughgut" was applied to them, meaning that they had nothing in their guts but dough; this word "doughgut" became shortened into "dogie.") "Burnt cattle" are cattle whose brands have been burned over. The term "wet cattle" is applied both to cows with calves and to cows smuggled over from Mexico. A "sleeper" is an animal whose ears have been cut to mark, but who is not yet branded. A "maverick" is ordinarily an unbranded animal. The word "maverick," just as the word "dogie," is commonly applied to any cattle; going out "mavericking" or going out to hunt "dogies" means simply going out to round up range stock. A "pelon" is a cow without hair. A "huby" is a homeless animal. A bunch of cattle consisting only of steers is known as "beef." A "scarl" is an abnormal growth sometimes produced by dehorning. The cow names of "drifter," "sweater," "tailings," and "cut back" are also applied to men. A "sweater" has been defined as "about the sorriest piece of humanity that inhabits the range." He gets the name from sweating around the stoves of bunkhouses, eating up everything without offering to pay. "Tailings" is a little bit more respectable, and "cut back" is about on the same plane as "tailings."

Cattle going up the trail in the old days, in herds of from two to ten thousand head, assumed in a little while the form of a kite. At each tip of the wing of the kite rode reliable men called respectively the "right pointer" and "left pointer." Then along each side appeared the "flankers" who kept the cattle from roaming off. At the last, where the "dogies" and "drags" were found, were the "drag punchers." Behind these came the "wranglers," "roustabout," and cook. The trail bosses were the most responsible men; they rode in the lead of the entire herd, at the frontal tip of the kite; this was said to be "riding in the swing." At night the herd was "bedded down" on the "bed ground," wherever possible on the edge of a bluff or in the bend of some river, so that the cowboys on guard, or "night herd," would have the least amount of riding to keep the animals quiet. Usually there were two men on a night watch, lasting from two to four hours. They kept constantly in motion around the edges of the herd, singing songs as they moved, or giving cowboy yodels for their effect in keeping the cattle quiet. Some sudden noise, or a rainstorm, would sometimes produce a stampede, which almost always occurred at night. The cattle would rise suddenly and all start off in one direction, running aimlessly over anything that obstructed their path. I was told by a reliable cowboy that when one large stampeding herd came to a rocky gorge something like twenty feet deep, the cattle rushed headlong over the edge of the gorge, which soon was filled completely full of bawling and kicking cattle; latecomers in the stampede were then able to run across the gorge, level-full of struggling animals, without pausing. In order to control a stampede, cowboys endeavor to ride ahead of and on each side of the herd in such a way as to get the cattle running in a circle, or "milling." To do this they often utilize their "slickers"—or waterproof overcoats—which they either are wearing or have attached to their saddles. This is so common that the expression "slick 'em" is current, meaning to wave the slickers in the faces of the maddened brutes.

Prior to taking a herd of cattle up the trail from Texas to Montana or the Dakotas occurred the spring roundup, which might include a range of country one hundred miles in diameter. Of course in such a stretch of land there would be a number of cattle owners. These would all join forces and, after days of hard riding, would bring together in a single herd all the cattle running on this range. On the roundup ground the cattle were then "worked"; that is, the calves following their mothers were branded and marked with the brands employed by their owners, or they were cut into groups either for purposes of sale or for further identification. Those cut out were called the "cut"; the specially trained horses used for this work, so intelligent that you can remove the bridle after the animal to be cut out is indicated and the horse will separate the cow from the bunch with unerring instinct, are called "cutting horses," "carving horses," or "chopping horses." When fences became more common, the calves were cut out through a cutting chute or "dodged out" so they could be counted. Some cattlemen now employ a branding chute with an arrangement for holding the cattle while they are being branded called a "squeezer" or "snappin' turtle."

In preparing to brand an animal which has been roped and dragged near the branding fire, a cowboy throws it either by "tailing" or "flanking." In "flanking" the cowboy seizes the animal by the skin of the flank opposite him, at the same time throwing his arms over the animal's back; when the animal jumps with all four feet off the ground, the cowboy by a jerk throws it on its side, or he "bull dogs" it by twisting the neck, or "tails" it by giving a sudden jerk on the tail when some of the animal's feet are off the ground. I once saw a cowboy "flank" a calf in such a fashion that he threw it completely on its back with all four feet in the air. "See him sun his moccasins," said another cowboy who stood near. When the "flanker" and assistants have the animals stretched on the ground, they call out "hot iron!" or "sharp knife!" and the brander responds, "right here with the goods!" Ordinarily the brand is put on with an iron stamp carrying one, two, or three letters, arranged into various brands and marks. These marks and brands, like the "Flying U" and the "Lazy B," are so various as to require a separate discussion to give them adequate description.

A "running iron" is a branding iron made of a straight piece of iron with a curve at one end. This end is heated red hot and the branding artist is thus enabled to "run" any letter he wishes to put on the side of the animal. Some of the terms used in marking are "crop," "under hit," "over hit," "half crop," "split," "over slope," "under slope." A "jingle bob" splits the ear to the head and lets the pieces flop. A jug handled "dewlap" is a cut in the fleshy part of the throat, also used sometimes as a mark of identification. Roping a cow is sometimes referred to as "putting your string on her." If a cowboy ropes a cow without hitching his rope to the saddle, he "takes a dolly welter," evidently a corruption of the Spanish. To "fair ground" is to rope an animal by the head, throw the rope over the back while still running and then throw the animal violently to the ground where it will usually lie until "hog tied" with three feet tied together, "side lined" with two feet tied together on the same side, or "hobbled," both hind legs tied together. To tell the age of an animal, the cowboy "tooths" him, or examines the teeth, as is commonly done in the case of horses.

In a cattle outfit the owner is called the "Big Boss"; the lieutenant or right-hand man is called the "straw boss," "top screw," or "top waddy." The chief of any group of line riders is a "line boss," while the boss of a herd on the trail is the "trail boss." Ordinarily a cowboy is a "waddy," or "screw," or "buckaroo." A green cowhand is called a "lent" and his greenness is expressed by the word "lenty." He is also sometimes called "Arbuckle" on the assumption that the boss sent off Arbuckle premium stamps to pay for the extraordinary services of the greenhorn. The "stray man" is the cowboy's name for one who goes to the neighboring ranches after stray cattle. The "fence rider," also called the "line rider," is employed to ride fences and repair them. Before the days of fences, line riding was following an imaginary line between two ranches and turning the cattle back. The "line rider" has charge of a "line camp." In addition to the chuck wagon, a second wagon for carrying extra beds and bringing wood and water into camps sometimes goes along. This equipage is called the "hoodlum wagon," and the man who drives it is "the hood." The cabin where the bachelor cowboys sleep in very bad weather is called a "hooden." A "bog rider" is the cowboy who "tails" up the poor cows who get stuck in the mud. The chuck wagon is the cowboy's home; the chuck box is his store; the chuck box lid is his table. After a meal, if a forgetful cowboy happens to put his tin plate and cup on the chuck box lid instead of in the "roundup pan" (a tin tub for washing dishes), this constitutes a "leggins case"; that is, he is laid over a barrel and treated to a dose of leggins in the hands of the most athletic cowboy. The chief man about the camp is the cook, his pay usually equalling that of any of the men, and his expertness in preparing food remarkable when one considers that his cookstove is a hole in the ground; his cooking utensils, skillets and pots. Naturally the cook has many names applied to him. He is called a "sheffi," "dough roller," "doughie," "nero," "cooky," or "biscuit shooter." His invariable cry when calling the men to a meal is "Come and git it!"

I think I may claim that these few samples of cowboy lingo

are characterized by simplicity, strength, and directness—and, it may be added, accuracy. I knew a saloon once in the West known as "The Wolf," and another aptly named with a big flaring sign on the outside, THE ROAD TO RUIN. Out in Arizona there is a town called Tombstone, and the leading paper of that town has named itself the Tombstone *Epitaph*. Let me add a few of the cowboy's miscellaneous expressions. Of a tall man he does not like, he says, "He's just as long as a snake and he drags the ground when he walks." Of a fool he says, "He has no more sense than a little nigger with a big navel"; or "He don't know dung from wild honey." Although a cow is one of the stupidest of animals, when a cowboy says that a man has "good cow sense" he means to pay him a high compliment. When he means a thing is easy, he says, "It's just as easy as getting a slut." Washing the face is "battling out your countenance" or "washing the profile"; bathing, "washing out your canyon"; vomiting, "airing the paunch." An "eyeballer" is a person who pokes into other people's business; going courting is "goin' gallin'," "sitting the bag," "sittin' her"; "cutting a rusty" means doing your best; moving fast is "faggin'," "leffin' here," "sailing away," "dragging his navel in the sand," "goin' like heel flies are after him." A very small town is "a wide place in the road." A "two-gun man" is a man who uses a gun in each hand, often at the same time. A man quick at retort is said to have a "good comeback." "Telling a windy" means telling a boastful story; a "goosy" man is a man physically nervous. When a man plays the deuce spot in a card game, he is said to be "laying down his character." To "fork a horse" is to ride him; when a man is without information, he tells you, "I ain't got any medicine." "Antigodlin" means going diagonally or in a roundabout way. The "roustabout" is a man of all work about a camp. "Sweating a game" means doing nothing but sitting around looking at a card game. "Tie your hats to the saddle and let's ride" means to go on a long hurry-up roundup. The boss's house is referred to as the "White House." When a fellow makes a night of it, he is said to have "stayed out with the dry cattle." When a delicate situation arises, it is said to be "the hair in the butter." The water on the plains is sometimes so muddy that the cowboy says he "has to chew it before he can swallow it." When he has gained a little more experience on a proposition, he says he "has taken a little more hair off the dog." When there is room for doubt about his knowledge, he is said to know as much about it "as a dog does about a side saddle." A man who is good at roping is said to "sling the cat gut well." Damp, freezing weather is characterized as "cold as a well digger in Montana." Riding on a freight train in place of paying regular fare on a passenger train is said to be "saving money for the bartender."

Living in isolated groups, visiting but little except among these groups, rarely going to town, shy and timid as a result of long days of solitude, the cowboy develops his own form of speech. His words, phrases, and customs therefore easily become community property—his language a dialect of his own. In closing this discussion I cannot refrain from giving you one or two cowboy graces repeated indiscriminately either before or during a meal, and I shall end with some of the cowboy's most characteristic dance calls. On some future occasion, if I am invited, and if I am provided with just the right kind of audience, I engage myself to read a paper on "Cowboy Profanity." There is a certain wholesome strength, cleanliness, and variety in the cowboy's profanity, and even his vulgarity, that I do not believe is equalled by any other race of men.

Here are two cowboy graces:

> Eat the meat and leave the skin
> Turn up your plates and let's begin.

> Yes, we'll come to the table
> As long as we're able,
> And eat every damn thing
> That looks sorter stable.

The rhymed dance calls are chanted between the shorter calls and are supplementary to them.

> Swing your partners round and round;
> Pocket full of rocks to hold me down;
> Ducks in the river going to the ford
> Coffee in a little rag; sugar in the gourd.

> Swing 'em early, swing 'em late;
> Swing 'em 'round Mr. Meadow's gate.

Ladies to the center, how do you do;
Right hands across, and how are you!

Two little ladies, do ce do,
Two little gents you orter know.

Swing six when you all get fixed,
Do ce, ladies, like kicking up sticks.

Chicken in the bread tray kicking up dough;
"Granny, will your dog bite?" "No, by Joe."

Swing corners all,
Now your pardner and promenade the hall.
You swing me and I'll swing you;
All go to heaven in the same old shoe.

Same old road, same old boy,
Dance six weeks in Arkansaw.

Walk the huckleberry shuffle and Chinese Cling,
Elbow twist and Double L swing.

Everybody dance as fast as you can;
Catch your partner by the hand.
Two little sisters form a ring,
When you form it, everybody swing.

Meet your partner, pat her on the head
If she don't like coffee, give her cornbread.

Bird hop, crow hop in,
Right hands up and going again.

Girl after boy!
Chase that rabbit, chase that coon,
Chase the baboon round the room.
    Reverse!
Chase that rabbit, chase that squirrel,
Chase that pretty girl around the world.
    Promenade!
All hands up and circle round
Don't let the pretty heifers get out of town.
    Everybody dance!
Swing your pardners, swing 'em one and all
Corral them pretty mavericks up and down the hall,
    Whoop-pee, everybody prance!

Four ladies domineck, four gents shanghai,
Then build your hopes on sweet bye and bye.

Do ce, ladies, ain't you old enough to know
That you'll never get to heaven till you do ce do.

1. Frank Stewart Hastings was manager of the huge S M S Ranch from 1902 to 1922. An educated man, he contributed some fine articles to the *Breeder's Gazette* which were collected and published under the title *A Ranchman's Recollections* in 1921.
2. "Aermotor" is the brand name of a windmill.
3. "Navy" refers to Navy Cut Plug chewing tobacco.

At the seventh annual meeting of the Texas Folklore Society, held at San Marcos on April 27 and 28, 1917, Lomax read this paper. In the first volume of The Trail Drivers of Texas *(printed for the Old Time Trail Drivers' Association by the Jackson Printing Co. in San Antonio, 1920), J. Marvin Hunter included the second half of Lomax's paper, beginning with "Prior to taking a herd of cattle up the trail," under a title of his own invention, "Cowboy Life in West Texas." Reprintings of* The Trail Drivers *have also included the article. Dobie had a mimeographed copy of "Cowboy Lingo" in his Lomax file, and it is from this that the present text is taken. Three notes have been added by the editors. At the eighth meeting of the Society, which was held in 1922 after a lapse of five years since the previous meeting, Lomax again read his paper on "Cowboy Lingo."*

The Cowboy: His Cause and Cure

EUGENE MANLOVE RHODES

THE MOST FASCINATING THING in the world is the most difficult to put on paper: a hard day's work. Backache, hunger, thirst, heat, cold, dust, danger—you may write the words, but how many will understand them? In these white-collar days, few men have ever been really tired, fewer still have been really hungry; and as for thirst—

You sometimes meet a cheerful, twinkling person, tolerant of small annoyances, mildly amused at our small pleasures, glowing with a private content at the most inopportune moments, and, upon insufficient provocation, flying into a state of intense calm. You probably list him as a philosopher. In a way, you are right. He is a man who has known absolute thirst, once or often, and hence has formed a new standard of values.

Now the cowboy—the 'sclusively old-time cowboy—did work which was more striking, more packed with interest, than the sometimes misjudged activities of his infrequent vacations. Because that work was done, for the most part, in loneliness and privation, few writers were so hardy as to acquire first-hand knowledge of it. You find the cowboy's work touched upon but seldom in fiction. If work is mentioned at all, it is usually the obvious and external phases of it, such as calf branding or steer shipping.

Even when the writer knows, the reader does not. "Them longhorns lit out down the hill and old Bill after them, like hell on a holiday." But if the reader has never seen any old Bill fall off from any little old hill after any little old longhorns, nor observed holiday procedure in the locality mentioned, he will have no conception of what there befell, the color and thrill and dash, the reckless, flashing, simultaneous impossibility of that headlong miracle.

It was in his daily work that the cowboy was at his best. Something of that work I would tell you, what and how and why. But my space is sharply limited; so first you are to hear a little of the why. For the cowboy's code, admirable in the main, foolish in spots, sometimes vicious, was unique in one respect. 'Sclusively among codes and creeds, it was observed. Such as it was, they lived by it—and died by it.

Humility was not headlined in the cow countries. With the cowboy, the cornerstone of character was pride. He was proud of his skill, swiftness, daring, hardihood, endurance, and loyalty.

Let me set down a few sections of the code, as they come to mind.

Your loyalty was to the job, not to your employer. You might fall out with your employer; you might privately resolve to evidence your dissatisfaction by deleting your employer, in due time. But you were not supposed to quit the job until another man—another good man—was ready to take your place. "To quit a man in a tight" was the unforgivable sin. This, of course, had its origin in the days when herds were trailed a thousand miles to market. As a corollary, any purposed deletion of your employer, as noted above, must hold over till the trail's end; else the herd might lose *two* good men. This worked out well; animosity weakened with time, and at any trail's end, you generally felt pretty well pleased with the world.

There was another side to this. *Provided the job could spare you,* you were supposed to put up with no harsh talk from foreman or owner. At the first rough word you said:

"Who, me? Hell, I done quit twenty minutes ago."

You were held to that order of words. You must not say, "I've quit," but "I've done quit." And it must be twenty minutes, neither more nor less. So spake the fathers. The idea was that you were supposed to know your job and to have done your best in a difficult and ticklish business; when you failed, no reproaches were due. This also worked out beautifully. You did not often quit your job in anger—perhaps never in a lifetime. What happened was that no one used tall talk to you. It was a wise idea, which might spread to advantage.

Again, you might never have seen your employer. You might work for a stock company, or an absentee. You worked for the job. You stayed with the stampede; you might not know how to swim and might have grave doubts as to your horse—but you crossed the flooded river with the herd; you went sleepless through stormy nights, as you "rode 'round them." More common, less exciting, but quite as hard, was the chance where some emergency brought you a double or treble share of work. Some part of a plan has slipped up; it is up to you, man and horse, hungry and tired, all but exhausted—thirsty in the South or chilled in the North—to save the situation. You can save yourself much suffering by quitting. But you don't stop while you can wiggle; you don't "lay down on the job." It isn't done.... (And soft-handed people sneer at ideals! That sneer is "the cry of the blind eye, *I cannot see*." To graft a wild apple with a Baldwin shoot—there is pure idealism. And it works.)

It followed that "the alibi" was unknown. When you came in without what you went after, you made no excuses. At most, you jerked a thumb at the pinnacles, with the casual and indolent explanation: "I wasted 'em." No post mortems. You were supposed to have done all that any man could do. Proud? You were trusted—who would not be proud?

You might give a burlesque account of your "water-haul," grossly exaggerated, for campfire use, a few days later. But you made no excuses.

Better still—whatever your misadventure, no matter how painful the experience—you *did not complain*. There was a good reason for this and that reason was not because you were such a fine fellow. It was because your audience knew all about it: exposure, fatigue, hardship, suffering—the bunch had been there. To people who did not understand, you would have complained fast enough. Speaking to your tough-fibered peers, *you formed the habit of not complaining—and kept it, later*. It is a good habit.

The blurb was as unknown as the alibi. Men said—without emphasis:

"He'll do to take along."

That was enough. "He'll do to ride the river with"—"He'll make a hand." When such comment was passed upon Bud Keyes, Bud was labeled for life. He was trustworthy. Others might be more skillful, but Bud counted as a man complete. "Top hand" referred to seniority of service, not to skill—except with a new outfit.

For another sample of the highest praise, consider Johnny, the boy who herded the saddle horses through the long nights. "Is Johnny a good night hawk?" "He holds the horses."

Superlatives were not permitted on the range, with one exception. To be "a cowman right" did not refer to character, but to uncanny skill, ultimate wizardry of hand, and utter concentration upon every detail of the business. I have known one or two who, so far as can be judged, never forgot the fleshmarks of any cow they had once seen. A cow would be poor, her hide woolly, the brand indistinct, the earmarks dubious or ragged; two men would claim her. To throw her down to "pick" the brand would injure her, as she is already in bad shape.

"Leave it to Bill McCall. Hi, Bill—is this bag of bones a K B or a Circle Seven?"

Bill glances over his shoulder. "She's Jim's. Saw her at Hopewell Tank last year." Jim took her.

Because you know your business, the writer who would put you to paper meets a serious difficulty when he comes to dealings between you and the foreman. In practice, the foreman said, when no other was by to hear:

"Charlie, I reckon you might go to represent with the V Cross T, tomorrow." If there were extra horses in the *caballada*, not in your mount, but which he was willing for you to take, he mentioned them. That was all. He didn't suggest that you leave Jug who was lame, Tiger who was thin, or Rebel with a cinch-gall. He didn't tell you what to do or how long to stay. You were supposed to know your business. If the V Cross T work made an early shipment of steers, you were to use your judgment, to ship steers of your brand if you thought best. If you needed an extra man to drive back, you hired him.

But the writer is forced to explain. His readers, if any, would not understand. They do not know what is meant by the large verb "to represent." They do not know what you go to the V Cross T to do; they must be told. So the writer must put into the foreman's mouth, for the reader's helping, detailed instructions such as no foreman would give and no waddy would take.

"Representing" is given as a sample, only. It was the same with other work. You were told to take seven peelers and work Hueco Hills. Details were left to you. "Hank, you go with the wagon to Cedar Spring." But Hank was not told where to make camp, where to get wood, and so on. That was up to Hank.

As a curious by-product—because beginners *must* be given precisely such detailed directions as must *not* be given to the old hand—all "medicine" was given privately, except general orders, such as arranging watches for night guard. The old hand had been learning since he was three years old. Later would be too late.

I worked on the range twenty-five years, and in that time I did not hear any man told what to do. If it was obvious, a gate to be opened, bars to lash fast on a pen of cattle, wood to be rustled for a branding fire—the nearest man did it, untold. When the boys came in at night—too tired for any type to tell—if beef was low, the first four men killed a beef. The horse wrangler was supposed to keep the cook in wood and water; sometimes he was prevented, for reason good. In such case, the first men to reach camp rustled that wood and water. No one asked them to do this. Some strange instinct seemed to tell them that the cook would need wood and water.

The foreman was supposed to know his business, too. He had hard problems of ways and means. He must ask no counsel, make no public planning; he allowed himself no indecisions; and for what went wrong, no other took the blame.

Another reticence—a small matter, but occasion for comment—was the way a bunch of cowboys would shut down "talking shop" in the presence of outsiders. It has been variously attributed to an oafish bashfulness and to a fine modesty. We were not bashful and we were not modest. I am clear on that. For the reason of those depressing silences, I am not so sure. It was probably because strangers didn't speak our language. They didn't understand some of the words—and half of the other words didn't mean to them what they meant to us.

So much—and only a small part—for the tradition of work. For the etiquette of homicide, it was one with the age-old code of the *duello;* a real or apparent equality of opportunity, and no backing down. This phase has been done and overdone. Since the Great War, some of us are not so bloodthirsty as we were, anyhow.

Cowboys carried arms, and were anachronistic in the matter of using them on their fellows. They needed guns for other purposes than man-killing; but, packing guns, they used them in anger, when another man, quite as willing to shoot, could have reached no weapon until he had a chance to take a second thought—and until the target had time for a few thoughts, as well.

There has been mutiny upon the high seas before now, and piracy—but the finest thing sailors have done has been to drive their ships across the sea. There *was* gunplay amongst the cowboys; but what cowboys did best and most was to work the cattle. It was not unnatural to write up the fighting days of the cowlands; but the skill, the daring, the fine faithfulness, and the splendid fun of the working days has been neglected.

Andy Adams wrote of those working days, truthfully and lovingly. At that time, gore was what readers wanted. Today, they may be willing to read of that work of yesterday.

You should read George Pattullo's "The Horse Wrangler," about "little Dick, who never lost a horse," perhaps the best Western short story written, true to life, reflecting all that was best of the cowboy spirit. I don't know if it has been published in book form. If not, let us make demand that it shall be. It would be shameful that so fine a story should be forgotten.

You who write today the stories of our yesterdays—can't you give our grandchildren something to remember of the cowboy, besides gunplay? A little about their work?

No shirking, no alibis, no bawling out, no post mortems, no whimpering, no passing the buck, no blurbs, no pouter-pigeon posings; "Let me at it" rather than "Let George do it"; such material for a novel should at least possess the merit of novelty. So much youth and pride and skill, gay daring, unswerving loyalty—surely all these are worthy of a better fate than forgetfulness.

Whatever was fine in the cowboy was because he was interested in making the best possible job of his work, with an unexplained indifference to the financial rewards of it. As it happens, his pay was at all times laughably inadequate to the "service rendered."

Time and chance cured the cowboy. But when you look around you and find any man doing notable work in any line—try to get him more interested in his pay than in his work. That will cure him.

Impertinent Postscript—for which I profess myself "puhsunally responsible, suh."

Can that be "what's wrong with the movies"? Is it possible that anyone in the movies thinks more about making easy money than he does about making a good picture?

Rhodes's article was published in Story World and Photodramatist *for August, 1923, under the title "The Cowboy in Fiction." It was republished in* Writers' Markets and Methods, *May, 1933. Rhodes sent the late Walter Prescott Webb a copy in 1924, with several changes and additions in his own hand. He said he had originally entitled his article "The Cowboy: His Cause and Cure." This whimsical title has been restored in the present reprinting, which also incorporates Rhodes's few revisions. The Texas Folklore Society is grateful to W. H. Hutchinson, who now represents the Rhodes heirs in literary matters, for permission to use the article here.*

The American Cowboy

ANDY ADAMS

THE IMPRESSION SEEMS a general one that the sole duty of a cowboy is to herd cattle. This idea is no doubt largely gained from reading. In our tenderfoot days, we have all thrilled over the rejuvenated story of the cattle king and the highwayman; the former, when attacked, remonstrated with the latter over his mode of existence, resulting in tears of penitence, and the robber going home with the cowman to accept a job of herding cattle on a Texas ranch. A beautiful old story, which will probably be retold, with new settings, to future generations. The brutal truth, however, should assign a more plausible motive than that of herding the festive cow. Why not let him marry the ranchero's daughter? As range cattle were never herded, the latter suggestion is more probable; and then look at the great possibilities in showing man's love for his fallen brother. If the wild horse on the boundless plain, rather than forsake the range where he was born, permits himself to be walked down and captured by men, when he is domesticated for generations, what would be the necessity of herding him? If the fox and deer, either capable of outrunning the hounds, could only eradicate that innate love of lair and range, they need never sacrifice their lives to the circling pack. The ox still knows his master's crib. Then why herd the eternal cattle?

The truth is, range cattle were never herded. The livestock industry in the West and Southwest, constantly yielding to the encroachments of agriculture, found no permanent abiding place, until the arid regions were reached. The scarcity of water in the range country is the best herdsman; and when the old West was an open range, the ranchman met fewer losses by straying and thieves than under modern fenced conditions. There are many reasons to believe that the ox was man's first domesticated animal, and to this day the two are inseparable. The question naturally suggests itself, If the cowboy did not herd cattle, what did he do? There are many things that a farmer does besides plow and sow. In fact, only a small portion of his time is consumed with seedtime and harvest; yet he is a busy man for twelve months in the year. So with the ranchman. A calf, from the moment it is born, has natural enemies. The maternal parent may ward off the lurking wolf, yet at the same time a fly may deposit its larva, and the life of the new-born calf is in jeopardy. On the ranges of the Southwest, men ride constantly on the watch for the ravages of screw worms among young calves. Should the weather be damp and showery, so as not to permit the wounds to dry up within a few hours after birth, the opportunity is seized by the blowfly, and without man's assistance, the little one's life is lost within a few days. Carrying in his saddle pockets a preparation for the extermination of insect life, the cowboy rides the range, and in a single day, may save the lives of ten young calves.

One season of the year safely past, another commands his attention. Like the farmer, the ranchman always finds work to do. With his increasing herds, it may be necessary to build new corrals. Cattle are the embodiment of innocence and strength; and while their owner and his help may live in the crudest of shelters, when he builds for his beast, he builds for his own and the next generation. Choosing some location in the open and near timber, a trench is dug six feet deep, palisades of some durable wood are cut fourteen feet long, frequently requiring two yoke of oxen to drag them to the site, when they set upright in the open ditch. This extra strength may seem uncalled for, but our ranchman is a practical one, and having seen corrals built out of lumber and leveled to the ground by cattle stampeding within, he makes sure that his work will stand. Like the house that is builded on a rock, when his corrals are full of beeves and the lightnings flash, in the frenzy of a stampede the animals may throw their united weight against his palisaded wall, only to be hurled back like the angry waves that beat upon a rocky cliff. The supreme test of a corral comes in holding stampeding beeves, and numerous instances might be cited where heavy cattle threw themselves against the enclosure with such momentum as to form a scaling ladder with their own bodies, allowing the rear animals to pass over the prostrate ones and escape; yet the structure stood. In southern Texas, there are corrals built out of live-oak palisades, which have been in use over forty years, yet today will hold a thousand longhorn steers through any night, bearing mute testimony that its builder avoided the sands.

The cowboy, of necessity, was a versatile man. In a winter camp in the North, I saw a patchwork quilt made from old trousers and neatly lined with a bed blanket, every stitch of the work being done by an idle cowboy. Again, on the lower Rio Grande, I heard the blessing of the saints invoked on the head of a lad who had repaired the sewing machine of a poor, devout Mexican woman. In a brief article like this, it is possible to notice but a few of the cowboy's duties. In turn, he might act as engineer, carpenter, or machinist, as there were earthen tanks to build in preserving the scanty water supply, houses to erect, while the windmills and pumps of a ranch were in constant need of repair. In advance, in working in a well in the far South, we always lowered a man with a lantern and hatchet on the lookout for live snakes. Not a desirable task by any means, but with a pump out of order and a thousand suffering cattle lowing in their thirst, there was no alternative but to go down, kill out the reptiles, hoist the piping, and repair the machinery. In an arid country, moisture attracts snakes, and many a fine well has been taken possession of by them, requiring a strenuous fight to recover it from its creeping possessors.

The actual work with the cattle, performed by the cowboy, might not require over half his time. But slight as were his days of recreation, his presence was ever required on the ranch, for there was the unseen to be guarded against. Some of his work was done under circumstances requiring unlimited patience, and then again with a rush where all the comforts of life were left behind. In the Cherokee Strip, now part of Oklahoma, I have seen a prairie fire break out from the reflection of the sun on a tin can, throwing its signal column of black smoke into the sky, instantly summoning every man within fifty miles. Or it might occur at night, from different causes, with its brilliant horizon, the flames leaping upward, visible at the distance of twenty miles, while every breeze was saturated with the smell of burning grass. Under such circumstances, horseflesh was never spared in reaching the actual scene. The first men to arrive would begin back or counter firing as it was called, much the same as city firemen blow up blocks in the pathway of a conflagration, taking every advantage of arroyo or dry wash, and with saddle blankets, beating out their own fire on the leeward before it could gain headway. If a wide enough belt could be thus burned, in advance of the main conflagration, it might check the fire, or jumping the emergency guard, break out anew on its course. Within two or three hours after a prairie fire had thus started, there might arrive fifty to one hundred men. Being plainsmen as well as cowboys, they knew what to do. Frequently several light cow brutes were killed, beheaded, and split down the spine, leaving only the hide to hold the body together. The carcass of the animal was then turned flesh down, ropes were fastened from a fore and hind foot to pommels of saddles; and riding astride the burning grass, the body was dragged over the fire, virtually rubbing it out. Other men followed on horseback, to beat out any remaining flames and relieve the mounts by pulling on the ropes. This process could only be applied on the flanks of the main conflagration, and on the leeward of all counter firing, as no one dared to dispute the sway of the fiery monster, except well in its advance. Such a fire might last three hours or three days, at the termination of which, the men would ride for the nearest camp for rest and refreshment.

The most systematic work with cattle which ever fell under my observation, was that of the roundups during the palmy days of the Cherokee Strip. The range was about sixty miles wide by two hundred long, and almost exclusively devoted to the maturing of young Texas steers into marketable beef. It had a grazing capacity of from one and a half to two million cattle, requiring about two thousand men and twelve to fifteen thousand saddle horses. When a lease was finally secured, by an association of cowmen, from the Cherokee Nation, it was allotted and fenced into pastures, ranging in size from ten to two hundred thousand acres. The roundups usually took place in June, or as early after shedding their winter coats as the brands were readable. Under orders of the president and secretary, by authority of the directors, an annual call was made for a general roundup of the Strip. The work was done in three divisions, known as the eastern, middle, and western; and a meeting place and date were appointed for each department. Several days before the appointed time, the men began to gather at the different rendezvous. Every ranch or cattle company usually sent two or three men to represent it on each of the three sections, to which were added the local help, owners, and special inspectors from other associations, until the number might reach, in each division, five or seven hundred men on the morning of starting. Although the range was enclosed, there were winter drifts where the cattle leveled down barb-wire fences as easily as they crossed creeks in summer. The object of the roundup was to return these wandering animals to their owner's range. The evening before the start, a captain was elected for each division, and every man present was subject to his orders. At the expense of the association, a general commissary of several wagons and cooks, augmented by ranch outfits, went along, carrying blankets and provisions. The local help on each range usually drifted all their cattle into one end of the pasture, in advance of the roundup, and on its arrival, a few hours' work and all strays were cut out and taken along. Two or three separate ranges were thus worked in a single day; and whether fifteen or thirty thousand cattle were passed upon, hundreds of alert eyes scrutinized every brand. The strays were carried along with the roundup, both they and the saddle horses being night-herded by shifts of men. The work of the annual roundup of the Strip sometimes required thirty days; and then the men returned home with their cattle, and the stock-taking was over until another year.

I dare say my boy readers have been disappointed in this all too brief article concerning the life and work of the American cowboy. Whence come the old, old stories of the cowboy's romance, I know not. Cowboys, perhaps, *have* scalped Indians, but on the other hand the Indians have scalped the cowboys.

If I have any word to say of the life of these range riders, it is that no harder life is lived by any working man. And that I know whereof I speak, rest assured, for I have been myself a cowboy. For years, I roped, threw, and branded cattle, and the little "fun" in the business made no appeal to me. It is perhaps, after all, not the work, but the life in the open, under the blue sky of day and the purple star-flecked sky of night, that held us to the life. The range was no place for a weakling, though I dare say a weakling might have thrived and waxed strong under the strenuous regime of its life in the open. But all the men who were my friends in my cowboy days were, physically at least, kings among men. All and all, of my brothers of the cattle country I may say:

One man to his trade and another to his merchandise. Those who knew the cowboy best, know that amid the prosaic details of his daily life, he often displayed patience, courage, and even heroism, which entitled him to respect and admiration. And when his history shall have been truthfully written, it will show that this man bore his burden among other pioneers in reclaiming the old West.

This article was published, accompanied by some fine photographs, in the Pilgrim, XI *(February, 1905), 7-8. Andy's hyphenation has been modernized; otherwise the article is reproduced as it originally appeared. Andy's punctuation respects rhythmical demands first of all. The dangling constructions have been allowed to remain. Theodore Roosevelt, who wrote several books about the ranching country and had the advantage of a Harvard education, did not always succeed in making his participles and gerunds behave either.*

Andy was writing against certain misconceptions of the cowboy's life and work that had been popularized by newspapers, magazines, and dime novels.

The "association of cowmen" that Andy refers to was the Cherokee Strip Live Stock Association, which had the whole Strip or Outlet under lease from 1883 through 1890. Andy seems to have had some cattle of his own in the Strip for a while; his brand there was the Barb Wire, a horizontal line with three short vertical lines to represent a strand and barbs.

The Texas Folklore Society thanks Andy T. Adams of Denver and the other Adams heirs for permission to republish this article.

The Cowboy's Code

PAUL PATTERSON

IN NO OTHER PROFESSION since knighthood was in flower is there a greater number of unwritten laws than those governing the cowboy calling. And no cowboy since Ab Blocker ever adhered more rigidly to the code than did—and does—my brother John of Stiles in Reagan County.

When Rufe Bishop of the JM in 1917 cut fifteen-year-old John Patterson his first mount of horses, long gone were the long trails and open range, but still fresh as horse tracks in this morning's dew, still stout as a new Manila "ketch" rope, were the behavior patterns, the etiquette of an equine-oriented society—the cow country code of behavior as laid down by old-timers of Charlie Goodnight's day and earlier.

These cowboy do's and don't's were not only unwritten laws, but unspoken ones. As far as I can determine they were never heard, or overheard, around a cow camp or bunkhouse. They were absorbed, as a saddle blanket absorbs sweat, or acquired just as a grain-fed cow pony acquires a hump in his back on a frosty morning or a cow-camp cook contracts crankiness.

First and foremost among a bucked-off cowboy's don't's was never to let a horse jerk loose and get away. This is rule No. 1. Here was a throwback from the open range days when a loose horse might mean a walk of 200 yards to 200 miles, both distances being equally distasteful to a cowboy.

Since John never was considered among the contest class of bronc riders, adherence to this rule was extremely hard to come by. Even so, he has appeared back in camp still a-horseback as regularly as the best of them—still a-straddle such outlaws as Mogollon, Donegone, Yellow Jacket, and scores of others just as snaky.

This writer has witnessed many of these struggles—John dragging by a bridle or hackamore rein and some old spoiled outlaw tromping and stomping at him for fifty yards in an effort to break away.

There was the time out west of Girvin when a cold-jawed horse shed his bridle and sold out across the alkali flats. Sizing up the situation, John stepped calmly down and eared the critter to a stop, which takes considerable doing for two men, much less one, especially when this one is considered awkward by some standards.

At the age of fifty-eight, the code still stamped indelibly upon him, he held onto the reins of a young half-bronc that threw him and knocked out most of his upper teeth. Only on two occasions did his medicine fail him—once at the Jigger Y when a horse fell with him, knocking him unconscious for ten days (and he was carried by wagon ambulance thirty miles to Odessa), and again down at the 7h when old Yellow Kitten fell on him, breaking his leg above the knee. He couldn't have mounted anyhow. Besides, the old pony would go in and make his report.

This outmoded code, this hold your horses in spite of hell or high water, is not a family characteristic, however. Yours truly, in his brief cowboy career, took frequent long walks rather than face the hazard of another hard fall. Only once was I ever known to come in a-horseback after such an experience, and this was not of my own making. On my way back to the John Lane Headquarters a little sorrel warped me hard against the hard side of a hillside and then had the gall to stand when I made a lunge at him, in what appeared to be an effort to live up to the code, but what was in reality a move calculated to booger him off—so I could walk the remaining six miles in safety and comfort.

Nor was this "hold 'em, cowboy" as widespread as one would suppose. It was an exclusive fraternity indeed, as Tom Wilson, ex-wagon boss of the Bar S, will assure you. He tells of a big, loud kid that Noah Schrier hauled out to the old 7D's.

It was during World War I and the outfit was extremely short on manpower and long on horse. The good, grown cowboys had gone "over there" and left 300 to 500 horses in the remuda to grow fat and sassy from lack of use. What's more, those old 7D's already had a reputation for having more power per horse than any remuda around. With this in mind Noah asked the kid: "You jist got *one* saddle?"

"Why, shore," said the kid, half on the prod at such a damn fool question. "Whoever heered tell of needin' two saddles?"

Noah had. But he let this big kid with the loud spurs and voice to match find out the hard way. The wagon boss, not through compassion but through caution, cut the Big Loud Kid the gentlest horse in the outfit. Even so, before you could say "Jack Robinson" the kid was stretched flat and windless and the old pony was high-tailing it for the Middle Concho brush with the kid's *one* saddle.

Noah could have said "see there" but he kept his counsel, figuring there would yet be a more appropriate time. Shortly the kid had his wind back, though not so much as formerly, and was calling for another horse—with the cook's saddle. You had to hand it to him, the Big Loud Kid was game and he had a little more modesty than before.

Even so, the curtain parts on Scene II—identical with Scene I—a big kid flat and gasping for wind, a big blue roan cracking stirrups together above an empty saddle as he lines out for the Middle Concho brush. There was, however, one slight addition—a big fat cook cussing a blue (roan) streak.

"See there," said Noah. But his heart wasn't in it, having gone out to a child too young to leave its mother. The boss likewise seemed somewhat softened by such a sad spectacle.

"You ain't the only one, son. Makes seven, all told, with their saddles to hell and gone out yonder sommers," he said, the 360-degree sweep of his arm taking in the 700 square miles of the 7D's.

Tom Wilson's account, as narrated above, leads us to the conscientious cowboy's rule No. 2, namely, never inquire as to the killer quirks or cold-blooded qualities of any horse the boss cuts to you, regardless of the degree of apprehension you might feel. Besides, such information to an inquisitive new hand is generally inaccurate, unreliable, exaggerated, and calculated to induce terror —especially if the newcomer is the blow-hard type.

For this type Bud Barfield of the 7f's had a stock sizing up of the first horse he cut to him. "You better watch him. He's the one that killed *that* woman," he'd say gravely. If the cowboy in question was of the completely insufferable variety Bud would add as a sort of coup de grâce, "And drug pore Charley to death."

Had "pore Charley" been some gullible greenhorn it was still enough to clabber the blood of the bravest, but the "pore Charley" Bud had reference to was the great Charley Lyons himself, who was dragged to death while working for this very outfit. And for all the blow-hard knew, it was by this very horse whose hot, loud breath was being emitted with such fearsome snorts against his neck this very minute.

Rule No. 3 in the code, the lacing of your kack on anything the boss drug out, was a noble attribute indeed in a cowboy but was a definite strain on a wagon boss's disposition, and an obvious drain on precious man-and-horse hours. Horses running loose with saddles added little joy to a boss's eighteen-hour day. Being keenly aware of this was what made John so determined to hold his horses, according to the first rule.

Rigid adherence to rule No. 3 was an attribute the Big Loud Kid shared with all responsible hands, Brother John not excepted. In fact, John was, and still is, as much a stickler for No. 3 as for No. 1. From that distant day when Rufe Bishop cut him old Mogollon, he is yet to turn one down, though he is his own boss now. Of course none is as salty as old Cement or Bay Hippy or Mogollon, but they have been snaky enough to have knocked out his uppers and broken an arm within the last two years.

In his late forties and during World War II, when horsebreakers were hard to come by, he and Pete Hollowell (another overage cowboy) in the course of one day took seven unsuccessful seats on a bronc.

"John," asked a neighbor, "how's that thoroughbred coming along?"

"Well, he keeps one of us in the air most of the time, but he's a-comin' along nice!"

Until cowboying became automated, John, in strict observance of rule No. 4, took great pains to relieve a man on day herd early, which act required the hasty bolting down of his dinner. Even now, with his uppers knocked out, he can have his meal bolted and be up from the table before the rest of us are halfway through the first slab of cornbread.

The same rule applied to night guard. The late arrival was far more intolerable than the hand who lingered too long over the cook's noon offerings.

My Uncle Fisher Pollard once took drastic measures against a cowboy who consistently and persistently relieved him late. One cold night he pitched a loop to his guard partner, who secured the same to the tarp-covered cowboy still sleeping in his wind-protected spot. Wheeling off at right angles, Uncle Fish spurred for a fast fifty yards across the lumpy, bumpy plains. Thereafter he was promptly, if not sooner, relieved at guard.

Rule No. 5 had to do with a cowboy's bed. When vacated of a morning (which was generally still night), his bed must be rolled and stacked by the wagon with care and, in some circles, loaded on. Otherwise a cowboy might have to commute some fifteen or twenty miles back to last night's camp site if he wanted to sleep in his own bed. While there were no restrictions on the size of his roll, he was limited as to how long he could stay in it. As one heavy-eyed cowboy's lament went, "It shore don't take long to stay all night on this outfit!" A pallet could range in bulk from the vast Montana roll of the cook down to Alvin Reed's hat and saddle blanket; from Billy Rankin's three-or-four passenger mattress down to Uncle Henry Record's frazzly tarp and one little bitty Filipino wonder[1] thereunder. It was all according to how a cowboy catered to comfort—whether he preferred it in the "sacking" (the modern term) or in the packing.

As Uncle Fish tells it, the Texas-New Mexico line didn't have as much as a three-wire fence to deflect the razor edge of polar blue blizzards, and cozy comfort was at a premium, especially for the light rollers. One bitter night while Montana-roll addicts were snoring snug in their soogans Uncle Henry Record lay a-shivering beneath his hen-skin tarp and Filipino wonder. Along toward morning Top Heard rode in off guard.

"T-T-Top," Uncle Henry muttered, "th'ow a set of chain

harness, a cow chip—or somethin'—on me. Jist anything a-tall to add a little weight."

Once in the Marfa country an old cowboy was asked if he had ever slept cold.

"No," he said, "I've never slep' cold—but I've laid awake cold a hell of a lot of nights!"

Another seldom-violated statute was rule No. 6, which forbade doing a-foot whatever could and should be done a-horseback. Illustrative of this was an incident that occurred during Joe B. Johnston's childhood visit to the Jigger Y. Late that evening Joe Lane and Guy McLaughlin had ridden in, and the latter was in the process of unsaddling.

"Don't unsaddle. We haven't milked yet," said Joe Lane.

"That's so," said Guy, recinching and stepping back into the saddle. Shaking out two wide, quick loops, they built to a thin high-horned cow that had been walking the horse-trap fence. To little Joe B. she seemed mighty snaky for a milk cow, for she left there like an arrow shot from a bow. But she was soon stretched out between the two mounted cowboys, who were hollering: "Joe B., come whey this heifer!"

"Whey her your ownself," countered Joe B., spurning the battered bucket they had pointed out to him. He didn't like the way the critter was walling her eyes, bellering, and lolling out her tongue.

"Aw, come on, Joe B., it takes both of us to keep her down."

After further urgings, which had begun to sound like threats, Joe B. relented. Taking roundants on the sharp horns, he moved to the "udder" end, took hold and squeezed with might and main. But nary a drop.

"Might as well let her up," said Guy. "She's done taken up her milk."

"I can't understand it; we didn't chouse her," Joe Lane put in.

Joe B. was too innocent to realize this was an act—a show put on to impress him with how wild and woolly the "Booger Y" was, and to demonstrate the efficiency of a mounted cowboy. In reality, cowboys of this day and time had sooner be caught in hand-me-down boots than milking a cow—either a-horseback *or* afoot!

The cowboy's attitude toward this nester-introduced, woman-enforced chore may best be illustrated by an experience Brother John had in the employ of a branch of the 7f's with Uncle Tom Richardson as boss. John and Uncle Tom, in addition to their regular duties, were holding down the job of Aunt Mattie, who was on a long-deserved *paseada*. This proved quite a chore. And more. Slop the hogs, feed the chickens, gather the eggs, locate and relocate the setting hens, milk three cows, strain this morning's milk, skim last night's milk, churn day before yesterday's, and so on.

"Dammit, John," Uncle Tom lamented, "gimme the old days. All a man had to do was make up a batch of bakin' powder bread, roll a cigarette and he was ready to ride."

Respect for fences came to be part of the code (rule No. 7). Whereas old-timers cut them down, along with the builder on occasions, latter-day cowboys came to look upon fences as a necessary evil. And cowboys like Lee Reynolds, who moved lots of stock, looked upon them with something akin to affection. Fences, in the form of horse traps and nesters' pastures, had virtually eliminated the need for dreary night guard and the bothersome nighthawking of remudas. As a result, cowboys of Lee's day were careful to leave an outfit's fences in good shape after passing a herd or remuda over.

Once our old friend Lee Reynolds and another cowboy were, as Lee put it, "carrying a little bunch of ponies acrost New Mexico." The code had not yet covered New Mexico simply because fences hadn't. Having grown soft in Texas' barb-wire enclosed civilization, Lee was beginning to feel the strain of night after night of horse guard in New Mexico.

Finally, and suddenly, there stretched across their path a two-wire drift fence which lost its ends, eventually, on the horizon to east and west. Reining up, Lee solemnly surveyed same and said sourly, "Must be their weanin' trap!"

According to rule No. 7, once their horses were across, they fixed this "weanin' trap" fence back up, which would have been a powerful big job, Lee said, if he hadn't had a couple of "steeples" in his pocket. (To most people a steeple is what goes on a church, but to cowboys it is what holds a wire to a post.)

The same unwritten law applied to gates. Now a man could get shot almost as readily for leaving a gate open as he once could for building one. Old Man Rawls ranched eighty miles down toward the border from Marfa and was separated from this mecca of civilization by *one* lone, lonesome gate—a big beautiful wooden one about forty miles out. Now he was in town to herd home a brand new automobile.

It was early in the horseless carriage age and the transition was coming hard. But came the big morning and the step seemed simple, what with the driving instructor starting him off, jumping clear, and leaving the deep wagon ruts to do most of the steering. However, Old Man Rawls's intensive two weeks' accumulation of driving, or rather *stopping*, know-how vanished into thin air when that big wooden gate loomed up. He plowed on through and/or over it. One thing was in his favor, though. The impact killed his motor, and this probably saved him from a watery grave in the Rio Grande seventy-five miles or so on down the road. Carefully, painstakingly he patched up the gate, stood it up and closed it, cranked up—and backed back through it.

The early twentieth-century cowboy was a person possessed of a colossal and in some ways lopsided pride. Rule No. 8 has to do with clothing. The cowboy's pride was more pronounced at both ends than in the middle. His britches might be baggy and his leggings frazzly, but he had to have a Stetson (sometimes pronounced *STUD*son) hat and shop-made boots.

Brother John's psyche still bears the ugly scars of the pair of boots Papa bought him ready-made at old Arkansas Taylor's in Rankin.

"No wonder old Mogollon throwed wall-eyed fits," he says, convinced to this day that it was those store-boughten boots that outlawed him. John's first two months' wages went to H. B. Dorsey, a skilled Midland bootmaker. The next paycheck went to Wadley-Wilson for a hat—a Stetson, of course. As for his middle John wasn't so finicky, except that he wouldn't be caught dead in a pair of bib overalls (which old-timers pronounced *overhauls*). Only those who were real low down—or real high up—on the social totem could get by with wearing overalls. No greater breach of etiquette could be committed—except, perhaps, showing up at some roundup wagon riding a mare.

Deeper than a cowboy's pride in his appearance was the pride he had in himself as a person. Rule No. 9 required him to quit if he had been offended. He would "bow up" at the least provocation, roll his hot roll and ride, call for his time over a slight so slight that he himself couldn't pinpoint it. What's more, this rule wouldn't permit him to reveal the exact nature of his grievance—if he knew it.

Careful, tactful, thoughtful, and wise as the old-time boss was, he couldn't keep from twanging a sensitive chord now and then. He knew the chief taboos, however, and gave them a wide berth. For example, no wagon boss in his right mind would order, or even implore, a cowboy to saddle or unsaddle his (the boss's) horse. This practice might have been prevalent in early California, down in Old Mexico, in the Deep South, and now on TV and the wide screens. But in our part of the country you adhered rigidly to the demands of liberty, equality, and fraternity—fraternity, that is, provided your liberty wasn't curtailed or your equality questioned in any way at all.

The code-conscious cowboy took a special pride in his ability to endure, or rather ignore, pain; to make light of contusions, concussions, dislocations, and fractures—simple or compound. He'd never admit to being hurtable, much less to hurting. This was rule No. 10. Brother John, having lain out with a broken leg all of a winter day and up into the night, and having to spend another six weeks in a San Angelo hospital before the leg could be set, felt sorrier for the hurried, harried nurses than he did for himself. As for pain, a broken leg was more on the order of scaly dandruff, to hear him tell it.

Further illustrative of this attitude is the incident up at the Midland Fair when a bronc turned a cat on Cyclone Davis, which calamity occurred in the presence of scores of horrified spectators.

"My God, see if he's hurt," came an anguished plea from the crowd.

"Hell, see if the horse is hurt," remarked Will Gates, casually. "You know old Cyclone'll be all right!"

In Monahans when somebody rushed into a beer joint and up to Jack Lewis with the announcement that the latter's *compadre*, Bellcord Rutherford, had had his throat cut and was apt to bleed to death, Jack said, scarcely looking up from his drink, "Tell him to tie a tow sack around it and come on. His beer's a-gettin' hot."

And the time this same Bellcord had been shot (in anger, of course) with a .38 caliber pistol. Upon recovery he had grown rather plump, whereas he'd previously been somewhat on the lean side.

"Bellcord," Joe Bailey Rogers told him, "you shore are a-doin' good. If old Cody'd a shot you with a shotgun, you'd a got rollin' fat."

Rule No. 11, the most cherished and famous part of the code, was to keep your word and take the word of others unless they were known liars. "His word was his bond"—there is no better way of saying it. Everyone was presumed to be "a man of his word" and those who showed themselves not to be were severely condemned.

Once Zack Monroe went with a bunch of hands down into Kimble County to pick up the first of 10,000 yearlings the *Quién Sabe* Ranch had bought from the 7D's—by oral agreement. The first night out the herd stampeded through the cedars, breaking legs, necks, backs, and horns and causing considerable loss for somebody. Since such an eventuality was not covered in the oral contract, a heated argument arose over who would assume the damages. But it was a controversy in reverse. A part owner of the 7D said the 7D would assume the loss, since it happened in the country they had under lease. Old Man M. Halff, owner of the *Quién Sabe*, argued that it was the *Quién Sabe's* responsibility because they had already received the herd. Evidently they came to a peaceful settlement, for Zack said thousands of cattle changed hands between them after that, with never a written contract.

Dick Poage, former 7D wagon boss, died in Big Lake at the age of eighty-eight. The minister who preached his funeral pointed out that Poage was loath to affiliate himself with any particular church for fear he couldn't live up to its precepts. "Yet," the pastor went on to say, "Dick Poage's word was as solid as the

Rocky Mountains—absolutely and completely reliable." More reliable, we could add (from a church layman's fund-soliciting experience), than many signatures on a tithing pledge today.

And this verbal bond, in the old days, could be just as binding on a gambling man. George Teague tells of the time up at Midland when he casually bet Tom Owens $100 on a steer-roping contest and then forgot about it. In a few days there came through the mail a hundred-dollar check signed "Tom Owens." George and Tom, though quite contemporary, lap far enough back into the past to have acquired the code.

The last rule that I shall mention, No. 12, is this: Let there be no petty thievery. Lower than the low was the petty thief—lower than the sheepherder in *overhauls* and hand-me-downs. In the old West the petty thief was to the human race what the polecat was to the animal kingdom and the buzzard was to birds.

Pappy Taylor, a former freighter whose wagons bogged or broke down on the Angelo-Sheffield road for days at a time, never missed so much as a stick of candy. Ranchers left the latch string ever out. People of all kinds came and made themselves at home, and when they left they took nothing that wasn't theirs.

Merchants didn't lock their stores. There wasn't a lock on a store door from where the West began to where it ended. And nobody swiped as much as a can of sardines or a box of crackers.

Train robberies? Yes, by the score. And stage holdups—you bet—thirty times in six months between Abilene and Ballinger. Cattle rustling? Certainly. Some half a million head in thirty years. Horse thieving? Why sure—100,000 head in ten years! A westerner might hold up trains and stages and he might steal horses or cattle, but he wouldn't stoop to petty thievery.

The West's old days and old ways are no more, but there is in the making a New West Code, a set of unwritten laws, a book of etiquette to a great extent patterned after the old. This is the code of conduct being formulated by a new breed—the rodeo hand, the successor to the cowboy of old. This new breed has surpassed his predecessor in the physical skills—riding, roping, and so on. Thanks to the advances in medicine, vitamins, and better chuck, the cowboy sits taller in the saddle than ever before. Let us hope he will measure up to the old-timer in qualities other than physical—in integrity, in honesty, and in loyalty.

1. "Filipino wonder" refers to any flimsy, skimpy sort of bedding, and must have originated among cowboys returning from duty against the Philippine Insurrection at the turn of the century. The Filipinos, as I understand it, slept on fiber mats of some sort with no covering. Cowboys were impressed with a returning stranger who had heard the owls hoot and had a new word to add to their limited vocabulary. So "Filipino wonder" slipped trippingly on the tongue. My Uncle Fisher, who was too young to have made the Insurrection, was the only man I ever heard use the term, and so I know he must have picked it up from an older cowboy.

The Cowboy Enters the Movies
MODY C. BOATRIGHT

BY 1908, when the migration of the movies from the arcade to the improvised theater was virtually complete, the popular animus against the cowboy had disappeared, and the greatly augmented mass audience was ready to accept him as hero. Movies of cowboys were being produced, but other Westerns predominated. Films of white-Indian conflict, such as *Pioneers Crossing the Plains* (1908), in which the grandfather of the heroine takes the news of the Indian attack to her lover;[1] *In Old Arizona* (1909), in which the message reaches the cavalry by carrier pigeon; and *Custer's Last Stand* (1909)[2] are typical, and suggest the influence of Buffalo Bill's Wild West.

What is apparently the first stellar role played by a horse occurs not in a cowboy picture, but in a story about Daniel Boone (1907). Boone is taken prisoner by the Indians and is bound to a tree to await burning at the stake in the morning. During the night, when the Indians are asleep, his horse gnaws his bonds loose. Boone mounts and rides for the stockade, the Indians in hot but unsuccessful pursuit.[3]

Several cowboy pictures were produced in 1909: *Stampede*, "praised for its accurate depiction of Western ranch life," *Pet of the Big Horn Ranch*,[4] and *The Range Rider*, Tom Mix's first picture.[5] But the man who claimed with some justice to have invented the role of cowboy as screen hero was G. M. Anderson, who in 1903 had played in the history-making *The Great Train Robbery*. In 1948 he recalled that he had ridden a horse (he failed to ride him upon first attempt), been a passenger on the train who was killed, as well as the bandit who shot him, and as fireman he had fought with another bandit.[6] This exceedingly popular three-minute show, filmed in New Jersey, combined several elements that were to become the stock-in-trade of the horse opera: there was a violent crime; men were killed; there was a chase (a mounted sheriff's posse pursuing mounted criminals); the criminals were apprehended and brought to justice.

After acting briefly for other companies, Anderson, in partnership with George K. Spoor, founded the Essanay Company located in Chicago. In 1908 Anderson opened a studio at Niles, California, for the production of Westerns. He was looking for an actor to play the lead role in a succession of pictures—one who would be recognized by the audience and whose name would draw a crowd. Failing to find such an actor, he took the role himself. By appearing in chaps and spurs and by adopting the screen name of Broncho Billy, he proclaimed the cowboy. He was the first of the cowboy screen heroes. Between 1908 and 1915 he produced nearly five hundred one- and two-reel Westerns, more than anyone else, establishing the genre.

Important, too, was his decision to establish a studio in California. First, the atmosphere was then clear and smogless, and little time was lost on account of bad weather. Second, space was available without paved roads and telephone poles, and the scenery itself had an appeal independent of the story—an appeal later to be exploited by color films. A third advantage was the availability of cowboys from the ranches, expert riders and ropers who could be hired cheaply to form outlaw bands and posses. Harry Stephens remembers doing such work for the old Bison Company. He and other cowboys would ride over the hills as fast as their horses could run, shooting ahead for a while, and then turning to fire behind them. When the film was cut and put together, they were both the fleeing outlaws and the posse.[7] Anderson, never an expert rider, employed a cowboy for the distance shots, appearing only in the closeups. A cowboy could be hired to fall off a horse for a dollar, and bulldog another rider for two dollars.[8] With these wage scales, there was no reason to ration the number of redskins and bad men who bit the dust.[9]

In opening a studio in California, Anderson was abreast of the trends. William Selig had visited Los Angeles and decided to move there from Chicago. Other companies established branch studios at San Diego and Santa Barbara. The concentration in Hollywood began in 1913 when Jesse Lasky, Samuel Goldfish (later Goldwyn), and Cecil B. DeMille rented a barn on property fronting on Sunset and Vine.[10]

Most of the Broncho Billy films have been lost. Enough reviews and summaries of these and other cowboy films of the period remain, however, to indicate the development of the genre. As the most popular and prolific actor and producer Anderson was a primary influence in defining the roles the cowboy hero was to play. These roles are the ones that a cowboy might play without losing his identity—ones in which he could ride a horse, dress in cowboy garb, and use a six-shooter. Sometimes he drove cattle, but such work, if it occurred at all, was, except in a few early documentaries, purely incidental.

The three principal roles were the Good Bad Man, the Mounted Officer of the Law, and the Knight Without Armor.

1. *The Good Bad Man.* This character is in the tradition made popular by Bret Harte. Underneath the bad exterior lies a nobility that needs only to be awakened by the love of a good woman, a child in distress, a community terrorized by a brutal bully. The Good Bad Man may reform and be forgiven, or he may sacrifice his freedom or his life for another.

2. *The Mounted Officer of the Law.* He may be the sheriff, the deputy, or the Ranger who eventually gets his man.

3. *The Knight Without Armor.* The cowboy who, as private citizen, protects and avenges the weak, especially women.

These are the standard roles as they had evolved by 1913. There were also what were later to be called "off-beat" pictures, particularly comedies, in which the cowboy was the anti-hero, often the victim of the tenderfoot.

In order to illustrate the sources of information as well as to indicate what the movies meant to their reviewers, I shall quote rather extensively from contemporaneous reviews containing summaries of the action.

1. The Good Bad Man

The Outlaw and the Child (1911). A story which has for a background the great Mojave desert in California. The principal character is a little girl, scarcely more than a baby, daughter of the sheriff. She is found by an outlaw [Broncho Billy] whom the sheriff is pursuing and is taken to her father's home. The terrible sufferings in the desert are too much for the man and he succumbs before he can be aided. The ending is commended. It never seems quite right for a sheriff to break the law by allowing an outlaw to escape, as has been represented in some cases, merely because he performed some service for which the official might have felt indebted to him. This ending is more satisfactory. The sheriff is left under no obligation and the outlaw is removed from the society which he menaces.[11]

The implication of the review that the bad man usually escapes punishment is borne out by the files of the *Motion Picture World*. More typical is *Broncho Billy's Redemption* (1910).

Broncho Billy, our hero, in this instance, is a bad man of the first water, cattle rustler, black knight of the road, and his depredations number countless midnight raids on stray cattle bunches, stage holdups in lonesome mountain passes, and a few shooting-up affairs. However, Billy's record is getting too strong for even the sheriff of the county and a posse is organized to take the bad man in his lair. Yet Billy does not lack friends as is evidenced by the following note from an unknown friend.

Friend Broncho:
    The Vigilante Committee suspect you of cattle rustling. The Sheriff is on your trail. You will stretch hemp if you are caught.
                                                A FRIEND

[He rides away] . . . An hour later he draws rein at a prairie schooner outfit, pulled up under the trees in a little grove, the horses cropping the grass round about and a sweet faced girl cooking coffee over a campfire. In the wagon an old man is lying and he is informed by the girl that her "daddy is sick."

She gives him a cup of coffee and he rides away. She takes her father to a deserted shanty, where Billy visits her. Her father is in need of medicine for which she has a prescription. Billy takes it, promising to send her the medicine. He meets a Mexican to whom he gives the prescription and money. The Mexican, however, tears up the prescription and pockets the money.

Later Billy sees an unattended herd of cattle, and he cannot resist driving them away. He has not gone far, however, when he sees the wagon again and finds it empty. He abandons the stolen cattle and hurries to the shanty. There he finds both father and daughter unconscious. He places them in the wagon and drives speedily to town and stops at the doctor's office.

Then he turns to the sheriff and holds out his hands, but this officer of the peace hesitates . . . and finally ends by telling Billy he is free to go if he will promise to mend his ways. The bad man, redeemed, shakes the sheriff's hand and gives the promise.[12]

Other exemplifications of the Good Bad Man include *Man to Man* (1911), in which the bad man under arrest joins in fighting off an Indian attack, and, having the only unexpended bullet when the Indians are driven off, hands his gun to the sheriff, who lets him go;[13] *Jack Mason's Last Deal*, in which a gambler, finding out that the man he has ruined is the father of a girl he loves, plays a last game in which he lets his victim win back the money he has lost;[14] and *Why Broncho Billy Left Bear County* (1911), in which the bad man assumes guilt for a robbery committed by the father of "the girl who appealed to his heart and his rough chivalry," restores the stolen money, and, responding to the love of the girl and to the message of the Bible she has given him, changes his way of life.[15]

No detailed explanation is given for how the Good Bad Man becomes a criminal, but the implication is that he is basically a good man who needs only to be confronted with a situation that will call forth this latent goodness: a child or a woman or a sick man in distress with no other help available, the law and the outlaw attacked by a common enemy, the love of a good woman. The intensity of the internal conflict between the desire to remain free and the demands of humanity or love cannot be determined by the synopses. Nevertheless such conflict is assumed, and is especially evident in *Broncho Billy's Redemption*, in which the crucial decision is made.

2. The Mounted Officer of the Law

The Smuggler's Daughter (1912). Silas Gregg, a western mountaineer, makes a living by smuggling goods from Mexico. His pretty daughter,

Vedah, loves young Brant Graham [Broncho Billy], who is about to be sworn in as deputy sheriff. The opening scene shows him telling Vedah of his appointment, while Silas Gregg, in an adjoining room, listens to the story. Brant then leaves for the sheriff's office to get his badge. Silas comes into the room where Vedah stands happy over her lover's good fortune, and she tells him about it. Silas then joins his confederates in the barn.

Brant's first assignment is to identify and break up a gang of smugglers. He avows his love for Vedah, but she will not accept his ring without her father's consent. They go to the barn to look for him. Peeping in, Brant sees him and his companions handling smuggled goods. He tells Vedah that her father is the head of a gang of smugglers and that his oath and duty compel him to arrest him. He enters the barn with drawn pistol, and the smugglers hold up their hands. Then Vedah pinions his arms, and he is taken by the outlaws. Silas takes Vedah to the house, tells her that Brant must die, returns to the barn. Vedah mounts her horse and rides for the sheriff.

A posse headed by the sheriff, and accompanied by Vedah, ride furiously towards her home. Round the base of the frowning heights and through patches of forest, the mad gallop is continued until a halt is made in front of the Gregg barn. A rush is made into the smuggler's den, and none too soon, for one of the outlaws is aiming straight at Brant's heart. A wholesale arrest is made, and Brant is released and complimented for his courage.
    On arrival at the barn door, Vedah saw at a glance that her father was not present. He had determined at the last moment not to participate in Brant's murder, and returned to the house. There Vedah found him, and revealed that she had brought up the sheriff's posse and saved her lover. In his rage he almost strikes her, but, unheeding she begs him to mount his horse and fly beyond the border. She persists in her entreaties and he is convinced that it is his only hope. He is about to leave when she begs for a last kiss. He refuses. She begs again, and hurriedly he presses his lips to hers. Then he mounts and speeds away.
    When Brant joins Vedah, she points him to a horse and rider that appear as a speck on a steep slope in the distance. Silas Gregg has passed the border line. "I'm glad that your dad is safe across the border," said the deputy earnestly as he took her to his heart.[16]

The Sheriff's Decision (1911). Steve Jameson, a cowboy, is having a lonely meal on the range one day when suddenly he is surprised by a stranger, who rushes out of the bushes and begs, in an excited manner, for food. The newcomer is a Mexican and his strange demeanor and excited manner suggest to Steve that he may be a fugitive. Hastily bolting the food and water the young fellow runs on, while Steve looks after him curiously. Not until ten years later do they meet again. Steve, who is now sheriff of the county, is in love with a Mexican girl, Nita Sanchez.

There are other suitors, but Steve seems to be winning until

. . . One day a Mexican musician, giving the name of Manuel Garcia, comes to town and is taken by the boys to play for Nita. Nita soon loses her heart to the young troubadour and the two plan an elopement. As they leave the Sanchez home, however, they are surprised by the sheriff, who finally resolves to give up the girl to the man she loves. All this time Steve has been puzzling over the Mexican's face, which seems hazily familiar to him. Try as he will, however, he is unable to recall where he has seen the young Mexican before, until, when he arrives back in town, he is handed a telegram from the sheriff of a neighboring town, asking him to arrest one Manuel Garcia wanted for a murder committed some ten years before. Like a flash the truth comes to Steve and he recalls the chance meeting between him and the fugitive ten years before. Quickly turning his horse, Steve rides to the country parson's home, arriving just in time to stop the wedding and to arrest Garcia. Despite Nita's pleas to release her lover, Steve refuses to yield and drags the criminal with him to jail.[17]

In *A Romance of the Rio Grande* (1911) the hero is a Texas Ranger on the trail of a gang of Mexicans who are smuggling liquor across the border and selling it to the Indians. Finding that the drunken Indians have captured a rancher and his daughter, the Ranger's sweetheart, he gathers a posse of cowboys and arrives in time to save the rancher from burning and to overtake the captors of the girl.[18]

The role of the sheriff in *On the Mexican Border* (1910) is to prevent the cowboys of the Bar-B-Bar Ranch from lynching the Mexican abductor of the ranchman's daughter, whose sweetheart is not the sheriff, but the leader of the cowboys.[19]

In this respect the sheriff is not typical of the good peace officer of the movies of the period. For in the majority of my samplings the lawman is somehow emotionally involved. If the criminal is the father or the brother or the uncle of his sweetheart, he must undergo an internal struggle of love versus duty. Duty must always win, but the action is so contrived that the loved one or his sweetheart escapes punishment through no dereliction on the part of the officer. Thus he has his cake and eats it too. If the crime is committed by his rival in love or by a criminal not related to the girl, his urge to duty is reinforced by love, and when the guilty man is brought to justice he is likely to enjoy the double satisfaction of having done his duty and won his lady.

3. THE KNIGHT WITHOUT ARMOR

Circle C's New Boss (1911). Ethel Hanna resides in the East. Her Uncle William is a wealthy ranchman living in Arizona. One day a lawyer comes to Ethel and gives her word of her uncle's demise, and the further information that she is his sole legatee. With beating heart she calls her maid and packs her belongings and sets forth on a long journey to the West to claim her inheritance.

Her uncle had died in a wild paroxysm of rage brought about through the conduct of his foreman, Steve King, and some disorderly cowpunchers of the place. Steve, who is an unscrupulous fellow, is quick to take advantage of his employer's sudden death, so he immediately sets about confiscating some valuable documents, including the last will and testament of the old ranchman. The assistant foreman, however, one Harry Newton, a young cowpuncher of sterling worth, frustrates the evil designs of the foreman, and rescues his late employer's property from the hands of the villain.

Ethel arrives at the ranch in time to witness a quarrel between Steve and Harry. She interferes. Steve, unaware of her identity, brutally challenges her right to interfere. He does this to his sorrow, for the next minute he is discharged, and driven from the place by the cowpunchers under orders of their new mistress.

Harry is now made foreman, having won favor in the eyes of the girl from the East. He, in turn, appoints Jack Wilson his assistant, and Jack straightway falls in love with Hanna [sic] Ethel's maid, who has accompanied her on the trip to the West. In the meantime, the villainous ex-foreman plans to circumvent the new mistress and get her in his power. By a subterfuge he succeeds in getting her away with him on horseback. Then comes a wild ride, with Harry Newton and the rest of the boys in a fierce chase. Subsequently a fight to the death occurs, between King and Newton, in which the latter is victor. It is not to be wondered, then, that the fair Ethel bestows her hand and her fortune on the dashing Harry.[20]

The New Cowboy (1911). A Western picture the principal feature of which is the sound thrashing a bully gets because he forces his unwelcome attentions upon a girl and attempts to compel her to marry him. Her lover is informed of what is transpiring by her little brother. There is a wild ride and a good pommeling for the persistent suitor at the end. It is a novelty to see cowboys use their fists instead of firearms.[21]

The happy marriage of the girl rescued and her rescuer may be regarded as the normal ending of the two-reel films of the period. But the sentimental novels of Mrs. E. D. E. N. Southworth, Augusta Jane Evans, and their like were still being read; gift books containing "sad" poems were still to be found on parlor tables; young men and women still gathered around the parlor organ to sing "I'll Be All Smiles Tonight" and "They tell me, father, that tonight you wed another bride," or played "Hello, Central, Give Me Heaven" on the phonograph; and unlettered folk sang "Barbara Allen" and "Little Joe the Wrangler." It is not surprising, then, that the cowboy Knight did not always arrive in time.

The Cowboy and the Artist (1911). The story of how an artist deceived a single Western girl and apparently left her in hopeless misery. The discarded lover is asked by the girl to find the artist, who is lost in a canyon. He does so, bringing him back to the ranch. The artist has written a note directing whoever finds his body to notify his wife. This note the cowboy presents to the girl. The girl, realizing the enormity of the offense she has committed, turns to her mother for comfort, while the cowboy orders the artist to be gone.[22]

The Puncher's Law (1911). Tom Patterson, a young puncher, becomes engaged to Ethel Hastings, a pretty Western girl, just preceding Patterson's departure with the other punchers for the big fall roundup. A few weeks later, Ethel meets Jack Ferguson, a strolling gambler, whose apparently ardent and sincere love turns the girl's head. Following her promise to marry Ferguson, Ethel meets Tom at the roundup, and gives him back his ring. Heartbroken, Tom releases her and leaves the ranch. Only a few weeks elapse when the girl realizes her terrible mistake in marrying the gambler. She is ill when Jack tells her he has decided to leave her. Despite her pleas for him to remain he goes away. Some time later, Ethel locates her husband, and going to him begs him to take her back, but he thrusts her out of the house and the heartbroken girl, stumbling away, drops in the grass, where she is found in a dying condition by Tom Patterson. He soon learns the truth, and after the girl dies he seeks out Ferguson, and at the point of a gun makes him come to the shack and view the frail body of his former wife. Patterson then gives Ferguson the choice of a vial of poison or a bullet from his Colt, and the latter, seeing that escape from death at the hands of the enraged man would be fruitless, swallows the poison.[23]

In *Broncho Billy's Love Affair* (1912) Billy, a cowboy on the Circle C Ranch, and the foreman, Dan Wild, are both in love with the ranchman's daughter, Winnie Allen, who favors Billy. Wild gets Billy discharged, steals Winnie's engagement ring, and forges a note breaking the engagement. The unsuspecting Billy leaves the country. Several years pass. Wild takes Winnie's few remaining dollars, goes to town, becomes involved in a quarrel, kills a cowboy, and is himself wounded. Broncho Billy, who has now returned and been elected sheriff, arrests him. Wild, knowing that his wound is fatal, confesses his treachery. Broncho promises to see that Winnie will be taken care of.[24]

But the rule was for the Knight to arrive in time and save the woman. Sometimes, as in *The Mesquite's Gratitude* and *The Arizona Kid*, in both of which the women are Indian maids, the victim is a stranger to him, and his intervention is therefore prompted by a disinterested chivalry.[25] But generally he has loved the woman before the crisis, and has a personal as well as a chivalric and humanitarian motive in defending her.

The Cowboy as Non-Hero

Not all cowboys in cowboy movies are heroes. When the cowboy is a Good Bad Man, a Mounted Officer of the Law, or a Knight Without Armor, another cowboy may be the villain, and others may be subordinates of the hero and villain. There is little in the early movies to support the primitivistic idea that living in the great open spaces, riding a horse, and working with cattle will in themselves produce nobility of character.

The cowhand's provincialism, his rusticity, furnished a basis for comedy. Three basic plots exemplify this theme: (A) The Triumph of the City Slicker, (B) The Taming of the Bully, (C) The Tenderfoot Makes Good. These are illustrated below.

(A) *The Trimming of Paradise Gulch* (1910). The most absolutely new and original Western ever put in picture form. We find a little mountain tavern near the foothills where the cowboys and the rangers were wont to spend their spare time when they were not chasing a steer. One nice summer day the camp is all in turmoil; the stage had arrived and among its occupants was a young lady, demure and sweet, several residents thereabout and a smooth-looking chap of the city type who afterwards proves to be a vendor of cheap jewelry and is out for a harvest. Nell, the young lady in question, establishes a school in art, recognizing the cowboy clientele as excellent material to further her scheme. She soon has them all paying her homage—willing to take lessons in order to admire the teacher. They are suddenly seized with the idea of making her presents of rings and jewelry, little dreaming that the dark horseman in the background selling the rings was none other than her husband.[26]

(B) *Crazy Gulch* (1911). The cowboys of the I X L Ranch delight in seeing "Bad Bill," of Crazy Gulch, display his eccentricities. On this occasion, the cowboys are loafing in front of a saloon, when Bill rides up and cleans out the place. This pleases the boys, so they suggest that they go to the San Juan Sanitarium and have some fun.

Bill frightens a number of the patients; but when he attacks Percy, who has a mania for manicuring his nails, he meets his Waterloo, for Percy completely subdues him with blows. The cowpunchers now come up, salute Percy reverently, and assist Bill from the ground, while Percy resumes his manicuring and strolls away.[27]

(C) *Peaceful Jones* (1909). William Jones, a poor Eastern lawyer, goes to Arizona to grow up with the country. He arrives at Red Dog and puts up at the Palace Hotel. The proprietor of the Palace has a pretty daughter Belle, well named, as every man in the community is in love with her. Belle likes Jones largely because of his quiet, amicable manner, which wins him the nickname of "Peaceful" Jones. But when "Ugly Bill," a rival, strikes Jones with a whip and Jones fails to resent the insult, the girl calls Jones a coward and refuses to speak to him. Later a delegation of cowboys wait on "Peaceful" at his cabin and offer him a pistol with which to fight it out with "Ugly Bill." Jones refuses to fight, saying, "I am a peaceful man." The cowboys shove a rail under Jones and ride him out of town. A band of Indians out for trouble encounter the cowboys, fire on them, and a battle follows. The cowboys "drop" a number of redskins, but three of their number are wounded, and they draw lots to see who shall go for assistance. "Ugly Bill" is selected, and he has hardly started before he is shot. Now is "Peaceful" Jones' chance to show his real mettle. He rescues Bill, takes Bill's revolver and goes through the deadly passage for help. After two terrific hand-to-hand fights with the Indians, Jones comes up with a company of Uncle Sam's soldiers, who are engaged in signal practice. A word to the lieutenant and the soldiers dash to the rescue, and they come up just in time. Their ammunition gone, every man wounded, the cowboys are making their last stand. Just as the Indians dash toward them, the soldiers come up, led by "Peaceful" Jones. Two volleys from our gallant soldier boys drive the Indians up the cliff, leaving their chief and ten warriors with horses for the "Happy Hunting Grounds." And now that he has time to think of himself, Jones remarks quietly: "Boys, I guess I was hit," and the good-hearted fellow falls upon the ground. The soldiers pick up Jones and the wounded cowboys and carry them to the fort. A month passes, and Jones is the central figure at a celebration over his recovery. "Ugly Bill" is chairman, and he voices the sentiment of Red Dog when he says, "Peaceful, you're the best man in town." Then Bill leads the girl down to Jones and leaves them in each other's arms.[28]

The Anatomy of the Early Cowboy Film

There was probably more variety in the early two-reel cowboy pictures than in the features that succeeded them. Trends toward standardization, however, are clearly discernible in a structural pattern and a set of conventions. When Anderson began making his Broncho Billy movies, there was still a lively interest in mere motion—in a picture that moved. There was an interest in the western landscape, and Congress and the public were responding to President Roosevelt's demand for the preservation of virgin forests and natural wonders. There was also a popular interest, both promoted and exploited by Buffalo Bill, in horsemanship. The scenario writer or director could appeal to all these interests by providing a simple plot with plenty of riding through scenic country. In a few pictures the plot was nothing more than an occasion for presenting a rodeo on the screen. In one such picture, *Frontier Day in the Early West*, the exhibition of riding is followed by a horse race, suspense for which is created by one contestant's drugging the jockey of the young lady whose horse is reputed to be the fastest entry. The climactic scene shows her dressed as a man riding her own horse to victory.[29] In another, *The Broncho Buster's Rival*, a strange cowboy attracts the favorable attention of the heroine by his exhibition of bronc-riding. The hero shows him up as a bad man, and "the usual chase follows."[30]

The "usual chase" was in most Western films the most conspicuous and exciting part of the action, the chief variety being whether the spectators' sympathy lay with the pursuer or the pursued. The massive pursuit was typical of the military picture in which the cavalry, flag flying, arrived just in time to drive off the Indians with considerable slaughter, as the pianist pounded out martial music. In the cowboy pictures there were posses, but not infrequently it was one rider against another. A knowledgeable scenario writer need not limit himself to one wild ride. In *The Smuggler's Daughter*, already cited, there are three, but no pursuit. The girl rides to notify the sheriff; the sheriff and his posse ride to the smuggler's barn, arriving just as one of the outlaws is about to pull the trigger and send Broncho Billy to his grave; the chief of the smugglers, the girl's father, rides to make his escape into Mexico. Riding under an extreme handicap is illustrated by Indian Pete in *The Girl of the Triple X*, who with both hands tied behind him mounts his horse and reaches the ranch in the nick of time to prevent the lynching of an innocent man framed by his rival in love.[31] The running fight, although more common in the military Western, occurs also in the cowboy movie. In *The Half-breed's Plan*, the girl learns that the half-breed plans to rob her father as he returns with money from the sale of cattle.

Mounted on a fleet horse [she] gallops home and secures aid, and the cowboys by desperate riding rescue Dick and the old man, who are engaged in a running fight with their pursuers. One by one the desperadoes are picked off until they are all captured or wounded.[32]

Obviously the chief setting was the out-of-doors. The saloon, usually without the dancing girls, was an important interior, but it had not become universal. More frequent was the ranch home of the heroine. Barns, cowboy shacks (line camps), hotel lobbies, and schoolrooms occur.

The hero, whatever his role, did not have to be a paragon of puritanical virtue. He might drink and gamble and perhaps engage in the innocent pastime of shooting up the town. In *The Attack on the Train*, a cowboy being sent to jail for such an offense is rescued by his comrades, who hold up the train and release him. In *Broncho Billy's Last Spree*,[33] drunken and disorderly conduct is again treated with comic indulgence. Billy rides into town with his savage war whoop, staggers into the saloon, drains a bottle, and goes down the street. He rips off the coat of an old ranchman, makes an Englishman dance to the tune of his six-shooter, sends the hotel guests flying from the lobby, and breaks up a church meeting. The sheriff is notified, and Billy mounts the nearest horse and flees ahead of the posse. The sheriff finds him at home sleeping off his spree.

In the meantime an elderly lady arrives from the East looking for her son, William Jones. A photograph she carries shows that her son is Broncho Billy. The sheriff pretends that Broncho is sheriff and he the prisoner. The old lady gives him a Bible and admonishes him not to drink and to be a good man like her son. The sheriff goes on vacation after appointing Billy to serve as deputy for the duration of his mother's visit.[34]

Another film, however, is little more than a temperance tract. "A cowboy, committed to a two-year probation period by his sweetheart after a drunken debauch which resulted in his prospective father-in-law's death, becomes a parson and returns to marry the girl."[35]

The woman in the early cowboy movie existed primarily to provide the love interest, but she was not merely a passive creature to be awarded the hero at the end. My investigations confirm the finding of George Fenin and William Everson that the woman of the early Westerns "was shown as the full-fledged companion of the pioneer and possessed an inner strength that made her his superior."[36] The conventions of the cowboy movie demanded nubile women. Matrons are few, and mothers of marriageable daughters fewer. When they exist they either furnish opposition to the cowboy suitor, as in *The Cowboy and the Easterner,* in which the mother's opposition ceases when the eastern man is exposed as a coward, or they comfort the erring daughter as in *The Cowboy and the Artist.*[37] But more often the mother is just not there. The heroine is a ranch girl keeping house for her widowed father or unmarried uncle. The removal of the mother simplifies the action and implies a close relation between the girl and her father or unmarried uncle. It explains her love of the land, her joy in the out-of-doors, and her expert horsemanship. She rarely uses firearms, however. One of the few exceptions is in *Western Girls,* in which two sisters returning from town see two stage robbers dividing their loot. They slip away unseen and ride to the ranch, but finding no one there, they put on cowboy clothes, return, get the drop on the robbers and are bringing them into town with nooses around their necks when the sheriff arrives.[38] In another movie a girl being held for ransom effects her own escape, not only from the bandits but from the boarding school to which she was being unwillingly sent.[39] In another the schoolteacher insists upon a trial, which she conducts in the schoolroom, and prevents the lynching of an innocent man.[40] This is one of many movies in which the girl saves her man, usually, as here, her lover, but sometimes her husband or father or uncle. Most often she achieves this by a wild and desperate ride. In *The Mesquite's Gratitude* it is an Indian girl whom the hero has protected who takes a note to his friends.[41] In *The Cowpuncher* the girl sees her lover and brother under Indian attack and rides to the ranch for help.[42]

The villain as an artist in evil who glories in his art for art's sake is less frequent in the early cowboy movies than readers of the dime novels would expect. The most common misdeeds are crimes against property prompted by greed. Cattle rustling, strangely enough, is rarer than robbery. One scenario writer managed to bring in claim jumping, a tradition of the mining West, by making oil the mineral.[43] A character rare in her time, but one to become well known to later moviegoers, is the female gold digger. This one seduces a married man and drives him to the verge of suicide. His brother marries her, not for love of her but for love of her victim.[44]

About a third of the crimes attempted and committed are motivated by passion, equally divided between love or lust and revenge. The offenses of men against women include various kinds of unmanly conduct—excessive familiarity and the like, seduction, attempts to compel marriage, and extreme cruelty and wife desertion, examples of which occur in synopses already given.

Seekers of vengeance are usually rejected lovers or discharged cowboys or foremen. I find no example of the criminal returning to do in the officer who sent him up. The common acts of vengeance are kidnapping and framing. The victim of the kidnapper is usually, though not always, a woman, the female member of the love triangle, or the ranchman's wife, niece, or daughter, as in *Circle C's New Boss*, already cited, and *A Red Man's Bravery*, in which a friendly Indian overcomes the kidnapper and returns the girl to her sweetheart.[45] In *The Cattle Rustlers*, a couple of cowboys steal cattle and frame the foreman—the foreman who has discharged them,[46] and in *The Angel of Contention*, the sheriff makes a false charge of murder against his successful rival in love.[47]

Excluding racial conflicts to be noted later, the crimes and misdemeanors of the early cowboy movies are overwhelmingly individual crimes, individually motivated. Social conflict is apparent in only one film in my sampling. In *The Invaders*, a story based on a novel by John Lloyd, which is based in turn upon the Johnson County War of 1892, the conflict is between the large ranchman and the settlers. The writer, unlike Owen Wister, takes the side of the settlers. The cattlemen import a killer; a stranger, a tenderfoot from the East, appears and aligns himself with the settlers. The killer soon learns that the stranger is more than his match and plans to shoot him from ambush. At this point the cattlemen decide to import a hundred gunmen from Texas and drive the settlers off the land. The battle is beginning when, in accordance with historical fact, the army intervenes.[48]

The early cowboy movies show little hostility to Mexicans and Indians. There are Mexican criminals on the border and a half-breed Indian bandit, but even criminal Mexicans are capable of gratitude. In *The Lucky Card*, for example, a member of a gang of bandits, recognizing a victim as a man who had been a good Samaritan to him years before, helps him escape at the risk of his own life.[49] The majority of evildoers are Anglos. Hostile Indians provide crises to furnish suspense and afford opportunities for heroic action, as in the case of *Peaceful Jones* and *Man to Man*. But when Indians appear as individuals they are good, as in *The Girl of the Triple X, Red Feather's Friendship, The Mesquite's Gratitude*, and *A Red Skin's Bravery*. In *The Kid from Arizona* the gratitude of an Indian girl whom the hero befriended is the source of complication. As a token of gratitude she hands him a handkerchief which enfolds stolen money. Rather than betray her he flees, but when he is taken and charged with theft, she confesses.[50]

It is clear that violence was stock-in-trade for the cowboy Western from its beginning. Yet as one reads the synopses, he is impressed with their comparative moderation. In *The Invaders* casualties are limited to two men and a woman shot by mistake; in *The Red Devils*, a story involving an acrobatic troupe, cowboys, Indians, and cavalry, we are told that the soldiers "scattered" the Indians, but not how many if any were killed is indicated.[51]

In *Peaceful Jones* the Indian dead total eleven. In *The Halfbreed's Plan* all, an unspecified number, of the desperadoes are captured or wounded. In *The Cattle Rustlers* one rustler is killed and one escapes. Pistol duels to the death occur as in *Circle C's New Boss* and *The Sheriff's Sisters*, in which the victim draws first, but there are no sundown or high-noon ultimatums and no walkdowns with tense spectators waiting to see the show.

In a majority of the films a solution is achieved by something short of death. In *Broncho Billy and the Maid* there is a mutual wounding followed by a reconciliation; the fist fight, later to become a convention, is emergent. In *The Kid from Arizona* the hero, challenged by the bully to take off his gun, does so and wins the fight. Several innocent men barely escape lynching, one guilty one is lynched, and two sheriffs prevent lynching of guilty men.

In the early cowboy movie there is a rough, but only a rough, approximation to poetic justice; it was not yet a morality play in which the right always won, in which the good were rewarded and the evil punished. It has been shown already that "sad" endings were permissible, and that bad men sometimes went free as a reward for some noble act with or without an implied reformation. Death or imprisonment was by no means the universal doom of the wrongdoer. If he was the father of the heroine he almost invariably went free, though he might be removed from the community by a flight to Mexico. The girl in *The Blotted Brand* who altered the brand on her father's calves to that of her lover's, in order to hasten the time when her lover's herd would equal a third of her father's and he would consent to her marriage, received parental blessing.[52] Both the sheriff who gambled away the money he had recovered from a stage robbery and the robber who kept his promise to go to jail, but did not promise to stay there, went free. The gold digger came off pretty well in marrying her victim's brother. The Indians who were incited to hostility by liquor bought from a smuggler were punished, but the smuggler went free.

In *On the Border* Monte Joe, an Anglo, and Monte Pete, a Mexican, have been rivals in love. Pete is the winner. Later in Mexico Joe falls into Pete's power, and Papinta, the woman, helps him escape. "Joe realizes that it would be folly to leave the girl behind, so induces her to cast her lot with him. A thrilling dash for freedom closes this excellent story."[53] It is not clear whether Papinta will get a divorce, commit bigamy, or live in sin. Had a moral solution been demanded in those pre-Hays times, it would have been a simple matter to have Joe make her a widow.

1. *Moving Picture World*, III (July 4, 1908), 11.
2. George N. Fenin and William K. Everson, *The Western, from Silents to Cinerama* (New York, 1962), p. 56.
3. *Moving Picture World*, I (April 6, 1907), 74-75.
4. Fenin and Everson, p. 57.
5. Olive Stokes Mix (with Eric Heath), *The Fabulous Tom Mix* (Englewood Cliffs, N.J., 1957), pp. 68-69.
6. Ezra Goodman, "The Movies' First Chaps and Spurs," *New York Times*, October 10, 1948, sec. 2, p. 5.
7. Memoirs of Harry Stephens, unpublished.
8. *Time*, April 29, 1946, p. 94.
9. Philip Koury, "Rationed Violence," *New York Times*, October 9, 1949, sec. 2, p. 5.
10. Benjamin B. Hampton, *A History of the Movies* (New York, 1921), pp. 78-116.
11. *Moving Picture World*, VIII (March 11, 1911), 540.
12. *Ibid.*, VII (July 2, 1910), 25.
13. *Ibid.*, IX (September 2, 1911), 626.
14. *Ibid.*, VIII (April 22, 1911), 905.
15. *Ibid.*, XVII (September 27, 1913), 1371.
16. James S. McQuade, review, *Motion Picture World*, XIII (February 1, 1912), 233-34.
17. *Moving Picture World*, IX (September 30, 1911), 988.
18. *Ibid.*, X (December 9, 1911), 832.
19. *Ibid.*, VII (December 10, 1910), 1367.
20. *Ibid.*, VIII (May 12, 1911), 1089.
21. *Ibid.*, IX (August 26, 1911), 543.
22. *Ibid.*, IX (September 23, 1911), 892.
23. *Ibid.*, IX (September 9, 1911), 728.

24. *Ibid.*, XIV (December 28, 1912), 986.
25. *Ibid.*, X (October 19, 1911), 144; VIII (March 23, 1911), 662.
26. *Ibid.*, VI (May 28, 1910), 900.
27. *Ibid.*, VIII (May 12, 1911), 1088.
28. *Ibid.*, V (August 28, 1909), 295.
29. *Ibid.*, VI (April 9, 1910), 577.
30. *Ibid.*, VIII (May 27, 1911), 1208.
31. *Ibid.*, VIII (January 7, 1911), 36.
32. *Ibid.*, VIII (February 18, 1911), 378.
33. *Ibid.*, VI (April 9, 1910), 566.
34. *Ibid.*, IX (September 2, 1911), 632.
35. *Ibid.*, VII (August 13, 1910), 373.
36. Fenin and Everson, p. 40.
37. *Moving Picture World*, VII (August 27, 1910), 485; IX (September 23, 1911), 892.
38. *Ibid.*, XIV (December 21, 1912), 902.
39. "Billy the Kid," *Moving Picture World*, IX (August 5, 1911), 308.
40. "The Schoolmarm of Coyote County," *Moving Picture World*, VIII (March 23, 1911), 662.
41. *Moving Picture World*, X (October 14, 1911), 144.
42. *Ibid.*, VIII (June 10, 1911), 1327.
43. "The Claim Jumpers," *Moving Picture World*, X (October 7, 1911), 41.
44. "Men of the West," *Moving Picture World*, VIII (April 8, 1911), 788.
45. *Moving Picture World*, VIII (June 10, 1911), 1327.
46. *Ibid.*, VIII (March 23, 1911), 662.
47. *Ibid.*, XXI (July 25, 1914), 555.
48. *Ibid.*, XVIII (August 23, 1913), 827.
49. *Ibid.*, VIII (May 27, 1911), 1205.
50. *Ibid.*, VIII (March 23, 1911), 662.
51. *Ibid.*, IX (September 9, 1911), 621.
52. *Ibid.*, IX (September 2, 1911), 31.
53. *Ibid.*, V (November 27, 1909), 773.

Billy the Kid, Hired Gun or Hero

JOHN O. WEST

THE LINCOLN COUNTY WAR, which erupted with six-gun violence in New Mexico in the late 1870's, has provided historians with a vast amount of material to sift in arriving at the truth. Mixed with the partisan accounts of events furnished by both sides—and virtually no one could remain neutral and stay in the territory—is an enormous resource of folklore that has grown up about Billy the Kid. Without this war, the American pantheon of outlaw divinities would be lacking one of its shiniest halos, that of "Saint Billy the Kid," as C. L. Sonnichsen once called him.[1] Without this war, the cold-blooded killer might never have been heard of, and historians, folklorists, and garrulous old codgers would have had much less to concern themselves with.

Billy was, in every full account, a major participant in the Lincoln County War. Doubtless some people, convinced that Billy was ever eager to help old ladies across the street and to perform other Boy Scout duties, believe that the Lincoln County War is but another instance of the Kid's aiding his fellow man. They believe that he fought in the war much as knights of old went out to right the world's wrongs and to erase evil from the face of the earth. As evidence in support of this view, there are the recollections of Mrs. T. F. Ealy, wife of a minister who served in Lincoln during the bloody days of the 1870's. As she recalls, "McSween [leader of Billy's side in the war] seemed to have all the best people of the town with him."[2] In an attempt to give both sides, however, one must also note a different view, that "the better element rallied to the side of Murphy and Dolan," who were two fine young men.[3]

In the face of such contrasting opinions, we must accept the position that they were "all, all honourable men," or else believe what the evidently impartial judge wrote to Territorial Governor Lew Wallace: "The troubles have arisen from two contending parties both in my opinion equally bad, each having in its employ professional assassins."[4]

The history of the Lincoln County War is much too long and complex to relate here. Suffice it to say that there were two factions: Alexander McSween led one, and Thomas Murphy and James Dolan led the other. Reliable historians indicate that it was a war of economic interests. Murphy and Dolan resented the loss of business produced by the opening of a rival store by McSween and his intended partner John Tunstall. Both establishments also served as banks, and each had conflicting cattle interests as well. When Murphy and Dolan attempted to bankrupt the other firm through legal maneuvers, short tempers and quick trigger-fingers finished the job.[5]

Tales and reminiscences of old-timers have not presented a clear picture of the Lincoln County War. There is even variety of opinion as to who fought, and why. Some remember it as a cattleman-sheepman fight, which it was not. Others claim it was between Anglos and Mexicans, but Mexicans are listed among the participants on both sides. Several see it as retaliation by cattle baron John Chisum against organized rustlers presumably in the employ of Murphy and Dolan—but at least one modern researcher claims that Chisum did not take part in the war, and ordered his cowhands to stay clear of the action.[6] Nevertheless, the war was fought, and Billy the Kid was involved in it.

The purity of the Kid's motives in the Lincoln County War has been questioned frequently. A detailed account in the Las Vegas *Optic* for June 10, 1881—only a few weeks before the Kid's death at the hand of Pat Garrett—said that Billy was hired by Chisum, and that Chisum had failed to pay for services rendered; consequently, Billy rode up to a quartet of Chisum cowboys around a campfire, killed three out of the four, and sent the survivor to Chisum with the report that the Kid was allowing a credit of $5.00 per man, and would call the account square after killing Chisum himself.[7] This story, in one form or another, has been repeated in almost every account of the Kid's activities, although the origin of the debt, and the rate of pay, vary considerably. Usually Chisum has hired the Kid at from $5.00 to $15.00 per day—either to rustle cattle or to fight against rustlers. Governor Lew Wallace, in his autobiography, says that Chisum, besieged by rustlers, "recruited about 70 men—murderers, thieves, and dangerous men of all classes . . . ," without mentioning the Kid as one of them.[8] J. L. Hill, an old-time cowboy of untrustworthy memory, recalls that the Lincoln County War was between sheepmen and cattlemen, and that the Kid's first duty as Chisum's hired gun was to kill "Black Smith." (This name, as such, occurs nowhere else that I have seen in the lore of the Kid; however, the Kid is traditionally supposed to have killed *a* blacksmith!) Hill recalls, further, that Chisum was the leader of a gang of rustlers, and that the Kid was feared because he "was said to be a little weak minded."[9]

Nat Love, a Negro who claimed he was Deadwood Dick, reported that the Kid was rustling cattle *for* Chisum;[10] Ike Fridge has the Kid on the other side, raiding Chisum's herds.[11] In the account of another old-timer, John J. Callison, the Kid was rustling cattle from a ranch that turned out to be the property of the James and Younger Boys, and Billy barely escaped with his life.[12]

Perhaps the wildest account of Billy as a hired gun comes from Lloyd Lewis' book *It Takes All Kinds*; in that work old-timer Tom Blevins says that "Old Charley"—probably meaning John Chisum—hired the Kid at $10,000 a year to steal 10,000 cattle from "Blank"—probably meaning Murphy. In addition, the Kid was to get $200 per month for herding cattle and a bonus of $1,000 per man for killing Mr. Blank's cowboys.[13] For once, cattle were cheaper than men.

In the midst of all this confusion, perhaps there was one reliable witness—if *anything* he says can be believed. He was Brushy Bill Roberts, who at the age of 91 presented himself as the still-living Billy the Kid. His recollection was that Chisum offered him a dollar a head for retrieving cattle rustled by Murphy, and Chisum joined McSween in offering him $500 to join their gunfighters. Brushy Bill—or Billy the Kid, if you prefer—continues:

I gathered up some of the boys and hung around Fort Sumner picking up cattle which belonged to anyone who could round them up. We were accused of stealing cattle. So was Murphy and Chisum. The only difference between us and them was that they stole them wholesale and we just took them as we needed them.

As the war continued, Brushy Bill said, Chisum proved to be untrustworthy:

With Tunstall and McSween dead, Old John thought he could get out of paying us off, but he didn't, he didn't. We told him if he didn't pay us that we were going to run off enough of his cattle to pay what we thought he owed us. We cut cattle out of his herd and he didn't do anything about it. We got our share, and more too, maybe. But who knows?[14]

Implied support, partially at least, for both the debt and the Brushy Bill account exists in a newspaper interview with Billy the Kid, secured when the outlaw was in jail overnight in Las Vegas, New Mexico. The Kid's words are brief on this matter, but pointed: "Chisum got me into all this trouble and then wouldn't help me out."[15] In a long letter to Governor Lew Wallace, Billy told the same story: "J. S. Chisum is the man who got me into Trouble, and was benifited [sic] Thousands by it and is now doing all he can against me."[16]

In discussing Billy the Kid's short but eventful life, his chroniclers have made up for the scarcity of dependable details by accepting any fancy, and adding to it. Thus inspired, they go on to greater and more fantastic endeavors—even today when historical research has produced many dependable facts. One of the earliest books on Billy the Kid, written by Edmund Fable,[17] contains an account of what passes for the Lincoln County War—if it is scrutinized carefully with both eyes closed. Following is a brief résumé, with some of the more lurid passages in all their purple glory.

After a series of adventures which have convinced the Kid that all his efforts to lead an upright life have failed, he meets a group of herders led by John "Tontsill," whose "mild and gentle disposition made him the prey to the cattle thieves that swarmed the border." (The border, per se, was well over a hundred miles away.)

Billy is hired, and goes the next day with a gang of men to retrieve stock stolen from Tontsill; the boss is killed, and Billy flees. Back in camp, matters are taken in hand by one of the hired men—a fellow named "Chisom." His plan is simple:

Boys, they've given the old man his dose and left him dead among the cactus. . . . I'm damn sick of the thing myself and if stealing is to be the game in this country, and seems to be the only one that wins, why I'm in favor of going in with the rest of you, dividing the old man's cattle fairly among us all, electing a leader and take to the plains.

When Billy accepts the plan, the others also go along. After the first raid on a herd, Chisom takes the stolen cattle into Las Vegas to sell and turns the gang in to the sheriff. When one of the men returns out of loyalty to tell Billy, the Kid is furious, swearing vengeance on Chisom with an oath that recalls the splendor of the medieval curse: ". . . so long as I live I'll follow that man. So long as I live I'll follow his people. I'll kill his cattle. I'll kill his herders. I'll not spare anything until I have squared the debt he has created by betraying us all today." With the help of McClosky, the gang member who had revealed Chisom's treachery, the Kid captures two of Chisom's men, Morton and Baker, and ties them. The Kid seems ready to kill the two but McClosky objects to killing bound prisoners—so Billy shoots him from behind. Then he considers his situation:

In front of him were two living witnesses to his savage crime. Why should they live to tell the story of that night? Had they not deserved a similar fate?

. . . .

The moon at its height looked down on his cruel, savage face. Looked down on the pallid countenances of the two men bound to their horses. Its brightness caught a gleam from the glittering barrel of the leveled weapon as it was directed at the head of Morton. Crack! Crack! Its shrill notes rang through the night accompanied by the agonized cry of two dying men. The deed was done, and the Kid had added two more human lives to his list of victims.

Some time passes, and finally Billy's gang gets word of rising temperatures in Lincoln over a will leaving money to a woman represented by Lawyer "McSwain," money claimed by Murphy, Dolan, and Reilly. The ensuing trouble is called the Lincoln County War.

"I've a damn good notion to enlist," quietly interrupted the Kid.
"On which side," eagerly asked O'Phaller, who having finished his story, was now cooling his throat with a drink of brandy.
"On McSwain's, of course," answered the Kid. "For the woman every time."

Anyone familiar with the career of Billy the Kid can point out that three men named McCloskey, Baker, and Morton were killed—the latter two possibly by the Kid—but the circumstances were entirely different. Billy did have a friend, O'Folliard, whose name was garbled to produce O'Phaller. Likewise the *will* is a familiar matter in the events leading up to the Lincoln County War, but hardly as presented by Fable.[18]

Lest anyone think, however, that the author was an untruthful man bent on embellishing tales about the Kid, Fable's preface offers a disarming avowal of intent:

Whatever merit this volume may possess, attaches, in the estimation of the author, altogether to the accuracy of the events narrated and the correctness of the details connected with the career of "Billy the Kid." There has been no necessity to draw upon a vivid imagination to enhance its interest, for without any of the blazonry of humbug or the embroidery of fiction, the true history of "Billy the Kid" eclipses any border romance, and dims by comparison the tales woven from the realms of fiction.

With such wild tales as those of Fable being passed off as truth, there is little wonder that the story of Billy the Kid is filled with puzzles, inaccuracies, and downright lies. For instance, one old-timer claimed Billy killed forty-five men;[19] Fable's account lists only twenty-six; Sheriff Pat Garrett reduced the total to twelve.[20] But Ramon Adams, dependable bibliographer and student of the Kid's legend, counts only four killings by the Kid as certain, with six others as possible. Of the total of ten, three men were killed while unarmed, two were killed from ambush, and one was killed after Billy had rotated the half-empty cylinder of the man's revolver so that the hammer would fall on empty chambers twice before a cartridge was in position for shooting. Only four were killed on fairly even terms.[21] Despite the facts, the recurring total is almost always cited as one for every year of his life—usually "twenty-one men, not counting Mexicans and Indians." And even the exclusion of Mexicans from the total seems to have no point, since Billy's "biographers" (if they can be called that) almost unanimously note that he was always friendly with them, and New Mexico Governor Miguel Otero quotes a survivor of the Lincoln County War as saying, "In all his career, he never killed a native citizen of New Mexico."[22]

Concerning some of the feats Billy is said to have performed—both in and out of the Lincoln County War—a grain of truth sometimes exists, although the tale is more often one of vivid imagination or in the dime novel pattern. Even so, truth occurs in the least likely places. In Fable's book, for instance, Billy is said to have been arrested—unjustly, of course—as a lookout in a store robbery. He escapes from the jail through the chimney, a feat made possible because of his slight build. Such incidents smack of the dime novel; however, the earliest known newspaper account of his deeds, even before he gained notoriety, concerned his apprehension as a lookout during a robbery of two Chinese—and he did, in fact, escape from the jail on that occasion via the chimney. This news item is all the more striking when one notes that the Grant County *Herald* in publishing the story calls Billy by his almost-unknown real name, Henry McCarty.[23] Without such a source of verification, Fable's account of the arrest and escape would appear to be pulp-writer's fantasy, but it is almost accurate in all important details.

Adherence to truth, however, has never been a requisite for folk acceptance. When one has—or creates—a hero, outstanding exploits are a necessity, to be manufactured if lacking. One of the best feats accorded Billy is his ride of 81 miles at night, through desert, river bed, and danger, on his trusty gray horse. He was riding, according to the story, from Mesilla, New Mexico, to San Elizario, Texas, downriver from El Paso, to free a friend from jail, and took only six hours for the entire trip. Pat Garrett evidently told the story first;[24] Governor Miguel Otero swallowed it whole;[25] Erna Fergusson repeated the tale as gospel;[26] and Harvey Fergusson made the story even more fabulous by extending the distance to 125 miles in the same six hours.[27] Billy's ride of 81 miles in six hours averages thirteen and one-half miles per hour, on one horse. By comparison the records of the Pony Express, ordinarily held up as outstanding riding, become less glorious. The ride of "Pony Bob" Haslam of 120 miles in eight hours and ten minutes (average, fourteen and two-thirds miles per hour) is less impressive when one realizes that Haslam used several horses, while Billy used only one. The Pony Express had begun with remounts provided every 25 miles, but soon shortened the distance to ten or twelve miles, since even the finest stock the mail company could buy would not last 25 miles at top speed.[28] To add luster to Billy's feat, one writer even had the Kid stop off in Franklin (as El Paso was then known) to rest his horse; he even "had a few drinks of whiskey and fed 'Gray' some crackers, *there being no horse feed at the saloon.*"[29]

The hero's prowess with his chosen weapon must also be outstanding, and Billy the Kid had the required skill, whether it was with the sword he drew to fight his way out of a band of attackers in one early account,[30] or the more usual Winchester or six-gun. In one reported escape from a hideout surrounded by lawmen, Billy emerged from shelter with "two Winchesters and two six-shooters in both hands and the bullets was goin' so fast they was passin' each other in the air!"[31] Another tale suggests that Billy bore a charmed life: "The first man out with his revolver and snapped it twice at the kid. The kid out with his revolver and shot him six times before he touched the floor. He began to fall at the first shot."[32] Even in his final hour in Pete Maxwell's bedroom, when the "charm" had evidently worn off, Billy's speed was evident, according to an old-timer who speaks as an ardent disciple: "Garrett fired and the first shot hit the kid's heart, and the next went in the ceiling, above their heads. The kid fell and took out his revolver. They say if his heart would have beat one more time he would have killed Garrett."[33]

Pat Garrett, Lincoln County sheriff who killed Billy, supplied a vital element in the elevation of the Kid to outlaw sainthood—the Judas. Almost every chronicler claims that Pat and Billy had been friends, and the story is preserved in the familiar ballad: "Shot down by Pat Garrett who once was his friend,/ The young outlaw's life had now come to its end." Several writers have reported that Pat and Billy had been partners in a rustling operation only a few months before Pat turned lawman.[34] Governor Otero, Billy's most ardent supporter, explained that although Pat and Billy were "carrying on the same line of business," Pat was about to branch out in a new line:

> Pat was more cunning than the Kid. He saw an opportunity to make a big haul, so he quietly negotiated with Captain J. C. Lea, John S. Chisum, and several large cattlemen on the Rio Pecos for his election to the office of sheriff with the distinct understanding that he was to get rid of the Kid.[35]

Although Pat had difficulty collecting the $500 reward promised by the governor, private citizens made up a purse of about $900 for him.[36] The facts, of course, are never enough in a retold tale. The "Judas money" has been reported as high as $12,000 from the state and $32,000 from the cattlemen's association—a far cry from thirty pieces of silver.[37]

So Billy was killed, the Judas was rewarded, and the Kid's sainthood was assured—but someone is always trying to rock the boat. For example, when Jesse James came West incognito he ran into Billy, who suggested that they form a partnership. But the longer they talked, the more Jesse "became convinced that he wanted nothing to do with such a miserable piece of flesh." The Kid was no bank or train robber; he merely stole horses and cattle, shot unarmed men, and killed Mexicans and Indians. Jesse could see that they simply weren't the same type.[38] Such professional jealousy, of course, disenchants no true devotee of the Kid.

Recent efforts at enlarging the degree of Billy the Kid's sanctification, undertaken by the television industry, have only intensified efforts begun much earlier in Hollywood. Mr. Sonnichsen tells of one such attempt, in what was perhaps the earliest movie made of the Kid's career. Hired as technical advisor was Mrs. John W. Poe, an authority on the Kid by virtue of her husband's having been "outside on Pete Maxwell's porch while Pat Garrett was inside exterminating the Kid." The excesses of the movie script appalled Mrs. Poe. "Why, I knew that little buck-toothed killer," she said, "and he wasn't like that at all!" The movie director replied sympathetically, "I know how you feel, Mrs. Poe, but this is what the people want."[39] In support of Mrs. Poe's status as an expert, it might be appropriate to point out that although her husband had never seen Billy before the fatal night,[40] Mrs. Poe might have known the Kid.

Billy the Kid—hired gunman, or knight in shining armor? The known facts show him to have been a horse thief, gambler, cattle rustler, and hired gunman who shot men from behind. But despite the efforts of historians to search out the truth, the process of legend-making goes on, even to the point of causing people to brag about the dirty tricks Billy used—like "examining" the gun of a man he later expected to have a showdown with. Folks can't be stopped from believing what they want to. If they need a hero, they'll make one, no matter how raw the materials. And in the case of Billy the Kid, the materials are pretty raw.

1. C. L. Sonnichsen, "The Myth of the Old West," an address delivered February 19, 1963, at St. Edward's University, Austin.

2. Mrs. T. F. Ealy, "Recollections of Old Lincoln," *New Mexico*, XXXII (March, 1954), 43.

3. Arthur Chapman, "A Cowboy War," *Outing*, LVIII (April-September, 1911), 499.

4. Letter of Judge Warren Bristol to Governor Lew Wallace, October 5, 1878, quoted in William A. Keleher, *Violence in Lincoln County 1869-1881* (Albuquerque, 1957), p. 187.

5. Warren A. Beck, *New Mexico: A History of Four Centuries* (Norman, 1962), pp. 164-66; Keleher, pp. 31-108, *passim*.

6. Georgia B. Redfield, "Billy the Kid Rides the Chisum Trail," *The Cattleman*, XXXII (March, 1946), 32.

7. Reprinted in *Billy the Kid: Las Vegas Newspaper Accounts of His Career, 1880-1881* (Waco, n. d.), p. 22.

8. Quoted in Ramon F. Adams, *A Fitting Death for Billy the Kid* (Norman, 1960), pp. 214-15.

9. John L. Hill, *The End of the Cattle Trail* (Long Beach, California, [1922?]), pp. 43-44.

10. Nat Love, *Life and Adventures of Nat Love* (Los Angeles, 1907), p. 119.

11. Ike Fridge, *History of the Chisum War; or, Life of Ike Fridge* (Electra, Texas, n. d.), pp. 17-19.

12. John J. Callison, *Bill Jones of Paradise Valley, Oklahoma* (Kingfisher, Oklahoma, 1914), pp. 149-52.

13. Lloyd Lewis, *It Takes All Kinds* (New York, 1947), p. 102.

14. C. L. Sonnichsen and W. V. Morrison, *Alias Billy the Kid* (Albuquerque, 1955), pp. 29, 32.

15. George Fitzpatrick, "Interview with Billy the Kid," *New Mexico*, XXXII (September, 1954), 41, reprinting an item from the Las Vegas *Gazette*, December 28, 1880.

16. The letter is reproduced photographically in William L. Hamlin, *The True Story of Billy the Kid* (Caldwell, Idaho, 1959), Plates XXI-XXIV [pp. 372-75].

17. Edmund W. Fable, *Billy the Kid, the New Mexican Outlaw; or, The Bold Bandit of the West* (Denver, [1881]). Only one known copy of this work exists, that in the Boston Athenaeum.

18. Keleher's account, pp. 32-38 and 40-41, is reliable.

19. Lewis, p. 117.

20. Patrick F. Garrett, *The Authentic Life of Billy the Kid* (Norman, 1954), running count.

21. Adams, pp. 29-30.

22. Miguel A. Otero, *The Real Billy the Kid* (New York, 1936), p. 172.

23. Frazier Hunt, *The Tragic Days of Billy the Kid* (New York, 1956), p. 8; Adams, p. 11. Despite Fable's near accuracy, he calls the Kid *Bonney*, the most usual alias employed by Billy.

24. Garrett, pp. 31-35.

25. Otero, pp. 19-22.

26. Erna Fergusson, *Murder and Mystery in New Mexico* (Albuquerque, 1948), p. 52.

27. Harvey Fergusson, "Billy the Kid," *American Mercury*, V (June, 1925), 225.

28. Glenn D. Bradley, *The Story of the Pony Express*, ed. Waddell F. Smith (San Francisco, 1960), pp. 50, 73-74, 101.

29. Charles Siringo, *The History of Billy the Kid* (n. p., 1920), p. 20. (Italics mine.)

30. Quoted in Adams, p. 47.

31. James M. Cook and T. M. Pearce, *Lane of the Llano* (Boston, 1936), p. 89.

32. Will Hale, *Twenty-Four Years a Cowboy and Ranchman* (Norman, 1959), p. 42.

33. Lewis, p. 117.

34. Mary Hudson Brothers, *Billy the Kid* (Farmington, New Mexico, 1949), pp. 17-18; John M. Scanland, *The Life of Pat Garrett* (El Paso, 1908, 1952), pp. 16-17, leaves the same impression, as does Hunt, pp. 218, 232.

35. Otero, pp. 92-93.

36. Keleher, p. 304 n.

37. Lewis, p. 117.

38. Homer Croy, *Jesse James Was My Neighbor* (New York, 1949), pp. 145-46.

39. Sonnichsen, "The Myth of the Old West."

40. Garrett, pp. 143-44.

Laureates of the Western Range

EVERETT A. GILLIS

NOT ALL THE SONGS the cowboy sang came to him from the great anonymous resources of oral tradition. He knew songs, too, written by his fellow cowboys, who had for one reason or another turned their hands to the writing of verse about the life and adventures of the range. James Barton Adams, Charles Badger Clark, N. Howard Thorp, Phil LeNoir, Henry Herbert Knibbs, and others less well known published poems which became the familiar possession of range riders and trail herders, who memorized them and sang them, or copied them into their scrapbooks from newspapers and magazines, or treasured their favorites in dog-eared copies of the little paperbacked collections of the cowboy versifiers—thus absorbing them into their own oral tradition of songs and recited verse. Often enough, these same songs turn up in the standard anthologies of cowboy songs, having been discovered by field collectors, who return them by way of such collections once again to the printed page.

Frequently, as may be seen by comparing them with their originals, such pieces show the authentic stamp of folk usage. As Alice Corbin Henderson observes in her introduction to the 1920 edition of Thorp's collection:

> . . . songs originally printed, clipped from a local newspaper or magazine, fitted to a familiar air, and so handed down from one cowboy to another . . . [become] genuine folk-songs in the process. During the transition a certain amount of reshaping often takes place. Verses may be added or left out or the wording altered—these changes usually tending toward a greater simplicity and directness and a more graphic cowboy lingo.

According to John A. Lomax, cowboys often sent him songs which he recognized as having already been in print although his informants themselves were unaware of the author's name; one instance was "The Cowboy's Christmas Ball" by Larry Chittenden, an eastern newspaper man who retired to a working rancher's life in West Texas. Lomax also discovered several songs of N. Howard Thorp in oral circulation and published them in his 1910 edition of *Cowboy Songs and Other Frontier Ballads;* the best known of these, "Little Joe, the Wrangler," he had found in several Texas versions. Thorp had published this song, with four others of his own composition, along with a number he had collected, in *Songs of the Cowboys* in 1908. Another case of a published poem finding its way into oral tradition is a ballad generally known as "High Chin Bob," written by Charles Badger Clark, who spent four years in Arizona as a ranch manager, composing cowboy poems in his leisure moments. Originally published as "The Glory Trail" in Clark's volume of verse *Sun and Saddle Leather,* the poem appeared in *Poetry: A Magazine of Verse* two years later as a genuine product of the cowboy's singing art. Clark relates the incident in the preface to the 1920 edition of his book. After expressing his amazement at this unusual phenomenon, he modestly admits that the folksong version is "in some points more striking and easy than my more labored original, and I believe it is better known."

The printed sources through which authored songs of this sort were absorbed into oral tradition range from the published volumes of verse already mentioned to less ostensibly literary repositories: newspapers, popular magazines (especially Westerns), stock journals, scrapbooks, and the like. The following list of verse collections, all of which are typical, could be multiplied: Clark's *Sun and Saddle Leather;* Chittenden's *Ranch Verses;* George B. German's *Cowboy Campfire Ballads;* Curley Fletcher's *Songs of the Sage;* several volumes by Henry Herbert Knibbs; and Thorp's *Songs of the Cowboys*—the final edition of which included not only seventy-five songs he had gathered from oral sources in the course of his many years of collecting, but nearly thirty which he had himself composed.

Popular magazines such as *Adventure* and *Wild West Weekly* provided another source for the entry of printed songs into the folk repertory. These particular magazines carried special verse departments, which solicited both original material and authentic folksongs (usually referred to as "old songs") which their readers might possess—though the line drawn between the two in the minds of the editors of such "song corrals" might be conveniently thin. As part of his efforts in search of Western songs John Lomax frequently thumbed the pages of *Wild West Weekly* (he cites it five times in *Cowboy Songs* as a song source); and as some of his papers deposited in the Library of Congress reveal, he himself occasionally contributed folksongs to "Fiddling Joe's Song Corral" in this periodical. Fugitive poems from magazines undoubtedly found their way often—via the clipping process or in scrapbook versions—into the capacious songbag of the cowboy singers.

Newspapers, because of their wide availability to the general public and the frequency of their publication, were likewise suppliers of materials for the folk domain. Western versifiers, cowboy or otherwise, found the verse corners in daily or weekly newspapers good depositories for their literary efforts. Both Lomax and Thorp, as well as other collectors, cite newspapers as a source of many of the songs contained in their collections.

Not all the cowboy poets involved in the process just described were necessarily working cowboys. As a matter of fact, the term may be used to cover a variety of figures ranging from writers associated only loosely with cowboy life to the almost anonymous "stove-up" ranchers or cowboys who in their new-found leisure reminisce of the good old days in fairly passable verse. In between are the working cowboys themselves, who, whiling away the tedium of line fence riding or night herding, or inspired by some urgent event such as a stampede or the violent death of a friend, or perhaps simply spurred by the routine episodes of their day's work, make up a verse or two to some tune borrowed for the occasion from the traditional stockpile of melodies and afterwards sing their creation around at various gatherings until it becomes known by many. With this type, the process of creating is perhaps less obviously a matter of self-conscious verse-making than with the other two, and possibly it is the nearest of the three to the well-spring of the great body of anonymous songs comprising the cowboy song tradition.

Three figures will suffice to illustrate the types just mentioned: Clark, Thorp, and a cowboy balladist named Charlie Johnson, who is described by J. Frank Dobie in an article in one of the early publications of the Texas Folklore Society.

Although a westerner, having been born in Dakota Territory just before the turn of the century, Charles Badger Clark was a cowboy for only four years, when as a young man he managed a small ranch near Tombstone, Arizona. Here, he says, inspired by the vigor of ranching life and the wild beauty of the land, he began his writing career. After his sojourn as a cowboy, Clark returned to his native Black Hills. From 1937 to 1939 he was official state poet of South Dakota; he died in 1957. His two collections of verse, *Sun and Saddle Leather* (1915) and *Grass Grown Trails* (1917), contain sixty-two poems, the bulk of them lyrics, with several striking ballad-like pieces. On the whole, Clark's poems offer a fair cross-section of cowboy life and mood in pleasant, facile verse. At least three of them have been found in oral circulation as songs: "The Glory Trail," "A Cowboy's Prayer," and "A Border Affair."

The working cowboy turned poet is perhaps best illustrated by N. Howard Thorp, and we are fortunate to have his adventures in song-making and song-gathering recorded in "A Banjo in the Cow Camps," a chapter in his autobiography *Pardner of the Wind*. A New Mexican cowhand with a hankering after songs, Thorp in the spring of 1889 decided to drop his customary livelihood for awhile and drift through the countryside looking for opportunities to swap songs with whomever he might happen to meet—and to return to the homespread, as he informed his boss, "when he saw my dust arrivin'." This, one of the first of such adventures, took him some fifteen hundred miles through New Mexico and Texas cow country, and furnished him a handful of authentic range songs. His motivation and qualifications for the trip are described in his autobiography as follows:

Songs of the range had a special appeal to me. I was a singin' cowboy myself, by adoption, with a little mandolin-banjo that went where I went, and the songs I heard some cowboys sing were an authentic feature of the land and life that made it seem good to me. Sometimes on the trail or in camp I would think up a song of my own.

Several years later, in 1908, Thorp made a dicker, as he puts it, with an Estancia, New Mexico, printer to print two thousand copies of songs he had found in his travels.

I paid the printer six cents per copy. The book was printed on rough stock and bound in red paper. There were fifty pages, twenty-four songs. I advertised in some Kansas papers that published patent sheets, and sold a good many of the books at fifty cents apiece. They were fragile, and most of the copies probably were torn to pieces or lost long ago, the few that are left fetch twenty-five dollars or so from collectors.

Five of the twenty-four songs in the pamphlet were Thorp's own; in the much larger 1920 edition (the book most familiar to students of cowboy songs) the number of Thorp's own compositions increased to twenty-seven. In most cases Thorp did not make up the tunes to his songs. As he says of his compositions in his autobiography:

The cowboy hardly ever knew what tune he was singing his song to; just some old, old tune that he had heard and known as a boy. Very often the old familiar airs were used. Both "Little Joe, the Wrangler" and "Little Adobe Casa" were sung to the air of "Little Old Log Cabin in the Lane." "Sky High" was sung to the tune of "Solomon Isaacs"; "Overland Stage" to the air of "Song of Gambo-leer." "The Little Cowgirl" was sung to the tune of "Turkey in the Straw"; the people of Texas didn't know the national anthem, but they all knew "Turkey in the Straw."

Just how many of Thorp's own songs got into oral circulation is hard to determine. As already noted, five of the songs in the 1908 edition of Thorp's book were included by Lomax in his 1910 collection. (Thorp in his autobiography virtually accuses Lomax of lifting the songs bodily from his 1908 pamphlet; the 1938 edition of Lomax's book gives Thorp full credit for the authorship of the poems.) Many more of Thorp's songs, considering the nature and wide geographical distribution of his book, must have slipped into the folk domain. As Alice Corbin Henderson states in the introduction to the 1920 edition, *Songs of the Cowboys* in its first issuance had its chief sales, "not at the news stands or book stores, but, like the old broadside ballads, at cow-camps and the round-ups and cattle fairs."

The retired cowboy who turned to reminiscing in verse about the good old days may be illustrated by Charlie Johnson, a Texas cowhand and trail driver whom J. Frank Dobie used to meet at the annual Old Time Trail Drivers' reunions in San Antonio. Johnson knew many cowboy songs himself and usually brought a composition of his own to recite before the Trail Drivers' Association meeting. He was born and reared in South Texas in the brush country in the 1860's and spent many of his mature years as a working cowboy and trail driver. The songs created by such old drivers and waddies as Johnson are strongly sentimental and nostalgic in tone, typically summarizing the standard routines of cattle-country life rather than concentrating on a specific event as is habitual in folk ballads, though they are nonetheless full of concrete factual detail. As an example here is Johnson's own poem, "The Old Cowboy," published in 1925 in the *Frontier Times*.

> I rode a line on the open range,
>   When cowpunching wasn't slow;
> I've turned the longhorned cow one way,
>   And the other the buffalo.
>
> I went up the trail in the eighties—
>   Oh, the hardships I have stood!
> I've drank water from a cow track, boys,
>   When you bet it tasted good.
>
> I've stood night guard many a night
>   In the face of a driving storm,
> And sang to them a doleful song,
>   While they rattled their hocks and horns.
>
> But many a boy I worked with then
>   Is sleeping on old Boot Hill;
> For his last cow drive was made to Dodge
>   Over the Jones and Plummer trail.
>
> I've been in many a stampede, too;
>   I've heard the rumblin' noise;

> And the light we had to turn them by
> Was the lightning on their horns.
>
> They're building towns and railroads now,
> Where we used to bed our cows;
> And the man with the mule, the plow, and the hoe
> Is digging up our old bed grounds.
>
> The old cowboy has watched the change,
> Has seen the good times come and go—
> But the old cowboy will soon be gone,
> Just like the buffalo.

Charlie Johnson may be cited also in connection with another common aspect of the "authored" cowboy songs—the tendency to associate a song with a specific individual as its creator, whether he happens to be or not, with perhaps little or no grounds for the association. There may be several reasons for this. One, certainly, is a cowboy's own claim of authorship of a given piece. Johnson, for instance, Dobie reports, sometimes "made up songs," as he said, which were actually not of his own composition; but as Dobie points out about the ballad "The Cowboy's Stroll," which Johnson said he had made up, in the realm of folksongs "made up" probably means little more than "made over." "The Cowboy's Stroll," a song which was popular on the trail while Johnson was driving and which derived from a Confederate ballad entitled "The Rebel Prisoner," certainly may have been fitted to the cowboy format by Johnson himself. Such adaptations were common practice. Another possible reason why a specific name becomes attached to a song is that a singer may have learned a song from the singing of someone he has known or met and thereafter tends to associate the song with the latter as *his* song—to such an extent that he is felt to be its actual creator.

In these or similar ways numerous songs in the standard cowboy collections have no doubt been credited to certain people, most of whom are little more than names. Thorp himself notes of the song "A Cow-Camp on the Range"—"Authorship credited to Tom Mew, Oklahoma"; of "The Cowboy's Dream"—"Authorship ascribed to father of Captain Roberts, of the Texas Rangers"; of "The Rambling Cowboy"—"Author supposed to have been K.

Tolliver." Even the familiar "Cowboy's Lament" or "Streets of Laredo"—definitely a cowboy adaptation of an Irish stall ballad—receives such an acknowledgement in Thorp's volume, being accredited to a certain Troy Hale of Battle Creek, Nebraska. One such accreditation in Lomax's collection, of "The Zebra Dun," is just vague enough to be believable: "This song is said to have been composed by Jake, the Negro camp cook for a ranch on the Pecos River belonging to George W. Evans and John Z. Means." At least the ranch is specific. Another accreditation in Lomax shows more about the process of ascription than it does about the originator. His informant for "The Buffalo Skinners," J. S. McCauley of Seymour, Texas, wrote him of this piece: "Song made by Buffalo Jack. I don't know the author or how it come to be wrote, or anything of that kind, but they must have been somebody of that name for a starter."

The phenomenon of the cowboy poets—the "poet lariats" as someone has aptly termed them—offers an interesting sidelight on the rich tradition of Western range verse. Their casual launching of verses into the vigorous stream of cowboy song, though slight, perhaps ultimately furnished some of the songs and tunes cherished by the common hard-working cowboys who—to quote a stanza from a cowboy song—

> Galloped and sang
> The long day through,
> Shortened the trail
> By the songs they knew.

J. Frank Dobie on Folklore

PASSAGES COLLECTED BY
WILLIAM D. WITTLIFF

NO SINGLE CLASSIFICATION truly fitted J. Frank Dobie; none was broad enough. He was at once many things—cowman, folklorist, storyteller, writer, teacher, philosopher, naturalist, humanist, fighter for individual freedom and for everything he judged right and decent—all in his own maverick manner. He was a *paisano*—fellow countryman—to all who "would do to ride the river with."

But most people, in our time at least, will think of him first of all as a storyteller. In youth he "gloried in nothing but the pageantry of the past"; he filled himself with the traditional stories and legends—of animals and places and people of long ago—which were a part of that particular plot of earth he always belonged to. Ever reading, listening, observing, experiencing, understanding, and growing, he wove these tales into designs uniquely his own—all strengthened by a perspective that came to be universal in reach rather than merely regional. This was his genius; the result was art. He approached his materials as an interpreter rather than as a literal recorder, and his larger purpose was the enrichment of life.

Over the years Dobie made many statements about folklore in general. A number of these statements are brought together here. The arrangement is topical rather than chronological; it is designed to reveal a sequence of thought, beginning with Dobie's basic attitude toward the subject. The extracts are taken from his many contributions to the "Publications of the Texas Folklore Society" and from other sources. In folklore and storytelling, as in everything he did, he never ran with the herd.

1. I have never had any idea of writing or teaching about my own section of the country merely as a patriotic duty. Without apologies, I would interpret it because I love it, because it interests me, talks to me, appeals to my imagination, warms my emotions; also because it seems to me that other people living in the Southwest will lead fuller and richer lives if they become aware of what it holds. *1952*

2. There's nothing duller than praise. There's nothing more stupid than eulogy. *1961*

3. One night after Santos had told what was to me a gripping story about his experience with a *bulto,* a ghostly bulk, that held him flat on his back at a goat camp, I thought of how John A. Lomax had collected cowboy songs and ballads, and decided that I would collect traditional tales of Texas. Texas soon got too small for me, and other coherences came to supersede man-made geographical lines, and life inherent in tales extended itself. I have been listening for and to tales ever since, though I learned to have little truck with the literalists designated as scientific folklorists. *1961*

4. I do not mean that my ambition was ever to write "pure history." Pure history is a naked collection of documented facts; if the facts are patterned into pictures or directed into conclusions, purity is defiled. Yet I am more appreciative of pure historians than I once was. Most of them are teachers, and while they may not open windows they do not shrink intellects, like political school superintendents and academic flunkies of material power. They seek truth and discipline minds, and the pure histories they write are profitable to consulters. Nevertheless, excellence in historical writing comes only when interpretative power, just evaluation, controlled imagination and craftsmanship are added to mastery of facts. *1952*

5. I am a teller of folktales, and as a historian I have not hesitated to use scraps of folklore to enforce truth and reality. *1941*

6. . . . history has no more business interfering with legend than legend has interfering with history. *1930*

7. But what makes history, whether authenticated or legendary, live is that part of it that appeals to the imagination. *1939*

8. Here I am living on a soil that my people have been living and working and dying on for more than a hundred years—the soil, as it happens, of Texas. My roots go down into this soil as deep as mesquite roots go. This soil has nourished me as the banks of the lovely Guadalupe River nourish cypress trees, as the Brazos bottoms nourish the wild peach, as the gentle slopes of East Texas nourish the sweet-smelling pines, as the barren, rocky ridges along the Pecos nourish the daggered lechuguilla. I am at home here, and I want not only to know about my home land, I want to live intelligently on it. I want certain data that will enable me to accommodate myself to it. Knowledge helps sympathy to achieve harmony. *1952*

9. The assembling of the legends of my own state has been with me no light matter, though it has been a joyful business. *1924*

10. We are inheritors of a vast body of tales about cunning coyotes, matchless mustangs, fabulous mines, gigantic bears, phantom stampedes, daring riders, and scores of other phenomena characteristic of our land. We have a well authenticated horseback tradition excelled not even by that of the Tartars and gauchos; at the same time we have headless horsemen as good as any provided by the forests of Germany. We do not have to go to the Eskimos or to Grimm for folk tales any more than the Grimm brothers themselves had to go outside Germany for theirs. *1931*

11. If a piece of ground talks to me so that I want to linger on it, I yearn to hear in detail what it has to say—to learn something about the natural life it nourishes, to follow some of the tracks men have made over it. *1949*

12. You're not going to get tales that linger in the imagination except from people who have time to linger, time to stare at cows or anything else that comes along. In my experience, the best tale-tellers did not spend hours a day in a bathroom scrubbing themselves. *1961*

13. . . . I have always felt a distrust of regionalism as a cult; my ideal regionalist has all along been Shakespeare. *1955*

14. Good writing about any region is good only to the extent that it has universal appeal. *1950*

15. Truth is precious; so is an interesting story, even though the facts therein be overshadowed by fable. *1930*

16. The difference between an encyclopedia of facts and art using knowledge through understanding and craftsmanship is the difference between dull literalness and beautiful truth. *1961*

17. The basic differences within the hordes comprising the human race lie not in color, creed, cranial conformation, linguistics, or belief in the folklore of this or that nationalism. They lie in the realm divided between literalists and people with imagination. I am not a literalist. I do not write to satisfy literalists. *1947*

18. I like folklore because it has color and flavor and represents humanity. . . . *1932*

19. I look for two things in folklore. I look for flavor and I look for a revelation of the folk who nourished the lore. If the lore interests me, I want to know its history; unless it has something of flavor and fancy and smacks of the folk, then it is not likely to interest me. If a thing is interesting, that is all the excuse it needs for being. *1930*

20. Folklore has come to be of two kinds. First, there is the folklore, mainly narrative in form, with human and humanistic values, such as Grimm's *Fairy Tales,* the saga of Deirdre as told by Synge, James Stephens and other Irish writers, and the Uncle Remus tales by Joel Chandler Harris. The other kind of folklore has left humanistic values behind and seems to be recorded for the purpose of affording scientific analysis of plot motifs and folk mores. This kind of folklore is a scientific development of modern times; it has its value, but often the human values of it are as non-apparent as vitality is in a poorly stuffed bird. *1947*

21. Considered scientifically, folklore belongs to science and not to the humanities. When folk and fun are not scienced out of it, it is song and story and in literature is mingled with other ingredients of life and art, as exampled by the folklore in *Hamlet* and *A Midsummer Night's Dream. 1952*

22. Newspaper reporters not infrequently label me "folklorist." I am not a scientific folklorist at all, for after I have heard a tale, I do all I can to improve it. "Do not let your characters talk as they do in parlors but as they might talk." If the characters in an orally told tale do not talk effectively, the business of any writer

who adopts this tale is to make them talk better—with more savor, more expressively of both themselves and the land to which they belong. *1960*

23. I care next to nothing for the science of folklore, which some scholars reverence and which seems to consist of the tedious process of finding out, through comparisons and analogies, that nothing new exists under the sun. The "quavering ditty" that John Masefield's drunken sailor "sang all in a fo'castle tone" could no doubt be traced all around the world and back. To me it is much more profitable to trace "the progress of a king through the guts of a beggar." *1943*

24. My custom is to try to tell a tale as the original teller should have told it. Any tale belongs to whoever can best tell it. *1955*

25. I have an idea that I often know too much for what the average reader regards as good storytelling. *1939*

26. The folkier an anecdote is, the handier it is for passing on. All we writer fellows can possibly do with a story is to retell it, supplying an occasional variation. *1953*

27. There are just three essentials to a good story: humanity, a point, and the storyteller. . . . *1953*

28. Folklore has interested me to the extent that life and life's romance, vitality, flavor, humanity, humor, gusto, drama, songs with tunes and tales without ends, cowchips and stretching rawhide, Bowie knives and quilt patterns and hundreds of other factors of the land I belong to are inherent in it. Folklore to me is an expression of folks, the essence of a cultural inheritance. *1943*

29. I may be wrong, for I have never become a part of the machine age and, therefore, am not modern, but it seems to me that stories about simple times and simple people have more endurance and are more protean than the others. The best ones involve elemental humanity, and their point is never patronizing. *1953*

30. Our ancestors used to sing their songs; now we get a large percentage of singing over radio or from phonograph records, taking them in with about as much activity as a cabbage exercises when a butterfly wings a minuet over it. *1944*

31. The modern anecdote among Hollywood-adoring, radio-stupefied Americans is apt to smell of Hedda Hopper gossip, Walter Winchell pre-war smartness, radio jokesmiths, and beer-bottle horseplay. Old-time pioneer stock, people I have cultivated all my life, are the best tellers of character anecdotes that I know. And character anecdotes are the best anecdotes in the world. *1944*

32. As regards foolishness, there are divers professors of History—branded with more letters than Nig Add's old cow—who delight in nonsense but not one of whom will stand for a gleam of it in history. Folklore in the hands of scholars bent solely on comparative studies and analogues is fully as bad off as history. *1935*

33. Folklore . . . should express the life of the folk; it should reveal the social background; it should suggest raciness, flavor, color in character. If it does these things, its work will be substantive, even though no ballad or play ever makes use of the folk material preserved. *1925*

34. Nothing is superior to flavor and vitality. Folklore that is interesting—whether it be accompanied by footnotes or not—is good to print and preserve. *1930*

35. And folklore, like poetry, romances, music, and art, is meant to be enjoyed. *1932*

36. There are only three forms of folklore that people really enjoy. They are songs, tales, and pithy sayings. The remainder belongs to social history. *1951*

37. Unadulterated superstition is the lowest and dullest form of folklore. Imaginative power, not superstition, makes Hamlet's ghost harrow up thy soul and translates Queen Mab of the fairies into a reality a thousand times realer than any female of the human species pictured in a thousand Sunday newspapers. *1955*

38. Next to catalogues of superstitions, perhaps the most deadening form of folklore is the tall tale that has no other quality than tallness. It has come to be as American as congressional committees to preserve Americanism. As cheap money drives out sound money, it is running the genuine folktale out of circulation. Any adding machine can make one. These tall tales that have no other quality than tallness are as devoid of imaginative qualities, of humanity and charm, as jokes manufactured for the radio and Bennett Cerf's

books. They take their flavor from sawdust and the mass production line. They are never childlike in naturalness and simplicity; they are invariably puerile. I am not talking about tall tales validated by wit and ingenuity, though the best of these rate low unless they are seasoned with the salt of humanity. *1951*

39. Classifying all traditional tales as "tall" shows the debasing effect of jargon on the perceptive faculties. Properly, a tall tale is one of sheer exaggeration. It is usually short of wit and devoid of humanity. It is tolerable only when it brings out characteristics of situation, place, person or some other subject. The most ingenious tall tale ranks below any good anecdote of character, though the almanac-minded manufacturers of humor have driven the character anecdote off the air and out of films in favor of their product. *1955*

40. Jokes, laws, songs, stories, all forms of human expression except those bedded deep in human nature and truth, become obsolete. *1955*

41. Extraordinary folklore develops around only extraordinary characters, though not all extraordinary characters inspire it: Woodrow Wilson and William James, for example. At its best it is spontaneous, coming of its own will, as about Abraham Lincoln and Mark Twain. While such folklore is often false as to fact, it is oftener true to character, illuminating instead of betraying truth. Propaganda assimilated by a folk until it is part of their lore—Japanese belief in the divinity of their emperor, for example—never seems natural and never has charm. White-faced Hereford cattle have been of large economic importance to the western half of the United States; the Hereford is an extraordinary bovine; but there is no folklore of consequence about the animal. The coyote is extraordinary in another way. He is extraordinary as a character, quite aside from economic, political and like importances. He has something in common with Abraham Lincoln, Robin Hood, Joan of Arc, Br'er Rabbit and other personalities—something that sets popular imagination to creating. *1947*

42. The object of humanistic folklorists is not to destroy myths—excepting those held by the paid agents of standardized institutions—but to foster them! *1925*

43. Some tales seem to belong to all races—like ideas of decency to one's fellows. No matter what their origin, if they have vitality, they take the first ship out and travel across oceans and fasten themselves to fresh hosts. *1947*

44. If the science of comparative folklore has discovered anything, it is that the situations in most folk tales are common to all continents and races. *1947*

45. "Have you heard this one?" If it is a real story and not a jokebook gag, and if the teller is an artist, we want his variations just as we go to see *Hamlet* played by every actor who acts in it. *1953*

46. It is my nature to draw out of men anything strange or novel they have within themselves, whether the matter be fact or not. In truth I have no reverence for mere facts. *1935*

47. I have an enormous respect for thought. I surrender all to a storyteller—if he's good enough. It's the despair of a writing man who has known the best of storytellers that he cannot translate their oral savor into print. *1961*

48. The greatest defect in American literature is want of flavor, gusto; the only source for flavor and gusto is the soil. *1925*

49. The tempo of the earth is not the tempo of action. The tempo of the earth-dwellers to whom I have been listening for many years is the tempo of growing grass, of a solitary buzzard sailing over a valley, of the wind from the south in April, of the lengthening of a tree's shadow on a summer afternoon, of the rise and fall of flames in a fireplace on a winter night; it is the tempo of a staked horse grazing out from camp in darkness, of a coyote greeting moonrise, of a bobwhite making dawn more serene, of a lizard in the sun waiting for a fly, and of cows chewing their cuds after they have drunk; it is the tempo of a ranchman sitting on the front gallery and looking for hours and hours into space with latent hope for a cloud. This is not to say that folks who belong to the earth do not vivify action. They do, but somehow, in the phrase of Reed Anthony, cowman, they always appear to have "ample time." They may hum but their humming is not the humming of industry. They may be propertied, but their minds are not on drilling the guts out of the earth, damming up rivers, laying pipe-

lines across continents, converting the elements into bombs to annihilate nations. They may run, but they have a genius for soaking in and oozing out. *1955*

50. For me at least, the buzzard expresses better the tempo of the land than any airplane trying to run him down. *1950*

51. I'd like to use for a spittoon the skull of every radio jazz hound who scoots "Oh, b-u-r-y me not on the l-o-n-e p-r-a-i-r-i-e" into a skating rink whirl. *1944*

52. If the ballads of a nation are as important as its laws, its legends are almost as important as its ballads. Here I must confess a great hope that some man or woman who understands will seize upon these legends and use them as Irving used the legends of the Hudson and the Catskills, as Whittier used the legends of New England. People of Texas soil still have a vast body of folklore, and whoever will write of them with fidelity must recognize that lore as surely as Shakespeare recognized the lore of his folk, as surely as Mr. Thomas Hardy has recognized the lore of Wessex. *1924*

53. And what, some people are asking, is to be done with all this collected folklore? For one thing, a number of intelligent people read it and enjoy it and are instructed by it as they read and enjoy and are instructed by history. This folklore is a part of our social history, as legitimate in its way as the best authenticated state papers. *1927*

54. So there is not only fresh and entertaining folklore in the world yet, but there is thought and meaning to be wrung out of it. *1928*

---

1. J. Frank Dobie, *Guide to Life and Literature of the Southwest* (Dallas, 1952), p. 10.

2. Quoted by Isabel Gaddis in the *Texas Observer*, July 24, 1964, p. 18, as being from the *Texas Ranger*, 1961.

3. "Storytellers I Have Known," *Singers and Storytellers* (Dallas, 1961), p. 4. "Publications of the Texas Folklore Society" (hereafter abbreviated as PTFS), XXX.

4. *The Mustangs* (Boston, 1952), p. xii.

5. *The Longhorns* (Boston, 1941), p. xviii.

6. *Coronado's Children* (Dallas, 1930), p. 351.

7. "The Line That Travis Drew," *In the Shadow of History* (Austin, 1939), p. 13. PTFS, XV.

8. *Guide*, p. 10.

9. "Editor's Preface," *Legends of Texas* (Austin, 1924), p. iii. PTFS, III.
10. *On the Open Range* (Dallas, 1931), pp. x-xi.
11. "The Apache and His Secret," *The Sky Is My Tipi* (Austin and Dallas, 1949), p. 142. PTFS, XXII.
12. "Storytellers I Have Known," p. 6.
13. "As the Moving Finger Writ," *Southwest Review*, XL (1955), 297.
14. "The Writer and His Region," *Southwest Review*, XXXV (1950), 81; and *Guide*, p. 4.
15. *Coronado's Children*, p. 308.
16. "Ross Santee—His 'Cowboy,'" J. E. Reynolds Book Catalogue Number 66 (Van Nuys, California, 1961).
17. *The Voice of the Coyote* (Boston, 1949), p. 229.
18. "Muchas Gracias," *Tone the Bell Easy* (Austin, 1932), pp. 5-6. PTFS, X.
19. "Just a Word," *Man, Bird, and Beast* (Austin, 1930), p. 6. PTFS, VIII.
20. *The Voice of the Coyote*, p. 372.
21. *Guide*, p. 190.
22. *I'll Tell You a Tale* (Boston, 1960), p. xi.
23. "Twenty Years an Editor," *Backwoods to Border* (Austin and Dallas, 1943), p. x. PTFS, XVIII.
24. *Tales of Old-Time Texas* (Boston, 1955), p. ix.
25. *Apache Gold and Yaqui Silver* (Boston, 1939), p. x.
26. "The Traveling Anecdote," *Folk Travelers* (Austin and Dallas, 1953), p. 5. PTFS, XXV.
27. *Ibid.*, p. 10.
28. "Twenty Years an Editor," p. x.
29. "The Traveling Anecdote," p. 10.
30. Quoted by Wilmot Ragsdale in "A Texan at Cambridge," *Southwest Review*, XXIX (1944), 508.
31. *A Texan in England* (Boston, 1945), pp. 35-36.
32. "Prefatory Wisdom," *Puro Mexicano* (Austin, 1935), p. v. PTFS, XII.
33. "Forward Remarks by the Editor," "Publications of the Texas Folklore Society," IV (Austin, 1925), p. 7. (This volume had no title of its own. In 1964 it was reprinted as *Happy Hunting Ground*.)
34. "Just a Word," p. 6.
35. "Muchas Gracias," p. 5.
36. "Charm in Mexican Folktales," *The Healer of Los Olmos* (Austin and Dallas, 1951), pp. 1-2. PTFS, XXIV.
37. *Tales of Old-Time Texas*, pp. xiii-xiv.
38. "Charm in Mexican Folktales," p. 1.
39. *Tales of Old-Time Texas*, pp. xii-xiii.
40. *Ibid.*, p. xiii.
41. *The Voice of the Coyote*, pp. 246-47.
42. "Forward Remarks by the Editor," p. 8.
43. *The Voice of the Coyote*, p. 234.
44. *Ibid.*, p. 307.
45. "The Traveling Anecdote," p. 10.
46. *Tongues of the Monte* (Boston, 1935), p. 44.

47. "Storytellers I Have Known," p. 29.
48. "Forward Remarks by the Editor," p. 7.
49. *Tales of Old-Time Texas,* p. x.
50. "The Writer and His Region," p. 85.
51. *A Texan in England,* p. 225.
52. "Editor's Preface," p. iv.
53. "The Editor's Prerogative," *Texas and Southwestern Lore* (Austin, 1927), p. 6. PTFS, VI.
54. "Report, Sir," *Follow de Drinkin' Gou'd* (Austin, 1928), p. 5. PTFS, VII.

The Hat-in-Mud Tale

JAN H. BRUNVAND

I

IN HIS NOVELS AND STORIES Andy Adams included much material from oral sources. Fifty tales told around campfires have been collected from his books and unpublished manuscripts and brought together in *Why the Chisholm Trail Forks* (1956).[1] They are probably stories that Andy heard while he was working with cattle and horses or that he sought out after becoming a writer. They are presented as true-life narratives; the teller is almost always involved in or present during the action. They are oral tales but are not traditional in the way folktales are, though a campfire narrator could, if he chose to, appropriate the adventures of some other cowboy and retell them as his own. Only one of Andy's campfire tales is readily identifiable as the reworking of a folktale.[2]

In *The Log of a Cowboy*, along with the fairly formal storytelling at firesides, there is other more casual swapping of wisecracks, anecdotes, and jokes between the cowboys of Tom Quirk's outfit. Among these items we find echoes of oral narratives. The report, for instance, that General Price said about St. Louis, "I don't know as I can take it, but if you will give me Louisiana troops, I'll agree to steal it,"[3] sounds like the real thing. The foreman's remark about "the man who said if he owned hell and Texas, he'd rent Texas and live in hell"[4] refers to a popular tale and song. A similar item is the story of the woman who wrote home, "Texas is a good place for men and dogs, but it's hell on women and oxen."[5] A tall tale is implied by the remark, "The country was so bare and level that a jack rabbit needed to carry a fly for shade."⁶ A joke about a stutterer apologizing to a girl, "Y-y-you n-n-n-needn't g-g-g-go to hell; y-y-your b-b-b-brother and I have m-m-made other 'r-r-r-rangements,'" is probably also an oral one.⁷ But one of the clearest examples of a well-known folktale in *The Log of a Cowboy* is one that Paul Priest—nicknamed "The Rebel"—bunkmate of the narrator, tells one night as they ride one round together on night herd. He calls it "an old war story."

> They used to tell the story in the army, that during one of the winter retreats, a cavalryman, riding along in the wake of the column at night, saw a hat apparently floating in the mud and water. It the hope that it might be a better hat than the one he was wearing, he dismounted to get it. Feeling his way carefully through the ooze until he reached the hat, he was surprised to find a man underneath and wearing it. "Hello, comrade," he sang out, "can I lend you a hand?"
> "No, no," replied the fellow, "I'm all right; I've got a good mule yet under me."⁸

The same story without the Civil War setting is traditional in Texas. Mody Boatright gives this version in *Tall Tales from Texas*.

> You ought to have seen them flats before they begun makin' roads. When I first hit that country, they was jist fencin' off the lanes, and when I got a job, the boss put me to ridin' fence. One day I was ridin' along by the lane, and I looked over and there was a good, brand-new Stetson hat layin' on the top of a mud-hole. I thinks to myself, "That's a good hat, and I might as well have it as the next feller." So I got down and got a-holt of a fence-post to steady myself, and reached out to git it. Jist as I teched the crown a feller yelled out: "Hey, what you doin' there?" he says. Then I noticed for the first time that there was a man's head stickin' out of the mud. I asked the feller if he needed any help, but he said he was ridin' a mighty good hoss, and he guessed he'd make it through all right.⁹

In another Texas version the submerged traveler is standing on his mule.¹⁰ The story has been reported to me recently by a Texan who writes, "I have heard this told as the truth by Stockton Axson, President Wilson's brother-in-law. He gave it a very definite locality in Houston, at the end of the car line on the way to Rice Institute."¹¹ Axson, speaking in 1930, was illustrating how bad the streets were in Houston before there was much pavement. This story has been adapted to the Trans-Pecos region by changing boggy mud to wind-blown sand.[12]

The hat-in-mud story has had a life far beyond the time and region of these variants. A review of its genealogy shows how the brief anecdote in *The Log of a Cowboy* leads directly back to a mainstream of American frontier folk humor.[13]

II

The tale about the man traveling under deep mud has been collected in three states of the Old Southwest, and it apparently migrated through a fourth. One version appeared in Mississippi embedded in a lengthy supernatural legend that had traveled west with a North Carolina family first to Tennessee in the 1880's and later to Mississippi; it is told by a young doctor in the story.

Last time I came over this road, about Christmas, it was the worst I ever saw. Why, I picked up a Stetson hat in the middle of a mud-hole near the four-mile board, and, by George there was a man under it. "You're in the middle of a bad fix, old man," I said. "Hell," he said, "that ain't nothin' to the fix this mule's in under me."[14]

Vance Randolph reports the story both from Arkansas, in the vicinity of Eureka Springs, and from Rolla, Missouri.[15] In the first version the muddy traveler protests to his intended rescuer, "Let me alone, stranger, you're a-pullin' me right out of the saddle." The second version is the standard, "I've got a good horse under me" type. Lowell Thomas also received a version credited to Missouri from a correspondent in Eire, Pennsylvania, about 1931; here the traveler is only up to his knees in mud, but he says that he is on top of a load of hay.[16]

Since southern texts are plentiful while other western texts are rare and atypical, it seems likely that the hat-in-mud story entered Texas from these southern states, just as did many real cowboys, as well as the fictional Tom Quirk. A North Idaho account of "Mud in Moscow" describes freighting teams bogged down underground all winter but kept alive by hay and water sent down by cable.[17] A short reference to a deep-mud story collected in Calgary,

Alberta, describes a horse "gone altogether," but the event is laid in Toronto, here referred to as "Muddy York."[18]

The first known printing of Paul Bunyan stories in James MacGillivray's 1910 newspaper feature, "The Round River Drive," included a version of the mud story as adapted by Michigan loggers to fit their occupation and weather.

> Bunyan sent me out cruisin' one day, and if I hadn't had snowshoes I wouldn't be here to tell you. Comin' back, I saw a whiplash cracker lyin' there on the snow. "Hello!" says I, "someone's lost their whiplash"; and I see it was Tom Hurley's by the braid of it. I hadn't any more'n picked it up, 'fore it was jerked out of my hand, and Tom yells up, "Leave that whip of mine alone, d—n ye! I've got a five hundred log peaker on the forty-foot bunks and eight horses down here, and I need the lash to get her to the landin'."[19]

Another Michigan loggers' text printed some thirty years later corroborates its oral life in that setting minus any connection with Paul Bunyan:

> I was comin' down the road and I sees a man's hat a-layin' in the road. I gets down off my wagon and goes to pick it up. And what do you think? Under the hat is a man's head. I asks the man if I could give him a lift and he says, "No, I'm all right. I'm on horseback."[20]

Printed sources extend the history of the hat-in-mud story through the nineteenth century and farther into the South and East of the United States. These can conveniently be surveyed in reverse chronology. Harold W. Thompson quotes an 1876 Erie County, New York, historian who thought his version was the original one. It ends with the following byplay:

> "My dear Sir," says the first traveler, "won't you permit me to help you out?"
> "Thanks, no," is the reply. "I don't feel that I should leave my horse, who is underneath me, traveling on hard ground."[21]

The earliest and the best version of *The Arkansas Traveler* dialogue survives in a version printed at Little Rock in 1876, a revision of the original which was probably published between 1858 and 1860. The text, as given by James R. Masterson, contains a reference to "the damdest swamp you ever struck in all your travels; it's boggy enouff to mire a saddle-blanket. Thar's a fust rate road about six feet under that."[22] A rhymed version of *The Arkansas Traveler* published in 1926 rendered the episode in this form:

> Yes, in fac' is so d—n soggy
> Hit'll mire yer saddle blankit,
> An' thar's nare a way ter flank hit.
> Thar's a good road six foot under,
> But that does no good, by thunder![23]

This is apparently the sort of version to which Thoreau alluded from an unidentified source in *Walden* (1854):

> We read that the traveller asked the boy if the swamp before him had a hard bottom. The boy replied that it had. But presently the traveller's horse sank in up to the girths, and he observed to the boy, "I thought you said that this bog had a hard bottom." "So it has," answered the latter, "but you have not got half way to it yet."[24]

A similar version attributed to an Arkansas native of the same period was printed in the New York *Spirit of the Times* in 1856, but here the traveler himself alludes to the floating hat story.

> ... [had he] seen any hats floating upon the surface of the bog, where their owners had sunk down over head and ears. His reply was, that if I wanted to see that, I must go the other road.
> "Where is that?" I asked ....
> "Why ... It is just six feet under the old one."[25]

Constance Rourke refers without date to a nineteenth-century midwestern version which has the complete action of the usual joke:

> A traveler floundering through the mire of a cypress swamp in Ohio saw a beaver hat lying crown upward in the mud. It moved, and he lifted it with his whip. Underneath was a man's head—a laughing head that cried, "Hello, stranger!" The traveler offered his assistance, but the head declined, saying that he had a good horse under him.[26]

The earliest documented appearance of the story was in James Kirke Paulding's farce *The Lion of the West,* which was written in 1830, produced in New York in 1831, subsequently acted in England, but was not published until 1954, when a manuscript was found in the British Museum. Here Nimrod Wildfire—"the Kentuckian"—relates:

> Look you here now, tother day, I was a horseback paddling away pretty comfortably through Nobottom swamp, when suddenly—I wish I may be currycomb'd to death by 50,000 tom cats, if I didn't see a white hat getting along in mighty considerable style all alone by itself on the top of the mud—so up I rid, and being a bit jubus, I lifted it with the butt end of my whip when a feller sung out from under it, Hallo, stranger, who told you to knock my hat off? Why, says I, what sort of a sample of a white man are you? What's come of the rest of you? Oh, says he, I'm not far off—only in the next county. I'm doing beautifully—got one of the best horses under me that ever burrowed—claws like a mole—no stop in him—but here's a waggon and horses right under me in a mighty bad fix, I reckon, for I heard the driver say a spell ago one of the team was getting a leetel tired.[27]

This text has the hat and "good horse" of most later versions of the story, as well as the team and wagon of Lowell Thomas' tale (a sled in MacGillivray's), and a whip, such as is mentioned in the 1910 Paul Bunyan version. Thus, date, style, and motifs suggest that it is a primary early version of the anecdote.

III

These variants of the hat-in-mud tale would seem to bear out Mody Boatright's theory that back country American tall tales were largely a folklore "burlesquing the nonfrontiersman's conception of the frontier."[28] Nimrod Wildfire in *The Lion of the West* was "loading" an English traveler, "Mrs. Wollope," when he related the story; her reaction was, "What a geological novelty!" All of *The Arkansas Traveler* versions represent a reticent backwoodsman parrying the questions of a city tourist, and "a traveler" is frequently the straight man in later variants. In the text from the *Spirit of the Times* the Arkansan responded "with a leer and a grin of intense meaning, as if he enjoyed in anticipation the effect of the 'coup' before it had parted."[29] It is also obvious in this text that the tourist was anticipating that the joke would be sprung on him eventually by some regional humorist or other. Thoreau's version retains the same tone when a boy laconically guides a traveler into a deep swamp by answering too literally a question put to him.

Probably the story developed from simple exaggerations of the truth about mud in the back country to the more elaborate subterranean narratives. The complex layering of various buried creatures and equipments in some versions merely projects the humor of the basic frontier deep-mud brag; the got-a-good-horse-under-me ending of most longer versions continues the tradition of buoyant backwoods bragging as Boatright has described it.

The frontier theme along with early dates and a wide distribution of texts in this country supports the theory of an American origin of the tale, although one English text is known. It would be interesting to find an example here of what Norris W. Yates calls the "depurifying 'feed-back' process" of American yarns being Anglicized, printed, and then returned to the frontier when Stateside newspaper editors clipped English journals for anecdotal fillers.[30] But neither an American reprinting nor a direct Yankee source is known for the version that a *Notes and Queries* contributor submitted in 1854 from Newton Prodgers, "the true and only genuine site of the stupendous adventure of the Manchester Bagman, which the Yankees have appropriated with characteristic coolness, and pitched somewhere down in Alabama."[31] The text, a full one, most likely stemmed from some frontier-American source, or possibly from the English productions of *The Lion of the West*.

... [the story is] about a respectable farmer of our village, no way connected with the public press, who set to work one fine morning to dig out a riding whip, the tip of which he saw sprouting out of the middle of the road. After an hour's hard digging he came to a hat, and under that to his intense horror, was a head belonging to a body in a state of advanced suffocation. Assistance was procured, and after several hours of unremitting exertion, worthy of Agassiz or Owen, the entire organism of a bagman was developed. "Now, gentlemen," said the exhumed commercial to his perspiring diggers, who of course concluded their labours finished, "now, gentlemen, you've saved my life; and now, for God's sake, lend a hand to get out my mare!"

Let me add that the crux of the hat-in-mud story has recently been presented to Englishmen in Reg Smythe's comic strip, "Andy Capp," which is distributed in America as well as in England. Andy is standing on the curb and a friend is moving in water above his waist—both are drunk. Andy asks, "Want me t' see yer t' yer bus?" The friend replies, raising his hat, "No, thanks, I'm on me bike." This appeared in American papers on or about April 10, 1965.

IV

The little jest of Paul "The Rebel" Priest in *The Log of a Cowboy* seems to have reached the western cattle range just as inevitably as the young men themselves of the Midwest and South drifted there to become trail drivers. It was more fitting than Andy Adams could have suspected that Tom Quirk was regaled with this particular folktale; it had been told by the first frontiersman on the American stage, was alluded to in the original *Arkansas Traveler*, had been read somewhere by Thoreau, had achieved a vigorous oral life in the Old Southwest (being reported from there to the *Spirit of the Times*), was revamped by Michigan loggers (thence injected into the earliest Paul Bunyan publication), and eventually became known in the Far West. Even the wartime setting for the *Log's* version of the story fits the tradition, for from Australia recently has come a variant attributed to World War I, while in a World War II text the unflinching underground wayfarer becomes a soldier perched on the shoulders of another soldier who is driving a jeep.[32]

1. Edited by Wilson M. Hudson and published by the University of Texas Press, Austin. There are fifty-one tales in the book, one of which is told at a table in the back of a saloon.
2. "The Cat in the Jacal" is identified as a version of Type 326 by Hudson in *Andy Adams: His Life and Writings* (Dallas, 1964), p. 127.
3. *The Log of a Cowboy* (Boston and New York, 1903), p. 4.
4. *Ibid.*, p. 64.
5. *Ibid.*, p. 152.

6. *Ibid.*, pp. 131-32.
7. *Ibid.*, p. 27.
8. *Ibid.*, pp. 68-69.
9. (Dallas, 1934), p. 48. The joke is summarized in Boatright's *Folk Laughter on the American Frontier* (New York, 1949), pp. 76-77.
10. Mary Jourdan Atkinson and J. Frank Dobie, "Pioneer Folk Tales," *Follow de Drinkin' Gou'd* (Austin, 1928), pp. 75-76. "Publications of the Texas Folklore Society," VII.
11. A letter from Wilson M. Hudson dated December 20, 1963, from Austin.
12. Another Texas version has recently come to my attention. It appears in an undated paperback booklet, 4½ by 2¾ inches and with pages unnumbered, titled *After Dinner Stories By Joe M. Evans* (Hotel Paso del Norte: El Paso, Texas. Price $0.50). The following item was pointed out to me by a student at the University of Idaho who had purchased the booklet from Evans, a traveling "cowboy evangelist":

> The president of the El Paso Chamber of Commerce was introducing Captain Gillett as the speaker to a group of Masons. This happened in March when the wind was blowing and the dust had covered everything. You couldn't see the sun, just a typical Western day. He apologized to Capt. Gillett about the dust storm by saying, "We never have a day like this in El Paso."
>
> The old Ranger Captain had forgotten more about West Texas than the Chamber of Commerce President ever could learn. Capt. Gillett said, "I came to El Paso in 1879, and they were having sand storms then and have been ever since. I remember one time we were coming in off an Indian scout. The wind had been blowing for three days and nights and the sand had covered up the grass and mesquite bushes. As we rode along through the sand hills between El Paso and Alamagordo, we discovered a man's hat lying there on a sand dome. We got down to pick it up and found there was a man's head in it. We scratched the sand out of his eyes and ears and mouth with our fingers. He said, 'Get a shovel, I'm horseback.'"

13. References to the hat-in-mud tale were compiled by Herbert Halpert in "Tall Tales and Other Yarns from Calgary, Alberta," *California Folklore Quarterly*, IV (1945), 29-49, note 26, and in Ernest Warren Baughman, "A Comparative Study of the Folktales of England and North America" (Indiana University dissertation, 1954), under Motifs X1655.1 *Deep mud*, and X1655.1.1 *The man under the hat, which is the only thing seen above the mud*. In Stith Thompson's *Motif-Index of Folk-Literature* the numbers are X1655 and X1655.1, but Baughman alone is cited. See also Daniel G. Hoffman, *Form and Fable in American Fiction* (New York, 1961), p. 69n.
14. Arthur Palmer Hudson and Pete Kyle McCarter, "The Bell Witch of Tennessee and Mississippi: A Folk Legend," *Journal of American Folklore*, XLVII (1934), 56-57.
15. *We Always Lie to Strangers* (New York, 1951), pp. 253-54.
16. *Tall Stories* (New York, 1945), pp. 160-62.
17. Federal Writers' Project, Vardis Fisher, State Director, *Idaho Lore* (Caldwell, Idaho, 1939), p. 134.
18. Halpert, as in n. 13 above, p. 42.
19. From the *Detroit News-Tribune*, July 24, 1910, as reprinted by Harold W. Felton, *Legends of Paul Bunyan* (New York, 1947), pp. 335-41. The story is reprinted in Daniel G. Hoffman, *Paul Bunyan, Last of the Frontier Demigods* (Philadelphia, 1952), p. 40, and Richard M. Dorson, *American Folklore* (Chicago, 1959), p. 220. Both Hoff-

man and Dorson identify the story as a genuine frontier tale attached by writers to the largely ersatz Paul Bunyan lore.

20. Earl C. Beck, *Songs of the Michigan Lumberjacks* (Ann Arbor, 1942), p. 282; credited to Jim Vahey of Leaton.

21. *Body, Boots and Britches* (Philadelphia, 1939), p. 174; quoted from C. Johnson, *Centennial History of Erie County*, 1876.

22. *Tall Tales from Arkansas* (Boston, 1942), p. 189.

23. *Ibid.*, p. 216.

24. Chapter XVIII, "Conclusion," in *Walden and Other Writings of Henry David Thoreau*, ed. Brooks Atkinson (New York: Modern Library, 1937), p. 294.

25. From "An Arkansas 'Sell,'" *Spirit*, XXVI (1856), 230, as quoted by Norris W. Yates, *William T. Porter and the "Spirit of the Times"* (Baton Rouge, 1957), pp. 152-53. Partially reprinted in Masterson, *Tall Tales*, pp. 237-38.

26. *American Humor* (New York: Anchor Books edn., 1953), p. 40.

27. *The Lion of the West*, ed. James N. Tidwell (Stanford, Cal., 1954), pp. 35-36.

28. Boatright, *Folk Laughter*, p. 22.

29. Yates, as in n. 25 above, p. 153, citing the *Spirit*.

30. *Ibid.*, pp. 187-89.

31. V. T. Sternberg, "An Old-World Village and its Christmas Folk Lore," *Notes and Queries*, X:269 (Saturday, December 23, 1854), 501-3; reprinted in *Choice Notes from "Notes and Queries": Folk Lore* (London, 1859), pp. 196-97.

32. Bill Wannan, *The Australian: Yarns, Ballads, Legends, Traditions of the Australian People* (3rd edn.: Melbourne, 1958), "The Slouch Hat," pp. 79-80, and Sgt. Bill Davidson, *Tall Tales They Tell in the Services* (New York, 1943), p. 47. I have not seen the latter.

The Baby-Switching Story

JAMES T. BRATCHER

WHEN I READ Owen Wister's *The Virginian* as a boy, I recognized an episode in its tenth chapter from some other printed appearance—I had forgotten just where. The episode concerned a prank played at a ranch-land dance. It was an early custom to take the entire family to a dance and put the babies to bed on pallets in a spare room; in another room the grown-ups would frolic to music. In the novel, the Virginian and Lin McLean slip into such a room and exchange the wraps and pallet positions of the sleeping babies. Towards morning the drowsy parents collect the wrong children and return to distant ranches. On discovering the joke, they anxiously hurry back to the scene of the dance, specified as the "Goose Egg" headquarters on Bear Creek, Wyoming. While mothers see to the more delicate matters of "sorting the herd," the fathers condemn McLean, conspicuous by his sudden absence—one observing that he had not merely "swapped the duds; he had shuffled the whole doggone deck."

Some eight or ten years passed before I reread *The Virginian* and, with it, read the edition of Wister's *Journals and Letters* (1885-1895) that his daughter, Mrs. Walter Stokes, published in 1958. The 1893 portion of the *Journals* is devoted partly to Wister's visit that year to Brownwood, Texas, near where a friend of his, Fitzhugh Savage, operated a ranch. The budding writer of cowboy stories made it a point when traveling in the West from his home in Philadelphia to "jot down all shreds of local colour . . . and anecdotes" that struck him as being "native wild flowers" (letter to his mother from Wyoming, June 21, 1891). His *Journals* mark

THE BABY-SWITCHING STORY 111

the indebtedness of *The Virginian* to this material. Under the Texas entry for February 21 appears the story as Wister first heard it, if not the complete version of the baby-switching story as I had read it originally.

The story in Wister's journal is almost a tall tale, as narrated by a neighbor of Wister's host Fitzhugh Savage, Jim Neil, to an Englishman in the vicinity named Thoroton. Wister's note on the story follows:

> They had a dance somewhere—one of the regulation dances where the babies are all brought and piled in a corner while their parents jump about to music. After the thing had got going full swing, some unknown person got the babies and changed all their clothes—putting the linen of Mrs. Jones's little boy upon Mrs. Smith's little girl, and so on. In the dim light nobody noticed, and all went home with the wrong baby. Next morning there was the devil to pay, and for a week the whole countryside was busy exchanging and identifying babies.
>
> Thoroton believes this for a fact. Savage told me it was all Neil's invention. I maintained Neil's invention is not up to that high level and that he read the story somewhere. The other day he was over here again . . . and I shouted out to Savage to tell Neil that he got the baby story out of the back of an almanac, which Savage did. Neil said that it must be in the almanac for next month, then. But he admitted that he had heard the story down at San Saba.
>
> To devise a trick of that completeness clean out of your head while you were talking to an Englishman would indicate most unusual powers; and I think, that if the thing did not actually occur, somebody thought of doing it while they were actually at a dance with a pile of babies in sight. Then the flight of imagination would be one of which even I might be capable.

Wister's imagination proved fully capable of dramatizing the prank. "Today you can hear legends of it from Texas to Montana . . . ," he states in Chapter XI of *The Virginian*. (This sentence and Wister's literary appropriation of the story appeared first in March, 1896, in a segment of *The Virginian* published as a short story in *Harper's Magazine*; the sentence suggests that by this time Wister had again met with the story.) For purposes of the novel, he sets the prank in Wyoming. The foregoing excerpt establishes that Wister heard of it in Texas, however, and it seemed likely to me when I read the journal account that if such an event actually happened it happened in Texas, maybe near San Saba. This made at least two Texas contributions to our best-known novel of the West, for the journal entry for June 26, 1891, reveals that the prototype of the outlaw Trampas hailed from Texas, although it was in Wyoming that Wister met him.

Soon after I had read the journal account of baby switching, there came to my attention an article by Robert Welles Ritchie in the *Bookman* for January, 1917, entitled "Some Scenes of 'The Virginian.'" Ritchie, a one-time journalist who writes at second hand, but with compelling detail, vouches for the historical truth of the prank and places it in Wyoming. He writes: "The scene of the famous incident that has had a whole nation laughing for a decade and a half was Hank Devoe's ranch on the south fork of the Powder River." Following the say-so of old-timers in the area, Ritchie goes on to name the culprit, date the prank approximately, and mention certain of the victims:

> It was Frant Osborn, a hare-brained cowpuncher with a rich imagination, who turned the trick. In Johnson County, Wyoming, old-timers will still tell with reminiscent pride of Frant Osborn and the babies. . . . "He rode with the L X Bar outfit, did Frant, and in the winter of Eighty-nine, or maybe it was Ninety, he and a bunch of the boys from the L X Bar home ranch on South Fork rode over to Hank Devoe's to cut in on the dance. They must have stopped at Barrel Springs stage house, because they were prime. . . . And nobody knew until afterwards why Frant didn't dance much and why, when folks did see him ducking out to the lean-to shed, he looked so all-fired mysterious. No, they didn't know until they began to see his work! The Waterburys, for instance, they rode eighteen miles back home on Red Fork with a baby belonging on Meadow Creek; Mrs. Jim Bliss, on Dugout, didn't get her Jim Henry back for four days—and him teethin', too!"

Another and later article, this one by the former director of the University of Wyoming Library, N. Orwin Rush, indicates the persistence of the story in Wyoming and possibly a number of other states. Published in the *Papers of the Bibliographical Society of America* for the second quarter of 1952 (volume XLVI), the article commemorates "Fifty Years of 'The Virginian'" and thus, indirectly, the anniversary of the baby-switching tale in its widest-known form. The story, writes Mr. Rush, "has caused a great deal of speculation and controversy. Claims have been made from all sections of the country, from Kansas to California, that Wister took the plot for this tale from local incidents. At least ten different persons in Wyoming have been identified as those famous changelings."

Although a letter of inquiry to Mr. Rush, now director of the Florida State University Libraries, has brought the reply that his original notes for his article are no longer at hand, there is no reason to question his statements about either the "changelings" or various claims of origin. Wister indicated the broad currency of the story by 1896, and *The Virginian* would have inspired local claims and identification of the exchanged babies with living people. Mr. Rush, it should be noted, cites a report perpetuated in the *Rocky Mountain News* for May 18, 1935, that the prankster was a well-known Wyoming cowboy named William "Missou" Hines. Gene Gressley, current director of the University of Wyoming Library, has written me saying that the trick is often attributed in Wyoming to Hines, a former employee at the Searight Ranch, called the "Goose Egg," about twenty miles west of Casper. Wister sets the prank at the "Goose Egg" ranch in *The Virginian;* but I find no mention of Hines—or, for that matter, of Frant Osborn—in his *Journals,* which are usually explicit in naming his western friends and acquaintances. Hines was later famous in some oil-leasing fights in Wyoming, and apparently a good many exploits were attached to him. In his obituary in the *Denver Post* for February 16, 1943, it is stated (although obviously falsely, in view of Wister's journal entry) that he witnessed the prank with Wister. The obituary also points to a popular legend that Hines was Wister's model for the Virginian. Possibly he was, as were fully a dozen other contenders!

Whatever the truth of these particulars, at this point in my puzzling over the baby-switching story two conclusions or near-conclusions seemed warranted. For one, considerations, taken all around, favored the genuineness of the prank. Granting Ritchie's colorful style and the reliance of his report on local lore, the details of his testimony regarding place, time, trickster, and victims were not easily dismissed as part-and-parcel legend inspired by *The Virginian*, however widely read the novel. Dances were a common outlet for frontier social needs, and frequently babies were brought and put in a room to themselves. Liquor livened these gatherings, and of course cowboys and early settlers loved a joke. Wister was convinced of the plausibility of the prank, and indeed, given the ingredients just mentioned, it would be strange if such a trick had not occurred.

Assuming that it did—at least once—the weight of evidence pointed to Wyoming as the locale. Wister first heard of the prank in Texas in 1893, but the recent cattle drives from Texas to the northern plains insured word-of-mouth communication between Wyoming and Texas, especially of a "whopper" to pass on in the bunkhouse. In 1962 Mody Boatright told me that he remembered seeing a report of the prank, once shown to him in some notes on the manuscript reminiscences of a Texas cowman. The cowman—whose reminiscences I have not been able to trace—gave what he thought was the origin of the baby-switching story and said that Wister had sent him an "authorgraphed" copy of *The Virginian*. The prank may have been assigned to Texas in these memoirs; but in their absence a link stronger than Wister's journal entry was needed before placing the prank in Texas as well as in Wyoming.

The necessary link appeared a while back, as I was browsing in Florence Fenley's rich collection, *Oldtimers of Southwest Texas*. Miss Fenley, a respected newspaperwoman of Uvalde, has for many years reported the oral recollections of early settlers in her area. The reminiscences of Z. T. Vernor, whose family moved from Alabama to settle near Leesville, Gonzales County, in the 1870's, appear here in part:

> After we got established in our new home, we took up farm life and got acquainted with all our neighbors. There was no church near us, and the school was only a two or three-months' school. . . . There wasn't anything social except a dance occasionally, but law! when they *did* have a dance at somebody's house, they came for fifteen or twenty miles around, bringing their children in wagons or on horseback, whichever was most convenient.

One night, they had one of these big dances, and everybody came for miles around, of course. There were two good sized rooms that had been cleared out to dance in and they put the children in a house apart from this one they were dancing in. Women, young and old, were there and those with babies put them on pallets and let them sleep.

Some of the older men decided to have some fun that night, so they went into this house while the others were dancing, and changed the babies around on the pallets, even changed the clothes on some of 'em, then went on back and watched the dance.

When the dance broke, the women were all tired and ready to go home, and in a hurry too, so they just went in and picked up the bundle where they had left it, blankets and all, and left for their homes, some going one way and some the opposite direction. In a little while, they were miles apart and most of them didn't discover the mistake till they got home. Then of all the clamor that broke loose! No one knew where to go to find her own baby, and it was two or three weeks before they ever got their babies straightened out and back to their own parents. It was often told that maybe some of them never *did* get back to their own mothers.

In a letter to me, Miss Fenley writes:

Mr. Vernor was a serious old fellow, and the incident was not hearsay with him. . . . He laughed about it when he told me, because he remembered so many of the mothers. . . . I am of the opinion that whichever locality played the joke on those poor mothers first may have had it copied elsewhere. Mr. Vernor told me it actually happened in Gonzales County.

By Texas reckoning Gonzales County is not far removed from San Saba, where Wister's informant got the story, and it will be noticed that the Vernor account closely parallels Wister's synopsis of the story in the following particulars:

even changed the clothes on some of 'em/
changed all their clothes

When the dance broke, the women were all tired and ready to go home, and in a hurry too/
In the dim light nobody noticed

Then of all the clamor that broke loose/
Next morning there was the devil to pay
it was two or three weeks before they ever got their babies straightened out/

for a week the whole countryside was busy exchanging and identifying babies

Just recently Lon Taylor, who works for the Austin city-planning department, told me that his grandmother, Mrs. Sue Taylor, used to relate a baby-switching incident. His grandmother placed the prank at Round Rock sometime between 1882 and 1887, and attributed it to her brother, Will Border. In her telling of the story, a party was being given in Round Rock and babies were brought and put to bed, not in the house, but in wagons outside. Mrs. Taylor's brother, along with confederates, shuffled the babies around in the wagons. I have spoken to Mr. Taylor's other grandmother, who lives in Wharton County, and she placed the prank at La Grange. She added that this sort of tomfoolery often happened at early dances.

With Miss Fenley, then, I have come to suspect that the baby-switching prank—a natural enough practical joke, given the circumstances—occurred more than once, and in Texas as well as (by Ritchie's testimony) in Wyoming. Interestingly, however, the Vernor account in particular seems to add to more than a geographic picture. The motif of deception by means of exchanged children (K1847) figures in a number of European tales, whether it involves a fairy who steals a child from its cradle and leaves a fairy substitute (F321.1), dwarfs who exchange children in their cradles (F451.5.2.3), or a nurse who exchanges children so that a preferred child will be assured of wealth (K1923.1). (I have not found instances of the exchange being made solely as a practical joke.) Apparently this Old World motif saw its literal enactment in the New World in the last century, and possibly earlier. From (1) the historical occurrence or occurrences of the prank, we must infer spread of the story as (2) a news item and then as (3) an anecdote bearing kinship to what J. Frank Dobie, writing in *Folk Travelers* (PTFS, 1953), has called a "traveling anecdote." When the story appears in Wister's *Journals*, it does so as (4) a mildly inflicted tall tale with an Englishman on the receiving end. Next Wister incorporates it in *The Virginian* as (5) a story of a clever trick of his hero's, often retold from Texas to Montana.

But there remains one other indicated step in the history of the story—a regressive one. As I remember the story from wherever I encountered it before reading *The Virginian*, its outlines were the same as in the novel with this one important exception: two of the children, boys, never got back to their rightful parents. I hesitate to trust memory and insist that one grew up with all the advantages and the other did not; but if we consider the final sentence of the Vernor account ("It was often told that maybe some of them never *did* get back to their own mothers") as well as hints of mixed-upbringing implicit in Mr. Rush's statement ("At least ten different persons in Wyoming have been identified as those famous changelings") we see the story reverting in the direction (6) of K1923.1. That this motif, of a nurse who substitutes her own child for one of rich parents, was circulating in nineteenth-century America is indicated by Mark Twain's *Pudd'nhead Wilson*, which makes use of it. Thus in time, and encouraged possibly by *The Virginian* and *Pudd'nhead Wilson*, both widely read books, the baby-switching story appears to be reverting to a very old pattern. What probably began with an actual occurrence is in the process of assuming a shape long familiar in folk literature.

Since completing this article, I have learned that baby switching (although not as a prank) was commoner in popular productions of the later nineteenth century than I was aware. Along with Twain's *Pudd'nhead Wilson* (1894) and Wister's *The Virginian*, Gilbert and Sullivan's *H.M.S. Pinafore* (1878) and *The Gondoliers* (1889) made use of the theme, and exposed large audiences on both sides of the Atlantic to it. W. S. Gilbert's preoccupation with babies separated from their parents was not entirely influenced by his reading or by folklore. Gilbert was not exactly a "mixed child," as in his scripts, but when he was two, in Naples with his parents, kidnappers hoaxed the nurse who was tending him and spirited him away for ransom. It may be worth noting that Henry Fielding, another who took a literary interest in parent-child separation, has gypsy women furtively exchange a sickly child for a healthy one in *Joseph Andrews* (1742), Chapter XV.

Saved from a Bullet: Miraculous Escapes from Death

JOHN Q. ANDERSON

"IT DIDN'T HAVE MY NAME ON IT" is the simple explanation a man gives who has narrowly missed being killed by a bullet or cannonball in either war or personal combat. The momentary brush with death by violence may soon be forgotten, but not so the more dramatic situation in which the bullet actually strikes the man, yet he lives to tell the story. Such a story is told and retold, and because of its inherent drama it may in time be borrowed by other storytellers.

Over the years I have collected tales, most of them in print, told by men who have, by a strange assortment of objects, been saved from bullets. The earliest account I have found is dated 1664 and is related by the English antiquarian John Aubrey (1626-1697). Aubrey had the story from John Heydon, a practitioner of the occult arts who had seen men rendered invulnerable to bullets by such amulets as rings and pieces of gold with special powers. Heydon said that, when Captain Carol Fantom was shot by his own colonel, Sir Robert Pye, for stealing a horse, the bullets went through Fantom's buff-coat, set his shirt on fire, but did no harm otherwise. Fantom "tooke the bullets, and sayd to Sir Robert, 'Here take your bullets again.'"[1]

In view of the ancient belief that sacred objects have special powers, the Holy Word has, of course, often shielded individuals from bullets. The folk hero of the Midwest, Johnny Appleseed, who according to tradition was an heroic participant in the Battle of Tippecanoe (1811), was struck by two bullets while tending the wounded, "but the Testament he carried over his heart saved his life. One of the bullets lodged appropriately in Romans 14:8, which reads: 'For whether we live, we live unto the Lord; and whether we die, we die unto the Lord: whether we live therefore, or die, we are the Lord's.' "[2]

Being saved from bullets twice by a Testament seems doubly miraculous, but this was the experience of Captain John A. Ansley, a drillmaster in the Confederate Army, who on two occasions escaped death because the Bible he carried on his person caught the enemy's bullets.[3] Another Confederate did not escape so lightly. Dr. Edward W. Cade, surgeon with Walker's Texas Division in central Louisiana, wrote his wife about a neighbor and friend who was a chaplain: "He had a Testament in his pocket immediately over his heart. It was struck by a bullet that went through it and when it reached the flesh its force was expended, and it did not enter the skin but knocked him down and he was shot in the foot which will probably cripple him for life."[4]

In the same year, Johnny Green of the Orphan Brigade also escaped the fatal bullet twice, once with the aid of a Testament. He vividly recounts this experience at the Battle of Shiloh:

. . . just as I had loaded & was raising my gun to fire I fell from a bullit [*sic*] which struck me just over the heart. I felt sure it had gone clear through me & it flashed through my mind that I would live until the arterial blood started back to my heart, when I would drop dead, as I had once seen a deer do which my father shot through the heart. I rose to my knees, took a hurried aim & fired at a clump of the enemy. By this time I was surprised to find that I was still alive. But I felt my breast to learn the extent of my wound when I found one piece of the bullit laying against my skin inside my clothes just over my heart. The ball had passed through the stock of my gun, split on the iron ramrod of my gun, and the other piece had passed through my jacket & burried [*sic*] itself in a little testament in my jacket pocket.[5]

Lest it seem that the Civil War monopolized instances of Bibles saving soldiers' lives, I cite one from the Korean conflict. A small tract published by the Gospel Publishing House, Springfield, Missouri, contains the story of an unnamed American soldier who, in hand-to-hand combat with a Chinese Communist soldier, fended off an attack by bayonet only to be wounded with a dagger.[6] The

American is quoted as saying: "I felt the dagger strike me. I thought I was finished. And yet, though I felt it strike me, I realized it had not pierced my body. I wondered why. Then I remembered my Bible. It was a little zipper Bible, and I had it in my pocket. That little Bible had stopped the dagger!" After the enemy soldier was killed by a buddy, the American checked his Bible and found that the point of the dagger had pierced through the Old Testament into the New and had stopped at Ephesians 3:20: "Unto him that is able to do exceeding abundantly above all that we ask or think, according to the power that worketh in us." Similarly, the religious object has been used in fiction to avert the deadly bullet; in Pasternak's *Dr. Zhivago* a man's life is saved when a prayer roll of one of the psalms which he carried in his pocket stopped a bullet.

Books other than the Holy Word have been effective antimissile defense. Augusta Jane Evans' *Macaria*, a novel first published by a bookseller in Richmond during the Civil War, saved the life of an unnamed Confederate soldier in a battle in the retreat from Chattanooga. He had folded the novel, printed on large, coarse, yellow sheets, and placed it inside his coat where it stopped the bullet that otherwise would have killed him.[7]

In San Angelo in 1881 the *Revised Statutes* of the state of Texas probably saved the life of Justice of the Peace Billy Russell. During a disturbance over the killing of a Negro, there was a great deal of promiscuous firing, and a bullet came through Russell's window and lodged in the law book before him on the table. "After all," he said, "the printed statutes of Texas had to be good for something."[8] In 1923, during the Prohibition era, a Webster's pocket dictionary was even more useful to E. E. Townsend of Alpine, once a member of the Texas Rangers and then sheriff of Brewster County. In a gun battle with a bootlegger he was shot with a small-caliber gun, but the dictionary he had in his pocket stopped the bullet. The bootlegger had no such protection.[9]

Various metal objects have been even more prominent in soldier and frontier lore in stopping or deflecting bullets: coins, watches, belt buckles, cartridge boxes, sabers, and even other guns have been in the right place at the right time. For instance, during the Mexican War P. G. T. Beauregard was hit by grapeshot at the Battle of Chapultepec but was unharmed. He describes the incident as follows:

As I was looking through my spy-glass at Santa Anna and his troops . . . they opened upon us and the grape came rushing and whizzing around us . . . . a smaller grape which was lagging behind, came and struck the hilt of my sabre, then my side and stunned me severely for a while—taking all the breath out of my body—but I soon recovered my strength (partly due no doubt to a drink of good brandy or whiskey given to me by one of the general's aides) and I examined my side supposing I had a hole in it at least large enough to receive my fist—so severe had been the concussion! but it had only penetrated my coat pocket where my thick gloves and eye glasses had no doubt stopped its onward course![10]

Beauregard also tells about a Lieutenant Wilcox, who, in the siege of Mexico City, was struck by a musket ball "on the side of his Colt's revolver which was hanging to his waist belt." Knocked from his horse, the lieutenant was surprised to find that the bullet "had been flattened to about the thickness of a dollar and had printed on its side the name of the maker of the pistol and the place where it was made!"[11]

During the Civil War various pieces of personal equipment stopped bullets. Jess Douglas of the 5th Texas Rangers, fighting near Fort Smith in 1863, was shot in the stomach, but the ball hit the big brass buckle on his belt and passed around his side.[12] The remarkable Elder Horn, then a young man, had a more amusing experience. In his words:

I received a minié ball in the center of my abdomen and imagined I could feel where it passed out my back. . . . When I undid my belt cartridge box, my pants opened and the battered ball fell to the ground. It had cut two balls in my cartridge box half in two, had cut the top button off my pants, had cut a hole through my drawers, and had frazzled the shirt, but had only broken the skin.[13]

A civilian belt buckle saved a man's life in Lampasas County in 1882. At a dance at the Tom H. Kirby ranch, north of Senterfitt, four young men from Shaw Bend, twenty miles up the Colorado River, came down to break up the affair. In the fighting that followed, Constable O'Brien was shot in the abdomen. "Boys, I'm done for," he cried, but when he unbuttoned his shirt he found no wound—the buckle of his belt had deflected the bullet.[14]

A silver dollar once saved the life of Jim Bowie. J. Frank Dobie tells how Major Morris Wright, with whom Bowie was in a "difficulty," hit Bowie in the chest with a bullet which was checked by the dollar in Bowie's vest pocket.[15] Another silver dollar saved an unnamed Denton County man who during Reconstruction was being chased by a band of robbers. He outran them and got home, but was shot in the thigh as he dismounted; "a silver dollar in his pocket turned the ball, causing only a flesh wound."[16]

Lieutenant George Stormfeltz of Terry's Texas Rangers during the Civil War seemed to live a charmed life; he had several horses shot from under him, and on one occasion escaped with a slight wound when his watch stopped a bullet that might have killed him.[17] At the Battle of Amelia Court House another Confederate, Henry Douglas, was knocked from his horse by a spent musket ball which struck a button on the breast of his coat.[18]

In the turbulent aftermath of the Civil War in Texas some former Confederates turned outlaw; such a one was Ben Bickerstaff, who terrorized portions of East Texas until he came to a violent end at Alvarado in 1869. Connected with that incident is the stopping of a bullet by another gun—and that in the hands of a Methodist minister named Powell. Notified that Bickerstaff and a companion were coming into town, the men of Alvarado armed and hid in stores around the town square. Bickerstaff, mounted on a mule, was knocked from his mount by the surprise blast from the men's guns; his right hand disabled, he raised on his elbow and returned the fire with his left. One of his bullets went into the muzzle of the Reverend Powell's gun, but the preacher was unharmed. With forty-two bullets in him, Bickerstaff took more than half an hour to die; he was later buried in a nameless grave in Alvarado Cemetery.[19]

The many-lived Johnny Green, already cited as having escaped death in the Civil War because of a Bible, was miraculously spared a second time. As he describes the incident:

[At Chickamauga] I was running toward the enemy, as was our whole line [when] a grape shot struck me in the groin; it in some manner whirled me clear around and threw me flat on my back. I thought my entire leg was torn off, but I looked down & saw my leg was not gone. I felt with my hands & found no blood, but there was a grape shot in my pocket. It had force enough to tear through my pants, but struck the steel clasp of a pocket book which I had in the pocket of my pants & this stopped it. The clasp was doubled around the ball.[20]

Plug chewing tobacco, whether "Star," "Razor," "Brown Mule," or some other popular brand, was as effective as metal objects in stopping bullets. Captain Bill McDonald, whom Boyce House called "one of the greatest and most picturesque of that great and picturesque body of man hunters, the Texas Rangers," confronted "Bucko" Matthews in Quanah and put "two bullets in the space of a half dollar just above the heart—but Matthews had a thick plug of tobacco and a heavy notebook for protection and was unharmed."[21]

A plug of tobacco in the rear pocket, rather than the front, saved S. P. Hardwick from a serious wound—or at least from great embarrassment—during the wild days of Sweetwater, where Marshal Bill Gilson had killed two or three men before he himself was killed. Hardwick got into a fight with a man named Cooksey, then lost his nerve. As Hardwick ran out the back door of a saloon, Cooksey shot him, but a plug of tobacco in Hardwick's hip pocket stopped the bullet.[22]

Another tale of the saving plug of tobacco was sent to me in a letter by Joe Jenkins, retired postal employee of Houston. The story concerns his Grandpa Schooler's experience at the Battle of Mansfield, Louisiana, during the Civil War.

Grandpa showed her [his wife] a package of her letters that she had written him and which he had been carrying around in his pocket all the time and that bundle of letters once probably saved his life when a spent bullet lodged in among them. Grandma loved her fun, so she says, which pocket, hip or breast? . . . Grandpa swore up and down and sideways that they were in a shirt pocket. . . . After the war at one of those reunions I spoke of, Uncle Josh Stewart, who was in my Grandfather's company, swore that it was a plug of tobacco that saved Grandpa Schooler's life and that most people carried plug tobacco in their rear pocket.[23]

But a package of letters *did* save a Confederate soldier's life—love letters. Val C. Giles told about an officer in Hood's Texas Brigade who carried his sweetheart's letters, tied with a blue ribbon, in a black morocco notebook fastened in the inside pocket of his uniform. He added:

A Minnié ball struck him on the left breast above the heart. His sword flew from his hand and he fell heavily to the ground, apparently dead. But he was not killed. The bullet never entered his body, but embedded itself in his bundle of love letters. . . . The bullet passed through eight or ten of them. . . [and] lodged against the last one received.[24]

Instances of men being saved from bullets by unusual means are not confined to the Civil War and the wild frontier of the last century. Certainly one of the most widely publicized occurrences involved Theodore Roosevelt in 1912. On October 14 of that year he was campaigning in Milwaukee, and on the way to the hall where he was to speak he was shot in the right breast by a fanatic, John Chrank. Ignoring a physician's advice, he insisted on going ahead and giving the speech; later, at a hospital, examination showed that the bullet "had entered the right lung, its velocity spent by passing through an overcoat, a spectacle case, and the folded manuscript of the speech he was to make."[25]

Twentieth-century tranquilizers relieve the shock of men who today escape the fatal bullet. In October, 1961, the United Press reported that Deputy Phillip Maiville of Lansing, Michigan, in a battle with two gunmen who had kidnaped two other policemen, was struck by two bullets, one of which glanced off a checkbook in his left pocket and the other off his badge. Rushed to a hospital, Maiville was found to be unharmed but "was sent home and put under sedation."[26]

Along with tales of people saved from bullets, I have also collected a few examples of close calls and unusual missiles. For instance, eyewitness Joseph Martin told this story of the American Revolution:

A woman whose husband belonged to the Artillery, and who was then attached to a piece in the engagement, attended with her husband the piece the whole time. While in the act of reaching a cartridge and having one of her feet as far before the other as she could set, a cannon shot from the enemy passed directly between her legs without doing any other damage than carrying away all the lower part of her petticoat. Looking at it with apparent unconcern, she observed that it was lucky that it did not pass a little higher.[27]

Perhaps the most unusual missile shot from a gun was not a bullet at all—it was a tooth! And the victim did not escape. French Major André Labruyère, wounded three times in a rebel ambush near Trementines, France, had no bullets left. He took from his pocket a tooth that had been pulled the previous day, loaded it into his pistol, and shot dead a rebel leading an attack; the others fled.[28]

The ubiquitous Johnny Green, mentioned earlier as having escaped two bullets, found himself freed from an embarrassing situation at the Battle of Atlanta by another Yankee bullet. As he climbed over the top of a rail fence, his canteen strap hung and left him suspended on the fence facing the Yankees. Unable to touch the ground with his feet, he could not disentangle himself, but of a sudden an enemy bullet grazed his shoulder, cut the canteen strap, and liberated him.[29]

Elder Horn tells an anecdote of a Confederate soldier who almost died of fright when hit by a strange missile. Drilling with his outfit in an overgrown field while an attack was imminent, the soldier stepped on an old sulkey rake tooth hidden in the grass; it flew up and hit him in the back. Falling, he cried out: "Oh Lord, take me home boys, I'm dead."[30]

No collection of tales of miraculous reprieves from death would be complete without mention of J. Frank Dobie's account of Bigfoot Wallace and the hickory nuts. Arming himself for battle with Indians, Bigfoot filled his loose-fitting buckskin suit and his hat full of hickory nuts, all of which were shelled by Comanche arrows in the ensuing fray. Even Bigfoot himself modestly admitted, "I guess this was the most remarkable experience I ever had with Indians."[31]

Finally, these stories of men who did not die despite being hit by bullets seem to suggest that man's life is indeed ruled by caprice, in spite of his conviction that he is captain of his own soul. Whether he has called it chance, destiny, fate, or accident, man has been awed by that unseen power which decrees life or death in combat.

When differences were settled by hand weapons, such as rocks, clubs, and spears, the death-dealing missiles could be observed; but the longer range of projectiles from firearms made the bullet seem to appear from nowhere. The greater the mystery, the greater the drama. How in future wars some will escape the deadly rays, radiation, and other yet uninvented terrors of nuclear war remains to be seen, but some doubtless will and live to tell their tales.

1. As cited by G. L. Kittredge in *Witchcraft in Old and New England* (New York, 1929), pp. 54-55.
2. Robert Price, *Johnny Appleseed: Man and Myth* (Bloomington, Ind., 1954), p. 81.
3. As told by D. S. Arnold to Lloyd C. Pyle, "History of Nolan County to 1900" (Master's thesis, East Texas State College, 1937), p. 174.
4. John Q. Anderson, *A Texas Surgeon in the C.S.A.* (Tuscaloosa, Ala., 1957), "Confederate Centennial Series," No. 6, p. 83.
5. *Johnny Green of the Orphan Brigade: The Journal of a Confederate Soldier*, ed. A. D. Kirwan (Lexington, Ky., 1955), pp. 31-32.
6. I found the tract on a bulletin board in the Academic Building at Texas A&M about 1956.
7. Mildred Lewis Rutherford, *The South in History and Literature, A Handbook of Southern Authors* (Athens, Ga., 1906), pp. 569-70.
8. Julia G. Bitner, "History of Tom Green County" (Master's thesis, University of Texas, 1931), p. 280.
9. Told me by Mody C. Boatright, Austin, April 13, 1963. At the same time Wilson Hudson said that he had heard of bullets being stopped by metal-covered Bibles carried by American soldiers in World War II.
10. *With Beauregard in Mexico: The Mexican War Reminiscences of P. G. T. Beauregard*, ed. T. Harry Williams (Baton Rouge, 1956), p. 89.
11. *Ibid.*, p. 98.
12. *The Annals of Elder Horn*, comp. J. W. Bowyer and C. H. Thurman (New York, 1930), pp. 47-48.
13. *Ibid.*, p. 48.
14. Jonnie Ross Elzner, "The History of Lampasas County, Texas" (Master's thesis, Southwestern University, 1950), pp. 110-11.
15. "Bowie and the Bowie Knife," *Southwest Review*, XVI (1931), 354.
16. Ed F. Bates, *History and Reminiscences of Denton County* (Denton, 1918), p. 124.
17. O. M. Roberts, *Texas*, in *Confederate Military History*, ed. Clement A. Evans (Atlanta, 1899), p. 636.
18. Henry Kyd Douglas, *I Rode with Stonewall* (Chapel Hill, 1940), p. 331.
19. Charles H. Bryant, "History of Johnson County, Texas" (Master's thesis, Baylor University, 1931), pp. 51-55.
20. *Johnny Green of the Orphan Brigade*, p. 95.

21. Boyce House, *Cowtown Columnist* (San Antonio, 1946), p. 235. Everett A. Gillis retells the incident in his poem "Ballad of Captain Bill McDonald" (Texas Prize poem, Texas Poetry Society, 1951).

22. As told by B. M. Jones, Sweetwater, to Lloyd C. Pyle, "History of Nolan County to 1900," p. 116.

23. April, 1962. Mr. Jenkins mentioned the incident in a letter to Sigman Byrd, who printed it in his column "Byrd's-Eye View," *Houston Chronicle,* July 2, 1959.

24. *Rags and Hope: The Recollections of Val C. Giles, Four Years with Hood's Brigade, Fourth Texas Infantry, 1861-1865,* ed. Mary Laswell (New York, 1961), p. 207.

25. New York *World,* Oct. 15, 1912, cited in Henry F. Pringle, *Theodore Roosevelt* (New York, 1931), pp. 569-70.

26. United Press International release, printed in the *Dallas Morning News,* October 29, 1961.

27. *The Spirit of 'Seventy-Six: The Story of the American Revolution as Told by Participants,* ed. Henry Steele Commager and Richard B. Morris (New York, 1958), II, 714-15.

28. Ripley's "Believe It or Not," *Houston Post,* April 14, 1963.

29. *Johnny Green of the Orphan Brigade,* pp. 148-49.

30. *The Annals of Elder Horn,* p. 49.

31. *Tales of Old-Time Texas* (Boston, 1955), p. 50.

Tobacco and Longevity

J. T. McCULLEN, JR.

TO AFFIRM that the individual who would live to ripe old age must learn to take tobacco well would be, perhaps, to invite controversy. To hazard this particular controversy would be unwise, for it is possible to name at least three long-lived men not known to have used tobacco. Tobacco being an American plant, it is reasonable to assume (mere assumption though it may be) that, without tobacco, Methuselah lived for nine hundred and sixty-nine years. Without tobacco, too, the ancient physician Galen reputedly lived one hundred and twenty-eight years (some say one hundred and forty),[1] primarily by drinking mead and massaging himself with olive oil. One writer asserts that Attila the Hun was, at an advanced age, still "hearty and strong"; and he might have remained so for several years more, had he not, at the age of one hundred and twenty-four, married "one of the most beautiful princesses of the age" and died next day of excessive wine imbibed during his wedding night.[2]

For two reasons, however, it is desirable to review information concerning the link between the use of tobacco and the attainment of old age. First, evidence that tobacco promotes long life has, of late, been somewhat neglected. Second, how to live a long and happy life is currently a topic challenged for primacy by only a few others; namely, domestic and foreign peace, elections, and the ill effects of tobacco. To survey a few accounts which call attention to individuals who have used tobacco and yet lived long lives is the primary objective of this writing.

Evidence most fundamental, but too prevalent to receive more than passing attention, accumulated during the first two centuries of modern tobacco culture. Tobacco was, when first introduced among Europeans, welcomed as the panacea for which the human race had pined ever since the expulsion of Adam from Paradise. Tobacco was therefore hailed as a cure for many diseases—yea, almost all diseases! So universal and unrestrained were early laudations that a few authorities natively inclined toward restraint cautioned physicians to speak more temperately, lest someone should doubt their testimonials on behalf of the medicinal benefits of tobacco. In 1610, for instance, Edmund Gardiner noted that some "doe commend it too much aboue measure, attributing to it so many great and excellent vertues, as I think is scarce possible to find in any one hearbe."[3] To some readers in the 1960's the idea that, because tobacco is possessed of health-giving properties, physicians have praised it excessively may be a trifle surprising. If so, to return to the decade of Shakespeare's birth will be to end this surprise. Concluding a twenty-four page treatise entitled *Of the Tobaco, and of His Greate Vertues*, which discourses of the first genuine miracle medicine of the modern era, Dr. Nicholas Monardes admonishes readers thus: "Lo, here have you the true Historie of Nicotaine, of the whiche the saied Lorde Nicot, one of the Kynges Counsellers, firste founder out of this hearbe, hath made mee privie aswell by woorde as by writyng, to make you (friendly Reader) partaker thereof, to whom I require you to yelde as heartie thankes as I acknowledge my self bound unto hym, for this benefite received."[4]

Three centuries later, during a tobacco controversy beside which current agitation is relatively mild, a leading British physician first examined evidence offered by both supporters and opponents of tobacco, then concluded, "To longevity I feel that smoking is eminently conducive."[5] In support of this conclusion, he cites examples of long-lived tobacconists, including a lady who died at the age of one hundred and ten and who had smoked for ninety years. Impartial in his approach to the controversy, he surveys a great mass of pronouncements concerning tobacco and health, the con as well as the pro. The latter include such discoveries as the following: Tobacco is the "best remedy known for the fidgets." Tobacco prevents lunacy, during which many unfortunate victims meet an untimely death by suicide.[6] Like authorities who, at present, recommend formulas whereby to achieve long life, he emphasizes the value of quietude, a state of being promoted and sustained by the use of tobacco:

Tobacco soothes and tranquillizes the nervous system—helps man through the cares and turmoils of life—cools down his excitement and makes him reflect before he speaks—enables him to endure philosophically a backbiting enemy, a scolding wife, or a bankrupt debtor—and, above all, encourages the habit of abstraction which is essential to profound reflection and deep thought. Blue-devils fly before its honest breath. It ripens the brain; it opens the heart: and the man who smokes, thinks like a sage, and acts like a Samaritan.

In short, he finds in tobacco mental and physical repose to arm one against confusions of a mad scramble for things material, as well as against the "jarring, discordant sounds of a hypocritical age."[7] No wonder, then, that he labels tobacco a promoter of longevity. No wonder he asks, "Who, I say, that has once felt the perfect abstraction from all these, that a pipe can bring, would not seek a second dose of such a potent and such a blissful medicine?"[8]

An American who surveyed arguments and sought truth to end the tobacco controversy raging a hundred years ago reached similar conclusions. Typical of his compatriots, he relied on statistics when considering particular diseases, such as cancer, and discovered it to be (excepting on the lip) twice as frequent among nonsmokers of the 1850's (females) as among smokers (males).[9] Like the Britisher, he was especially interested in the question of tobacco and longevity. In addition to emphasis on such points as tobacco's being a "great soother of domestic difficulties,"[10] he reported an experiment resulting in the conclusion that a moderate use of tobacco promotes longevity. Among sixty-seven people aged from seventy-three to ninety-three (the average age being seventy-eight), he discovered only nine nonconsumers of tobacco.[11]

To say whether today the percentage of tobacco users in this age group is about the same is perhaps impossible. The question does not matter, for the individuals to be discussed henceforth are, with few exceptions, centenarians. One exception is a special case which merits immediate attention. More than a century ago, Robert Southey made the following contribution to the history of science:

There is now in the possession of Mr. Walton, farmer, of Great Lever, near Bolton, a male ass, which is known to be nearly fifty years of age. He is named "Billy," and prefers tobacco to any other luxury; he is likewise very fond of a pinch of snuff. Our informant has within these few days seen Billy masticate a large quid of pigtail with as much *goût* as any Jack tar in his majesty's service. When he had finished the tobacco, a pinch of strong rappee was administered, which Billy snuffed without the least demur, and curling up his olfactory organ, delivered one of those charming solos so peculiar to his species.[12]

The life span of jackasses being what it is among those subsisting on ordinary fodder, this report alone will probably silence the doubts of those who wonder whether the use of tobacco affects longevity.

Returning to observations on smokers who have survived a century or more, one finds rewarding food for thought in a book published in 1799. While discussing longevity among human beings, the author names and comments on several who, prior to 1799, had developed the tobacco habit and also lived for more than a hundred years. These centenarians may be divided into two categories.

The first is restricted to confirmed smokers. Two died at the age of one hundred and one, the first in 1779 and the second in 1790. Of Fluellyn Pryce of Glamorgan, the old book states: "Herb teas were his breakfast; meat plainly dressed, his dinner; and, instead of supper, he refreshed himself with smoking a pipe of tobacco."[13] The second is John Michiel of the Hague, who was "a great and regular smoaker of tobacco" (p. 238). John Saunders of Stratford, near Old Sarum, died in 1799, at one hundred and six. "When the weather would permit it, he usually attended Sunday service at his parish-church, near a mile from his home: occasionally he would walk to New Sarum, and back again, nearly three miles; and to Old-Castle house, to drink a cup of ale, and smoke his pipe; and, being perfectly upright . . . , used no stick to assist him." He furthermore, "a short time before he died, was seen to run, in order to avoid a carriage in a narrow part of the road" (p. 288). Two others lived to one hundred and eight. William Thompson,

Esq., of North Keyme, Lincolnshire, died in 1783. "He enjoyed a good state of health, smoked two pipes, and drank some ale, on the day of his death" (p. 189). Richard Brown, of Peter-church, Hereford, died in 1794. Of him, our eighteenth-century authority on longevity declares, "In the instance of this old man, the assertion that smoking tobacco is prejudicial to health, is completely refuted, as he was seldom seen without the pipe in his mouth, and took his last whiff a short time before his death" (p. 263). Another centenarian whose death, in 1791, is recorded in this old book is Paschal Seria, of Valentia. Dead at one hundred and eleven, Seria had almost become the prototype of modern health addicts: "He subsisted, toward the latter part of his life, principally on vegetables, and frequently smoked tobacco" (p. 246). The last of this group is an American, John de la Somet, of Virginia. He died, in 1766, at one hundred and thirty. "He was a great smoker of tobacco, which, agreeing with his constitution, may not improbably be reckoned the cause of his uninterrupted health and longevity" (p. 90).

The second group reported by our authority consists of two individuals who, despite the fact that they are not identified as smokers, are pertinent to this study. The first is Don Carlos Felix O'Neale, of Madrid, a sometime governor of Havana. Don Carlos, whose death at one hundred and ten occurred in 1791 (p. 245), is one whose smoking habits may well be assumed. This I say because, once during my transit from Havana to the States, a customs agent convinced me that to think of Havana is to think of tobacco: "What? no cigars?" he asked. "In Havana one smokes cigars and drinks rum, and when he leaves Havana he leaves with rum and cigars. You should have a supply of cigars and rum for each member of your party: yourself, your wife, your daughter. One hundred cigars and one gallon of rum are duty-free for each of you— for even an infant in your arms." The second example is a Yankee, John Weeks, of New London, Connecticut, who died at one hundred and fourteen in 1798. According to the report, "A few hours previous to his decease, he ate three pounds of pork, two or three pounds of bread, and drank nearly a pint of wine!" (p. 286). If, as was affirmed during the seventeenth century, tobacco is a purge that never fails of its operation, upward and downward,[14] tobacco might well have lengthened the life of John Weeks far beyond his one hundred and fourteen years.

The fact that man is, by nature, a species more attentive to history in the making than to the wisdom of history already made is, to the individual genuinely interested in the question of tobacco and longevity, a distinct asset. Today hardly any old man or woman can become even an octogenarian without being probed for a magic formula certain to prolong human life. It is worth noting that, whatever the exact percentage may be, the aged who offer a toast on behalf of tobacco speak with voices heard round the world. So also go reminiscences of many who, with nostalgic admiration, recall old-timers. News of the current decade affords an instance. In a résumé of snuff-taking, Dick West states, "One of my grandmothers dipped snuff from the age of 12 until she died at the age of 92."[15] Another contemporary account notes the ninety-second birthday of Bertrand Russell, a man capable of still addicting himself to tobacco (if he does not have the habit already), merely because the masses have antitobacco nerves.

Inasmuch as comments on other tobacconists aged from eighty through ninety-nine would consume pages adequate to the making of a book, this article will rush forward with accounts of centenarians in the news in recent years. Three centenarians given world-wide publicity in a single week are, in part, responsible for the writing of this paper. Before accounting for them, however, it is appropriate to comment on a few others who, having not long since passed the century mark, also demonstrate the relationship between taking tobacco and living to ripe old age. The first is noteworthy because at his death at the age of one hundred and one he was the "oldest Christmas baby" in America. "Active until a month ago," reads a news report of June, 1958, "he attributed his long life to reading, drinking beer, and chewing snuff."[16] The second is Mrs. Nicomedes Suarez, of Lanus Oeste, Argentina, who celebrated her one-hundredth birthday in June, 1962. Though tobacco is not included in her announced formula for longevity, "Mrs. Suarez puffed contentedly at her briar pipe while she posed for news photographers," and explained, " 'My doctor has forbidden me cigars, but lets me smoke my pipe.' "[17] The third is "a tiny woman who loved cigars and children almost equally." A native of Puerto Rico, she died in Miami, Florida, at the age of "either 112, 114, or 115 years," still "swearing by 'spicy food, a good cigar, and a good drink of strong rum' as the sustaining forces in her healthy life."[18]

The three centenarians in the news of one week are "pipe-smoking Mrs. Mary Guess, who observed her 107th birthday Monday" and "says she has smoked a pipe for many years";[19] an "ancient Chippewa" of Warroad, Minnesota, who "celebrated his 120th birthday Thursday" and stated that "he likes to smoke a pipe";[20] and an old lady in Villanrique, Spain, "the oldest woman in Spain, a 116-year-old gypsy," who said she "could never have accumulated so many years unless she smoked." The reporter then lets her speak for herself: " 'A long time ago,' Candelaria Campos explained, 'a doctor told me cigarettes were good for the health, and since then, I've always smoked.' " Described as a "chain-smoking centenarian," she added, " 'They all say I ought to be dead by now, but it's not my fault if I can't die.' "[21]

A final instance: A Roswell, New Mexico, physician in 1964 reported the condition of a man aged one hundred and twelve years who "was back in the hospital for a checkup after a successful operation." Said the doctor, "He's in awful good shape." This centenarian had "told a newsman recently he still smokes two packs of cigarettes a day."[22]

Convincing though these testimonials may be, it seems wise to make certain concessions to antitobacconists. Two points in particular merit consideration. First, it is true that some few people not known to be addicted to tobacco do live long lives. Second, the use of tobacco can be a hazardous venture.

Roaming the Southwest in 1963 was an old man, aged one hundred and twenty-six, who accounted for his long life without any specific reference to tobacco. According to the reporter who brought this so-called "vagabond" to public attention, "He attributes his exceptional age to Indian herbs."[23] To question this testimony is as useless as to speculate on whether tobacco is still catalogued as an "Indian herb." However, unless the herbs included in this old man's fare are exceptionally strong, to the mind of some who observe the coloration of his beard may come reminiscences of juice from a plant not normally associated with teapots.

As yet, too, it is not safe to ignore all medical admonitions that the use of tobacco may actually endanger health. A testimonial which only the foolhardy would discredit appeared late in the nineteenth century in one of the most reputable medical journals published in England:

Still another catastrophe caused by the abuse of tobacco. Yesterday, on the Avenue de l'Opera, a gentleman was about to pick up a cigar that he had let drop. At the same instant an omnibus was passing. The driver had not time to rein up his horses, and the unfortunate gentleman was literally crushed. See whither the immoderate use of cigars may lead one![24]

1. Thomas Cogan, *The Haven of Health* (London, 1584), p. 252.
2. James Easton, *Human Longevity* (Salisbury, 1799), p. 3.
3. *The Triall of Tobacco* (London, 1610), A2ᵛ-A3ʳ.
4. *Joyfull Newes out of the Newe Founde Worlde*, tr. John Frampton (1577); Tudor Translations, ed. Charles Whibley (London, 1925), I, 98. The original source of this statement is *L'Agriculture*, by Jean Liébault, 1567.
5. George Sexton, *The Great Tobacco Controversy* (London, 1857), p. 30.
6. *Ibid.*, p. 31.
7. *Ibid.*, p. 45. Sexton adapted these observations from a passage in *Night and Morning*, by Edward Bulwer, 1851.
8. *Ibid.*, p. 46.
9. Malcolm W. Spenser, "Tobacco," *Atlantic Monthly*, VI (1860), 197.
10. *Ibid.*, p. 189.
11. *Ibid.*, p. 199.
12. *Southey's Common-Place Book;* Fourth Series, ed. John Wood Warter (London, 1850), IV, 393-94.
13. *Human Longevity*, p. 161. Subsequent references to this book are indicated parenthetically in the text.
14. James Howell, *Ho-Elaine: Familiar Letters;* 8th ed. (London, 1713), pp. 402 f.
15. United Press International release, May 18, 1964.
16. Associated Press release, June 2, 1958. "Christmas baby" refers to the fact that this old man was born Christmas Day, 1856.
17. UPI release, June 28, 1962.
18. AP release, December 12, 1962.
19. AP release, May 12, 1964.
20. UPI release, May 15, 1964.
21. Western News Service release, May 12, 1964.
22. UPI release, May 21, 1964.
23. AP release, June 3, 1963.
24. *British Medical Journal*, I (March 19, 1881), 454.

The Sanctified Sisters

A. L. BENNETT

THE AMERICAN FRONTIER was often the scene of the rise of new, and sometimes strange, religious sects. Cut off from centers of culture and official church discipline, settlers might break away from organized religious bodies to form hardly recognizable splinter groups. In their endeavor to "live the Bible," or to give outward shape and ceremony to what was directly "revealed," they gave birth to new faiths, or at least practiced a new symbolic behavior, however scant the theology or formal dogma. This was not, speaking strictly, folk religion, but it *was* indigenous. One of the most interesting of the new sects was established in Texas about the middle of the last century by a group of determined women who brought quiet consternation to the male population of their community.

It was in old Belton that this little band of women who came to be called "the Sanctified Sisters" overawed, subdued, and almost cowed the male citizenry. It is a kind of cosmic irony that the virile, adventuring husbands stood dismayed and helpless before a feminine assault upon that most radical principle existing between men and women—love. The sanctified ladies removed themselves from their husbands' beds, and by joining what they called "the True Church Colony" vowed to live a life of sinless perfection—that is, without love. This earthly battle of the sexes was enough to excite the mirth of the gods, but to those most intimately concerned it was no laughing matter. Though psychologists and sociologists may have secular interpretations, this feminine withdrawal was all done in the name of religion.

The soul and genius of the "sanctified" movement was Martha McWhirter, who came with her husband from Tennessee and settled on Salado Creek in 1855. George M. McWhirter established a mercantile business in Belton and in time prospered and became prominent in civic affairs. He built for his family what must have been one of the finest houses in the city. That house still stands (on a street about two blocks west of the main thoroughfare and parallel to it), a fine-looking two-story stone structure with good lines and good proportions. It was not until 1866, and after she had borne twelve children by her husband, that Mrs. McWhirter became convinced it was sinful to live intimately with him. Now this has its humorous side, but Mrs. McWhirter was not one to see the humorous side of things.

According to one account, Mrs. McWhirter's extraordinary religious experience came when she was near death in 1866.[1] She promised the Lord that if she were spared she would consecrate herself to religious endeavors. She claimed that she received "divine revelation" assuring her "in audible voice" that she was not to die—that she had a great work to do. This version differs slightly from that of George P. Garrison, University of Texas historian who lived among the "sanctificationists" for several weeks during the summer of 1893 and had daily converse with Mrs. McWhirter and her followers.[2] At the time they had established a profitable hotel business in Belton. According to Professor Garrison, Mrs. McWhirter in 1866 lost two children and a brother; these afflictions she considered to be a chastisement from God and she resolved to live a purer life. During a protracted meeting held in Belton she became anxious about her unconverted children, who seemed cold and indifferent to the exhortations of the preacher. As she walked home one night, a voice suggested to her that the revival meeting was the work of the devil. Against this suggestion she struggled and prayed, but while she was busy with breakfast the next morning she received a "Pentecostal baptism" and knew then that the voice of the night before was the Voice of God. From that time forward she professed "sanctification."[3]

Up to this time Mrs. McWhirter and her husband had worked together in the Sunday school and prayer meetings, he being superintendent of the Union Sunday school. The McWhirters were Methodists, but when the Methodists broke away from the Union meetings and built a church of their own, they enjoined the Methodists not to set up a separate Sunday school. When the Methodist pastor did organize his own Sunday school, the McWhirters kept to their original group. As the Baptists and other denominations built churches of their own, they left the Union church, which became the special meeting place of Mrs. McWhirter's followers. It was sectarian differences, says Professor Garrison, as well as the doctrine of sanctification that led to the establishment of the True Church Colony. The zealous leader would not submit to pastoral control, for through revelation she had authority from the Highest Source.[4]

Mrs. McWhirter was a woman of extraordinary powers and wielded an uncommon influence over her followers. They had dreams, visitations, revelations, and finally the "Pentecostal baptism"; they readily accepted the central doctrine of the True Church, that it was sinful for a sanctified woman to live in conjugal intimacy with an unsanctified husband. If both husband and wife were sanctified, they might live together under mutual restrictions—that is, without love's unholy rites. The consequence of the movement was that the Sisters engendered a peculiar hostility among the male population of Belton. They reduced their husbands to a state of celibacy, held their biweekly prayer meetings from house to house, and made those economic arrangements necessary to counter the economic sanctions that some of the husbands invoked.

George McWhirter was a sensible man and from the beginning would have nothing to do with his wife's fanaticism. He kept on living with her because he knew she was sincere, because she was his wife, but mainly because he loved her. In his view she was a victim of delusion. Mrs. McWhirter remained in her husband's house in the role of "servant," a status which evidenced the humility fitting to religious abnegation and which neutralized their relations as mates. Though George McWhirter was in easy circumstances financially, his wife would accept no money from him. She did, however, require a maid servant, whom she allowed her husband to pay some eight or ten dollars a month. The maid servant, who happened to need an economic haven, was one of the Sisters.

The situation that confronted the men involved was what Bigfoot Wallace would have called a "poser." You could not fight a Woman, and you could not fight Religion. Again, one with ears delicately attuned might have heard cosmic laughter. Some of the more romantically inclined men sought better fortunes in Central America; some initiated divorce proceedings; and some just fumed and burned. It did no good to invoke economic sanctions against women who were shrewdly working out their own economic viability. If men needed little here below, women needed less. Sunbonnets and cotton dresses, sometimes homespun, sufficed for attire; these and a little food were easily bought with the butter-and-egg and vegetable money they had at hand. If a Sister, unceremoniously evicted, needed a roof over her head, there was always Mrs. McWhirter with her two-story stone house, a perfect physical and spiritual haven. This was not the affluent society, and the only status symbols, for the Sisters at least, were treasures laid up in Heaven.

Their communistic practices were neither doctrinal nor deliberate; communism for them was a practical necessity. Their common fund began when one of the unmarried Sisters, a schoolteacher, laid down twenty dollars she had saved. Others contributed their butter-and-egg money. They took in washing, they chopped and sawed firewood, they went out in the city to do housework. These women, it must be emphasized, were not drawn from the poor and the outcast; nearly all of them had been used to well-to-do circumstances, and some of them were accustomed to luxury. So that when a call came in that a Belton housewife needed a girl or woman to come and "live in" and do housework, there would be a brief fit of quiet weeping, but in spite of the humiliation there would always be someone to volunteer to go out in service and bring the money into the common fund.

It was in the promotion of the Sisters' laundry business that an unhappy incident occurred. Their practice was to wash and iron clothes at one Sister's house on Monday and at another's on Tuesday. Mr. Henry, one of the affected husbands, strenuously objected to their making his house into a laundry, and the Sisters just as vehemently protested his objections. "Shoo out of here, you old hens!" he yelled. "Now shoo out of here every one of you!" Words flew back and forth, but mainly back, and in the melee of pushing, shoving, and shooing, Mr. Henry let fly sticks and stones, with the result that his wife suffered a deep gash on her head. Central Texas newspapers gleefully reprinted the news item from the Belton *Journal*. The story in the Gatesville *Advance* ran thus: "Mrs. McWhirter and three other female members of the Sanctification band in Belton have been fined $20 each for occupying Mr. Henry's premises as a laundry to raise funds for the Lord. Mrs. Henry and her daughter left their home after the trial and will cast their lot with the band instead of the ungodly Henry."[5]

It seemed that the ungodly Henry had the law on his side, and a refuge had to be found for Mrs. Henry and her daughter. Mrs. McWhirter shrewdly went to work. She took money out of the common fund to buy building materials, chose one of Mr. McWhirter's town lots, gathered her band about her, and raised a house for Mrs. Henry in a few days. Mrs. McWhirter's son and the sons of some of the other Sisters helped out, and the only money expended for labor was for two days of work by a professional house builder. Though George McWhirter protested in strong terms against his wife's taking his lot, the good man had to yield when she reminded him that she had brought some property to their marriage. It should perhaps be added here that Mr. Henry, a man of means, had a large house, and when the poor man died not long after the fight over making his house a laundry, his wife came back to occupy his home, to take in some of the unhoused Sisters, and to start a boarding establishment that prospered and grew into the even more prosperous hotel business the Sisters enjoyed during the last two decades of the century.

In 1880, after the sisterhood had been a going concern for about thirteen years, the husbands of Belton found an effective way to strike back. In February of that year two Scots brothers who had heard of the religious order and thought highly of it came to Belton and proceeded to affiliate. Heretofore no men had joined, although theoretically there was no reason for them not to as long as they were "sanctified" and kept to themselves. But when the Scotsmen took up residence with the Sisters, it didn't look a bit good. In fact, it looked downright scandalous. And when rumors began to float around (false, of course) that the two Scotsmen were enjoying a life of revelry and riot, it was time for "direct and precipitate" action. This was something a man could smash with his fist—that is, another man. So one dark, cold midnight a mob of husbands who had been deserted gathered with their sympathizers at the McWhirter house and demanded the Scotsmen. A pathetic circumstance the mob did not know about was that the Scotsmen's aged parents had arrived to visit their sons this very night. George McWhirter, loyal to the end, was guarding the house, as rumors of mob action had drifted to him. But he was overpowered after a few stray shots were exchanged, and the Scotsmen were seized. The unhappy pair were flogged within an inch of their lives and told to leave town and never come back. This was an unjust, as well as an unlawful, injury, for the Scotsmen were upright and clean-living. They had the courage, too, to let it be known that they did not intend to leave town. Thereupon the civic authorities took a hand; they had the men adjudged insane and sent them to the Austin asylum to get them out of harm's way. The authorities at the asylum refused to accept them, however, as it was plain that the two men were sane; but they did extract from the victims a promise to leave Belton forever.

This violence discouraged male membership in the True Church Colony. The grand jury investigated the affair and indicted the husband of one of the Sisters, but he was speedily acquitted when brought to trial.

Another setback came to the order a little later when Mrs. McWhirter did something very foolish. I have this story from R. B. James, of Belton, who remembers Mrs. McWhirter and her religious band very well. Late one evening a large crowd had gathered in front of her house. She had announced about the town that she was going to demonstrate her religious faith; she was going to prove to people that the Lord would take care of his own. Her faith was so great that she believed if she jumped off the roof of her front porch she would not fall, or that if she did, the fall would not hurt her. Perhaps she had a revelation that told her to do it. Down on the ground were her faithful followers and all the curious of the town. The flat roof to the front porch made a high platform. She came out of the second-story dormer window wearing a long, flowing robe, and after a prayer or two and a dramatic pause, she sailed over the banisters of the porch as if she were trying to fly. She fell right in front of the crowd. When the doctors examined her they found she had broken two ribs and both legs.

All of this was humiliating to George McWhirter, a man of good sense and great heart. He loved his wife, in sickness and in health. He expostulated with her when she took his town lots and built rent houses on them for the sisterhood, but to the public he defended her as a woman entirely sincere in her convictions, however deluded she might be. He continued to live with her under the "restrictions" imposed by her "sainthood" and guarded their house against harm.

He suffered her to bring other women into the house and endured many humiliations, but one night when she endeavored to bring a male convert under their roof he rebelled. She gave him to understand that the male convert must be admitted. This he could not stomach. He gathered his things and left the house forever, and he never saw his wife again. He took up his abode in his mercantile establishment. Two years later when he grew ill and lay dying, Martha McWhirter debated with herself whether she ought to go see him. She said that she was moved by natural affection to go to him, but that she was restrained by her religion. It was a firm rule of her order that the Sisters were not to seek company outside of the order. They welcomed people who came to see them, but they did not go out to visit. She resolved that if she received a revelation that she might be permitted to go see him, she would go, and she would interpret his sending for her as a revelation. But this revelation never came.

Nevertheless he was thinking of her at the last. "He made a will in her favor, and appointed her executrix, without bond, declaring his faith in her integrity, and his conviction that she would do justice to all their children, to those who had not followed her as well as those who had."[6] The evidence is that she was scrupulously honest in administering his estate of twenty thousand dollars, as in everything else. In an interview late in life, Martha McWhirter said: "Mr. McWhirter was devoted to me; he loved me through it all. He believed with all his heart in the sincerity of my new religion. For years he tried not to oppose me, and though living under the same roof he allowed me to follow the dictates of my conscience. But when the younger children grew into years of discretion he left me. I never spoke to him again."[7]

That such an organization could be kept together for so long a time was due to the force of character of this one woman. Under her guidance the order prospered, though the adult membership was never over fifty. The group established a flourishing hotel business, operated two or three farms, drew rent from several houses in the city, and operated a steam laundry in conjunction with the hotel. In 1893, when George Garrison lived in the hotel for several weeks, the sisterhood had assets of about fifty thousand dollars. There were at that time four male converts in the order. One was in New York trying to establish a piano business for the corporation; one was a hotel clerk, one the manager of the laundry, and one a carpenter. The other members were married women who had left their families, widows, unmarried women, and some young girls who had followed their mothers. They were embarrassed for a place to invest their surplus funds. Some of the money was spent on excursions to Mexico City and New York. Toward the end of the century they were seeking fresh ground, and for this reason visited the Great Lakes region and Washington, D.C. In 1899 they left Belton and established themselves in a house on Kenesaw Street in Washington. After Mrs. McWhirter died in 1904, the band dwindled in power and influence, and little more was heard of them.

An epilogue to this story makes a pleasant little tale in itself. Adah Pratt was born into the sisterhood in Belton, her mother presumedly having left her father's household only a short time before. Thus she grew up under strict religious guidance and knew hardly anything else, for the Sisters had withdrawn from society and had as little to do with outsiders as possible. They kept their own school, had their own dentist, and never took much stock in doctors. Adah, and the other girls too, might have been sent to a boarding school if there had been the proper revelation, but it never came. There were some books to read at the hotel—Tolstoy and Edward Bellamy—and some fairly good magazines. But most of Adah's guidance came from the Bible; the Sisters tried to "live the Bible" according to their own interpretation. A German boarder at the hotel one time taught music to the young ones, but when there developed a delicate feeling among the group—a collective insight or intuition—that something was wrong, the music lessons were discontinued.

When the group moved to Washington, Adah was a blooming nineteen, but a girl ought not think of marriage. She was tall, of a striking figure, and had a wealth of chestnut hair.[8] But to what avail? She was taught to beware of men and was never permitted to have acquaintance with any of them. As time went by she saw men, often noticed them, but had not paid any particular attention to any of them—until one day.

"There were ten children in the colony," she said, "all girls. Five of the girls grew up, and then slipped away to be married. Of course they were regarded as sinners. I thought them bad. But about a year ago I went down town with a girl friend and she introduced me to Mr. Hoover.

"Somehow or other I could not get him out of my mind. I found myself wishing I might see him all the time. I knew it wasn't right; at least I thought it wasn't. Later I met him down town again, and several times after that. Then he told me he was going to leave the city and asked me to write. I told him I would."

From her story it seems that Hoover, who was a hotel clerk, went to Chicago, then came to Philadelphia and wrote his intentions to Miss Pratt in Washington.

"I was crazy to see him," she said, "and then decided to risk the fear of my mother's displeasure, and give him a surprise party. So I slipped quietly out of the house in Washington and came to Philadelphia. When I found Mr. Hoover he was greatly surprised.

" 'Why, Adah, have you come up here to marry me?' he inquired.

" 'I don't know that I thought much about that,' I replied. 'I just felt I had to see you again.'

" 'Well, *will* you marry me?' he asked. It took me by surprise, although I was not wholly unprepared for it.

" 'I'm willing,' I said finally.

" 'Right away?' he asked. This took my breath away.

" 'Can't you wait until tomorrow night?' I asked him, and he said he would."

Ah, brave new world, that has such people in it!

1. Aline Rothe, "Texas Women's Commonwealth," *Houston Chronicle Magazine,* November 19, 1950.

2. George Pierce Garrison, "A Woman's Community in Texas," *The Charities Review,* III, no. 1, November, 1893. A photocopy made by the Library of Congress may be found in the Texas Collection at the University of Texas.

3. *Ibid.,* p. 30.

4. *Ibid.,* pp. 29, 30.

5. Issue of November 18, 1882.

6. Garrison, p. 32.

7. Rothe.

8. This story originated in Philadelphia and was distributed by the news services on April 18, 1908. The Gatesville *Star-Messenger* carried it in the April 24 issue.

Running the Fox

FRANCIS E. ABERNETHY

AN EAST TEXAS FOX HUNT is more than a hunt. It is a convocation that binds its following together with closer than Masonic ties. The wine is drunk and the bread is broken, but no blood is spilled. The race is the thing, and it is the running of it that is the measure of its significance, not the reward in the end. And the pursued is as important as the pursuers.

Two pickups with pens in the beds pull over to the side of a two-rut, red-dirt road and cut their lights. Men get out and talk and argue for a while, then open the gates to the pens and the hounds spill out—red bones, blue ticks, black and tans, lemon spotted. They scatter in the darkness, each yelping his own personal cry. Then the men wait until pretty soon an old bitch hits a hot trail and in singles and in groups the pack hearkens to her until all are pounding through the woods, pursuing the same quarry. The men get back to their trucks and drive the country roads, stopping silently to listen every few minutes, hunting the best seat in the house to hear the music of the pack. When they find that particular hilltop, they stop, build a fire to cut the chill, and listen and speculate and talk. This continues till the fox trees or goes in the ground. By that time it is usually around sun-up, and they start rounding up the dogs, driving, stopping, and blowing long, clear blasts on their horns. They don't miss work the next day, but a hunter can usually be distinguished by his sleepy look.

There are a lot of stories about the dogs and the men and the foxes that get together on these cold East Texas nights, and there is probably an element of truth to some of them.

A bunch of high school boys from Kirbyville were running lines on an old slough off the Sabine, and they were all bedded down around about midnight. They heard a rustling noise and some light feet running, and some of them looked up just in time to see this little gray fox trotting and picking his way right through the center of the camp.

That was something to talk about, and they did while they listened to a pack of hounds sounding and heading in their direction. The yelping got closer and closer, and all the boys were standing up when the pack went right through the middle of camp, muddying up blankets, scattering the food, and knocking pots and pans all over the place.

The boys cussed, straightened up some, and crawled back between their blankets. Just as they were dozing off, the fox loped through again, this time sort of grinning and looking them over. One of the boys missed him about a yard with a stick of firewood, and they all settled down to some serious listening to the pack, which sure enough was headed their way. They were about half ready when the dogs came pouring through the camp again, baying and squawling on a hot trail. This time they flung every pine knot and mud clod they could get their hands on, and the dogs ran on through with a yelp and a holler here and there.

That was all the sleep for the night, so three of the boys went off to run the lines and the rest put on the pot and went to straightening up the camp again. An hour later, after the talk had shifted from the fox to fishing, it happened again. At the time the hounds were out of hearing and nothing seemed to be stirring outside the ring of fire. Then the little gray came through like a hummingbird, ran just outside the circle of light, and was gone before you could say, "There's that damn fox!" Then the pack topped a rise about two hills away, and you could tell by the sound that they were running the same old trail. When they hit the camp, the camp hit them—skillets, firewood, clods, everything that could be thrown or swung—and that was the end of the race for that night.

Going home the next day, the boys stopped at a snuff-and-soda-pop country store, and the first thing they were asked was had they heard the race the night before. They allowed they had and the old man told them about Little Gray, the smartest fox in Newton County. Usually Little Gray led a long race over the ridges and treed when he got tired of the fun. Last night, though, he must've been in a bad mood. He took the pack through every baygall and briar patch in the county, seesawed through half a hundred bob-wire fences, and then must've led them over Baird's Bluff. Damn near killed every dog in the bunch!

There's another smart fox up in Sabine County. This one's named Rusty and he's old enough to be gray-headed. Everybody chased Rusty and they had a lot of respect for him. They'd even set up some ground rules for chasing him. They'd never run him more than once a week and usually kept him for the Friday night race, and they never ran him with more than twenty dogs in the pack. The fox hunters broke in the young packs on Rusty because they always knew where to cast so they could pick up a trail in a hurry. Rusty had his stomping ground and everybody knew what it was, and they put out dead chickens for him regularly just to keep him happy. They loved old Rusty and looked out for him; you might tell a Sabine County fox hunter that his favorite hound was a cold trailer, but just don't say anything about Rusty.

Well, Old Man Jim Hughes' boys came home a few days for their daddy's birthday a couple of springs ago, and as usual they spent every night out on a red-dirt hill listening to a race. The last day they were home they decided to run old Rusty, so Mr. Jim checked around and nobody'd run him that week, so that night they cast the dogs near Rusty's stomping ground and sat down to wait developments. Somewhere out in the dark old Rusty unlimbered and started circling, running figure eight's, and just generally cutting up. There were twenty dogs running true, not a babbler in the bunch, and Mr. Jim and his boys sat on a ridge around a fire and listened just like the king and his court at a concert.

There was just one outsider in this group. He was a young fellow from Beaumont who'd come up with Alec, Mr. Jim's youngest boy. This fellow had been hearing dog talk for three days straight and almost considered himself a fox hunter. He was dressed for what he thought a fox hunter ought to look like, and later on that night when he heard the dogs barking treed and everybody started off through the woods in that direction, he felt that now was his time to shine. He trotted off ahead of the family, who weren't running, just long striding, and chorused the dogs till pretty soon he found them, yelling and squalling and bawling and running as high up the side of an old bent magnolia as they could. And there sitting about twenty feet out on an old crotch limb was Rusty, completely unconcerned about all the noise going on below. He'd made a good race, had helped the dogs put on a good show, and was waiting for what he figured would happen next. The men would tie off the dogs, and he'd hop down and run back to his ground where he'd find a dead chicken hung up in a tree. That was the way things went.

But he or nobody else had figured on this young fellow from Beaumont, who as soon as he saw him, pulled out a .22 pistol and began firing wildly in Rusty's direction. Well, old Rusty took one surprised look and fell limp across the limb he was sitting on. The dogs hushed and stood still, some of them slinking off through the woods with their tails between their legs. And Old Man Jim Hughes, who'd just come up flanked by his boys, said, "Well I'll be damned!"

And that was about it. Luke Hughes tied the young fellow's hands with a lead rope, and Old Man Jim made a noose with another one. They'd already got the hanging rope over a limb, and I guess that would have been the end of the fellow if Rusty hadn't got to laughing so hard that he fell out of the tree.

There never were two old men who liked to fox hunt as much as Dad Wilson and Bert Tunstall from up at Woodville. They were both older than the courthouse and so deaf they couldn't hear it thunder. Every day you could find them on the square talking at the tops of their voices to each other and the other old-timers, and any time there was a big fox hunt on, Dad and Old Bert would be there talking dogs and trying to hear who was running. They judged most of the bench shows in Tyler County and kept a pretty good bunch of blue-tick hounds to run whenever they could get somebody to go along and help them around.

Dad's grandson Charlie took them out east of Hillister one

cold spring night, and they cast the dogs about nine o'clock. The pack struck a trail right off, so they drove to the top of a sand hill near the railroad right-of-way and fired up some pine knots and settled down to enjoy the race. Their conversation was always sort of short during the running and generally was about which dog was leading or which one was just babbling or running the trail the wrong way. And this was a cold, still night and you could hear the pack nearly all the time, especially when they topped a hill, even though they were taking the fox away.

"There's old Jug leading the race again," said Dad.

"Too coarse-mouthed for Jug," replied Bert. "Sounds like Sadie to me."

"Sadie ain't that fast."

"Jug never led anything but his tail."

And this went on till the pack had run out of hearing, and they were getting ready to get in the pickup to find a better stand. About that time, though, the T. & N.O. freight out of Shreveport topped a rise and blew for a crossing about a mile off.

"I-God," Dad said, "don't tell me that ain't Jug."

"You better gitcha a hearing aid," Old Bert told him back.

And that T. & N.O. kept coming up one hill and going down another, blowing at ever logging road on the line.

Bert said, "Damn, they shore are coming, ain't they?"

And the old man said, "They *shore* are."

By that time the freight had hit the hilltop and was blowing the long whistle for the Hillister crossing, and the ground was trembling and the trees were shaking, and the two old men just stared into the fire. It had passed in a couple of minutes, and you could barely hear the sound of the engine as the tracks took the train through Big Turkey Creek bottom.

Old Man Tunstall shook his head and spit into the fire. "Well, sir, I don't know whether that was Jug or Sadie leading, but, by God, *that* was a race!"

And Dad said, "I-God, it *shore* was!"

The immediate sources for the above stories were David Shepherd of Port Arthur and Mrs. Ruth Garrison Scurlock and Charles Merrill of Beaumont.

The Charcoal Burner

E. J. RISSMANN

A LONG TIME AGO, Rucker Mayes was a charcoal burner on my father's place at Cedar Valley in Travis County, down on Bear Creek. His wife Jessie and his daughter Vera helped him.

Burning charcoal does not mean burning it as we burn gas in the space heater or the central heating system, or as we burn wood and kerosene in our camp stoves. It has to do with the making of charcoal.

Back in the thirties, in my store in East Austin I sold charcoal — cedar charcoal — by the wagonloads and truckloads. Negro women there used it to heat their irons when they took in washing. Blacksmiths, too, used it in forges. Ella Mae, my wife before she died in 1956, said we'd recognize East Austin blindfolded, by the charcoal odor. When I knew the charcoal burners at Cedar Valley, their kilns were discernible for miles by the smell and the curl of smoke.

In the Great Depression years of the thirties, various suppliers brought charcoal to my small East Austin store, which in the main part was no larger than eighteen by thirty. There was Lonnie Roberts, dark in complexion, beady of eye, slightly stooped, and unhurried in talk and motion. His charcoal had to be good or he'd not sell it, and the Negro women asked for it by his name. He took most of his pay in trade. Things were cheap — many groceries for much charcoal. I'd retail a towsack of charcoal for fifty cents and a big paper sack for a dime. Who was making money then out of anything? I liked to handle charcoal — I liked the clean smell. Another reliable burner was Mr. Shirey. He'd done right well at something in town before the Depression struck. He, his wife, and their pretty daughter were too proud to go on relief, and so they burned charcoal. Lonnie Roberts was a preacher on the side, a good one, but Mr. Shirey had no other income. You'd have thought the family was going to church, so neat and clean were they when they brought in a load of coal. And it was good coal, too. There were others who supplied the good kind, but most burners produced "sorry" charcoal which would lose customers for me when I stocked it.

Once, in 1963, I decided I'd prefer cedar charcoal for my broiler. The kind made from oak and the briquettes sold in the stores were hard to light. I drove all over East Austin and found none. Out in the cedar brakes charcoal isn't being burnt any more.

On our place out there on Bear Creek, round half a century ago, the woods were full of charcoal burners, sometimes as many as eight families working there at the same time. Most were Mexicans, with occasionally a Negro family. Many of the Mexicans had their small patches of cushaws and corn. There were woodchoppers, too, of course; they chopped wood by the rick or cord. To people who'd come after it, my father sold cookstove and heater wood for twenty-five cents a rick and fireplace wood for a dollar and a half a cord. Most of the woodchoppers were working to make charcoal, though a few of the Mexicans also grubbed stumps for us when land was being cleared for cultivation.

Rucker Mayes and his family lived up there in the pasture, in the Stubbs house, seemingly far away though really only a mile, beyond the lazy, seepy branch clogged with mint and weeds. Stepping stones led to the other side. After that it was not far to where the Mayeses lived, in a one-story, one-room rock house, with an unfloored porch in front and a lean-to kitchen in the back. The room had a fireplace in the north and two beds in the south. Outside was a windlass, really part of a big log, set horizontally on posts, over what had been a bored well before marauding boys filled it with dirt and rocks. Part of its metal casing stuck out of the ground. In the big flat lay seep holes, standing full of water after rains. Here were cedars too, where roosted and nested wasps. We'd chunk the nests with rocks, and the wasps'd fly out at us.

We'd lie on the ground and play dead, and the wasps would go away.

I'd go up to the Stubbs place often, and find Mr. Mayes chopping cedar poles into lengths of about four feet. Mrs. Mayes and Vera would be peeling off the bark with "case" knives, like those for eating at the table. The cedar had to be green. The bark was saved for covering the kiln.

Some said Mr. Mayes was of Indian descent. And I suppose he was, for he had the high cheekbones and the piercing eyes of an Indian. He stood tall and lean, the way most men did who'd come up in those days on a diet of biscuits, cornbread, bacon, molasses, and beef or small game. The reason I mention Mr. Mayes's supposed Indian blood is that I liked Indians. To me they were a sturdy, romantic race, and I wished Mr. Mayes would fashion a bow and arrow so we could hunt buffalo. But there were no buffalo, and Mr. Mayes had other things to do.

Mrs. Mayes wore gloves when she peeled the cedar poles, and so did Vera. Mrs. Mayes prided herself on neatness and cleanliness; she kept her hands nice with gloves and protected her face with a sunbonnet. Why shouldn't she have pride? Her relatives were people of substance and self-respect around the Driftwood area. She had refinement, if little formal education; and she had drive and energy enough for two people. You could be nice-looking, clean, and neat, even if poor.

Charcoal burning was a way of making a living. It involved some capital: a wagon and team, an ax, a garden rake, a sprinkler, and a shovel or scoop. Money was hard to come by and there were but few jobs in town. The final refuge, of course, for poor folks was the Poor House. Austin had one of these, maybe out the Webberville Road. Only the old and helpless could get in, and they had to sign a pauper's oath. And it was not a pleasant place. The Mayes family had few resources other than the capital required for making charcoal, unlike my parents with their debt-free 1,100 acres, part of it adobe hills too impoverished to sprout a grassbur.

Rucker Mayes had a brother, Bill, who with his family lived in a tent, which I fancied to be a tepee. They were poor. When my mother'd stop by, they'd spread their only rug on the chair for her to sit on. Bill looked more like an Indian than Rucker Mayes did.

Usually the Mayes family kept several kilns in operation. After the cedar poles were chopped and peeled, a little pen, maybe twelve inches across and four feet high, was erected on the kiln site. It was made of dry sticks. The peeled cedar poles were leaned against it at an angle of about forty-five degrees. Round and round, in a circle, pole was leaned against pole, until the radius of the circle was six to nine feet or so. Then bark was laid over the poles and dirt was shoveled on until everything was covered except a hole at the top. Only at the top could air or moisture get in. The kiln was now ready to fire.

A shovelful of live coals was dumped through the opening into the little pen and dry chips were heaped over them. Once the fire was going, bark and dirt were dropped through to cover the inside. Being smothered, the fire could not blaze. Day after day it smouldered through the kiln, reaching from cedar pole to cedar pole and leaving charcoal behind.

A watch had to be set, to make sure the fire would only smoulder. Something might break loose, and the air might reach the fire. Then there'd be a blaze, which if not put out with more bark and dirt, or doused with water from a sprinkler — a can with a perforated spigot — would ruin everything. Too much blaze, or too much water either, would make the charcoal light in weight and lusterless. Good charcoal has a sheen like anthracite, and it "rings," when tapped, like a century-old cedar fence rail.

During the night someone was on duty as observer, or would wake up and go outdoors to take a look. The kiln might start to blaze, or a downpour of rain might sluice off the dirt, seep through the bark, and put out the fire. Shovel, water, and dirt — these were kept handy. It might mean a week or ten days, this keeping watch, until the kiln should reach its maturation. And with several kilns going, the charcoal burner could hardly count on getting unbroken sleep.

There were many ways, of course, for charcoal burners to make the time pass acceptably and agreeably. There were clothes to wash in the old zinc tub with the aid of a washboard, mending and darning to be done, and meals to cook. Visitors might come to pass the time of day or perhaps even to get up a play party. After checking his kilns the charcoal burner might venture going to church or prayer meeting. To while away the watching time there was always chewing tobacco or snuff dipped with a hackberry twig, Garrett's or Lorillard's in brown bottles with one to five dots on the bottom to indicate strength. Some liked their snuff weak and some liked it strong. The bottles could when empty be used as borders for rose beds or walks.

The Mayeses carried water in buckets from the creek when it was running, or they hauled it from our cistern, a juglike underground reservoir, kept full by rains pouring through gutters from the roof and filtered through charcoal. They hauled it on the wagon, in wooden barrels covered with towsacks secured by hoops. Mrs. Mayes used water freely at their house. She kept the family's clothes spotlessly clean, ironed, and starched, as far as it was possible—that is, when the coal didn't have to be gathered.

The fire having run its course, the coal was raked out in piles, and the bigger chunks were broken into smaller pieces. The sprinkler was kept handy to subdue any vagrant blaze. It was a hot and smudgy business. The charcoal dust flew in the air and settled on the skin, especially where cedar sap, so hard to wash off, had clung. It penetrated clothing and made the skin itch underneath. Rivulets of sweat ran down the face, leaving meandering streaks.

The coal next was shoveled into towsacks for marketing, the sack openings then being woven shut with Spanish dagger leaves, tough like sisal. The wagon had standards on the sides, and the sacks of coal were piled between, on the wagon bed. When the wagon was full Mr. Mayes was ready to take off for market, while Mrs. Mayes and Vera stayed at home to look after the kilns. Sometimes they went along. Mr. Mayes would wear his Sunday suit, with a gold watch chain dangling from his vest, and a black felt hat. His shoes were shined, with Mason's blacking, I think. He smoked a pipe, as did my father, and he'd stop by the house to visit on the way. He spoke in a slow drawl, which was indicative of his contemplative, unhurried way of life. My father's voice was more rapid. He was always in a hurry, his days never being long enough for all the things he had to do and wanted to do.

I feel sure that Mr. Mayes, on the long, slow trips to Austin alone, made up and practiced the singing play-party calls for which he was known roundabout Cedar Valley. I can hear him singing, with endless variations,

London bridge is falling down, falling down,
London bridge is falling down, my fair lady.

Mrs. Mayes and Vera were afraid of the night when they were alone, and sometimes I'd stay with them when Mr. Mayes was off to market. Mrs. Mayes would see prowlers among the cedars in the moonlight. There were no prowlers, of course — I don't think there were any — just clumps of cedars. It was comforting to have a man around, even though he was only a small boy, when came the night with its hidden terrors.

Rucker Mayes is dead and gone and so is his wife Jessie, but as long as I keep them in memory they haven't vanished altogether. Vera is old and I am not growing any younger.

Charcoal burning was a whole way of life. No one burns charcoal in the hills now.

Creeping Ignorance on Poke Sallet

JAMES W. BYRD

IN EAST TEXAS during the early spring, the folks cook and eat "poke sallet." Not all of the folks, of course. Only those who have maintained a belief in the folklore of their southern ancestors greet the season of spring by saying:

"I'm going out and pick me a mess of poke today. I'll pareboil it and have some greens, or I may dress it up and have a real good poke sallet."

Even in East Texas, this statement might not be understood by the so-called younger generation, especially the city dwellers, the immigrants from the north, and the educated whose heads are filled with nothing but "book learning."

In the field of folklore, there are many instances when printed records, the so-called scientific "facts," are at variance with folk "beliefs" or folk "lore." The case of poke is a prime example.

To begin with, the printed records all use the term "pokeweed," which I have never heard in folk speech. Note the unfavorable connotation of the word "weed." And that isn't the only word used with an unfavorable connotation. *Webster's New International Dictionary* (2nd ed.) defines "Pokeweed" as a *"coarse* American perennial herb (*Phytolacca americana*) with . . . white flowers and dark purple juicy berries. . . . Both the berries and root are emetic and purgative. The root is poisonous but the young shoots are sometimes eaten like asparagus." Thus, *Webster's* begins with an insult and ends with a falsehood when defining a succulent plant that gave aid and comfort to the early settlers of Texas and still does to their descendants.

One would expect more knowledge and more objectivity in a distinguished-looking book published by the University of Texas Press. In *Roadside Flowers of Texas* Howard Irwin discusses both the small pokeweed and the great pokeweed, with only the latter being admitted as edible. He says:

The Pigeonberry or Small Pokeweed is found rather commonly, in places abundantly, in woods in the rolling hills of Central Texas, south to the Rio Grande, west to the Trans-Pecos. It is distinguished from the Scoke, or Great Pokeweed, by wavy-margined leaves, pale pink flowers, and red fruit. The Scoke on the other hand is an inhabitant of low moist woods, principally in East Texas, and has flat leaves, white flowers, and purple berries. . . . The early spring shoots of the Great Pokeweed are sometimes eaten as greens but this is utility fraught with danger; the entire plant, especially the root, carries a poisonous substance, hence the water in which the greens are boiled should be discarded.[1]

Although he reluctantly admits it is "sometimes eaten as greens," Irwin would certainly discourage any cook by calling this "utility fraught with danger." He then reiterates the point with a warning against the poisonous root.

Fortunately, there were few reference books on the frontier or the diet of the early settlers would have been more restricted than it was. Guided only by folk knowledge, or "lore" handed down in oral tradition, the settlers prepared poke by recipes inherited from Tennessee mountain ancestors or obtained from Indian friends.

An Indian cookbook published by the Museum of the Cherokee Indian mentions poke as one of the early spring plants "that the Cherokee people have eaten for as long back as any of us know about and are still enjoyed by many today." Usually the plants are "parboiled, salted, cooked some more with grease, if available."[2]

Historically, Tennessee is a parent state for East Texas,[3] and many of the folkways of that state survive among East Texans. One Hunt County informant[4] tells me that her recipes came from some of the first settlers in the Ozarks, whose speaking and eating habits were patterned after those of relatives in Tennessee mountain areas. My informant had recipes for poke stalk pickles, fried poke, and poke greens.

Still today, she says, some of the mountaineers pickle poke stalks. They are the only pickles some of them will eat (or can afford).

The method is simple: "Use only tender stalks not over 6 inches high. Cut in 3-inch lengths. Trim off leaves. Cook in clear water about 5 minutes. Discard water. Cover again with salted water, and boil about 5 minutes. Discard water. Pack stalks vertically in jars. Cover with this solution: To each pint of vinegar, add ½ teaspoon mustard seed and 2 tablespoons sugar. Heat to boiling, pour over pickles, and seal."[35]

Another use for the stalk, she says, is to "strip it, cut in small pieces, roll in meal and fry. Tastes like okra."

These are exotic uses, however. The standard method, reported by dozens of East Texas informants, is to cook the young leaves as greens, often mixed with other wild greens or with domestic mustard greens and turnips. Some of the wild plants mentioned (lamb's-quarter, sheep shire, sorrel, rabbit lettuce, also called wild lettuce, and sour dock, also called curly dock) are similar to the list in the Cherokee cookbook, and it is probably from the Indians that the white man learned to utilize wild greens. In East Texas, these greens are cooked with salt pork, as turnips are cooked. They are served with cornbread and perhaps a homemade pepper-vinegar sauce. Poke greens are especially delicious, being more mild-tasting and digestible than turnips.

It is poke salad or "poke sallet," however, that has made the plant survive the creeping ignorance that besieges it on all sides—especially the northern side.

Webster's New International snobbishly defines "poke salad" as "greens from the pokeweed," labeling even that definition as "Rural, U.S." East Texas folk know, however, that it is usually called "poke sallet," "sallet" being explained by *Webster's* as an archaic and dialectal form of "salad."

An informant in Commerce makes poke salad that pleases the most discriminating taste. Mrs. J. B. Yates, who learned her method from family cooking near Wolfe City, says no recipe is needed. Simply pick the tops or tender buds. Wash them. "Pareboil" them about half an hour (this is the folk pronunciation, also archaic and dialectal, which means boil and drain, from Old French *parboiller*). The draining is to get rid of a strong taste as well as a supposed poison. Put in half a cup of bacon drippings. Cook until all water has been evaporated. For every two cups of cooked poke, stir in five beaten eggs and scramble. Add salt and pepper. Serve with cornbread.

Another informant, reared on a farm near Bonham, says this: Garnish the cooked poke with sliced hard-boiled eggs and strips of crisp bacon. Serve with creamed potatoes, cornbread sticks, and cold buttermilk—in an unhurried atmosphere.[6]

Recently an ex-Yankee reporter, writing in the Greenville *Herald-Banner*, questioned whether this can be called a "salad." *Webster's* says salad is a "cold dish of green vegetables . . . usually dressed with oil, vinegar, and seasonings; called also *green salad*." Then there is a bow to "Southern, U.S.," where salad is "cooked greens or poke salad with seasonings."

That salads are always cold is Yankee fiction, not fact. In southern cooking there is also a warm potato salad, seasoned with vinegar, pickles, and boiled eggs.

Obviously, frontier cooks seasoned salads with the oil that was available—bacon fat. "Wilted lettuce," a popular dish in the Old South, was made by pouring hot fat over fresh garden lettuce leaves.[7] And even in northern Pennsylvania, a *Dutch Cookbook* lists a hot salad called "Dandelion with Bacon Dressing."[8] In fact, the wild dandelion is so popular in the North that you can find it described in seed catalogues.[9]

From the point of view of word changes and associations, "greens" and "green salad" could have become so closely associated that they became interchangeable in folk speech—without the present distinction between "vegetable" and "salad" courses. In East Texas today, poke greens usually become poke salad only when dressed up with eggs and perhaps bits of bacon. This is the result of modern influence. Historically, in folk speech of Tennessee and East Texas, "sallet" is the word used in referring to any fresh greens. The pioneers also referred to "turnip sallet" and "mustard sallet."

It is easy to believe that the settlers of East Texas found poke greens a welcome change from their limited rural winter diet. But they weren't eaten simply because they tasted good. There was, and is, a widespread belief that they are a good spring tonic. More than half of my informants mentioned this as a reason for eating poke salad in early spring. One wrote, "It was a good spring tonic after a winter of meat and bread."[10] Another said, "It was good for blood in the spring."[11] Others said it was equal to a "round of laxative."[12] And what would *Webster's* think of this: "My great-grandmother served it to her family to rid them of poisons accumulated during the winter!"[13] A Dallas lady wrote, "Men felt it brought back youthful vigor."[14] A liquor store owner of Longview confirmed this. He said, "It made you feel frisky as a snake that had shed its skin."[15] A housewife from Greenville commented: "My mother made us eat it as a tonic. Seems our old family doctor had said years ago that if a family would eat a mess or two of poke salad each spring, then he would do their doctoring free for that year."[16]

In this belief, folklore is backed up by scientific fact. Before such words were popularized, a source of vitamins and minerals was found by the folk. Even before Hadacol, they had an iron tonic for their tired blood.

The belief that poke contained poisons was, and is, widespread. That is why it is parboiled (or pareboiled), sometimes twice. The overcautious cook loses much food value by cooking too long. The rumored poison in the poke leaves is a libel grossly exaggerated. Although all informants had "heard" that poke was poison, only one knew of an example. She had read in the paper of some babies who got sick from sucking on raw poke stalks left in the back of a car.[17] My statistics show the danger is not as fraught as some have thought. There must, however, be some poison there, for insects do not attack poke as they do turnip greens. Poke is blessed with a built-in insecticide. Its leaves are unmarred, whether young or mature.

The most poisonous part, the root, has also been useful to man, or so the folks think. Several reported that the boiled root was a good treatment for the seven-year itch.[18] Beaten poke root was made into a poultice for "boils."[19]

The dark purple juicy berries have been put to even more uses. "Sure cures" for rheumatism and arthritis are made from them. They are put in the chicken water to keep parasites off the chickens, and to cure certain fowl diseases. They make excellent bird food and will attract wild birds. They make a useful purple dye. Their juice is ideal for turning youthful palefaces into redskins. Historically, their principal use was for homemade ink. Southern writer William Faulkner recorded that use in a story set before the Civil War.[20]

When we consider the aid and comfort this humble plant gave our pioneers, it is time to strike back at Yankee publishers and their carpetbagger representatives flooding the South. Some scalawags are now joining them. When I mentioned the poke plant recently, a native East Texas boy said, "Don't that grow mostly around outhouses?" Another said, "No, it grows mostly around the barns and the hawgpens." They are as ignorant as *Webster's* when recording that it is "eaten like asparagus." Poke grows, of course, wherever the soil is rich—along fence rows, roadsides, and lake dams. I was told in Hunt County that raccoons eat the berries and scatter the seeds far and wide. It can be found in April growing in the most sanitary soils. As for eating it like asparagus, experienced cooks laugh at such ignorance. Asparagus, grown easily in East Texas, is boiled briefly, standing on end with the tips out of the water, probably in an old coffeepot. It is then served with a cheese sauce. There is no comparison to poke in cooking, serving, or tasting.

Texas-born Dwight D. Eisenhower once classified T.V.A. as "creeping socialism." I have borrowed his phrase to explain the status quo of the poke plant in East Texas. Falsehoods have crept into northern-written dictionaries and reference books—slander is being published by our universities—libelous rumors are invading the oral traditions. Today even the folk are mixed up on poke. Someone must stop this creeping ignorance on poke sallet. It should be done by the Texas Folklore Society; if not, then by a much-need Texas Poke Lore Society. Membership would be open to anyone who could prove he was a proud possessor of a pure, palatable pint of pickled poke.

1. Mary Motz Wills and Howard S. Irwin, *Roadside Flowers of Texas* (Austin, 1961), pp. 108-9.
2. *To Make My Bread, A Cherokee Cookbook,* eds. Mary Ulmer and Samuel E. Beck (Cherokee, N.C., 1951), p. 47.
3. Barnes F. Lathrop, *Migration into East Texas, 1835-1860* (Austin, 1949), p. 35.
4. Mrs. Jerry Poteet, Greenville, letter dated June 22, 1962.
5. Sallie Hill, "Recipes for Centennial Cooks," *Progressive Farmer*, May, 1961, p. 68.
6. Interview with Mrs. E. M. Sherer, Commerce, April, 1963.
7. *South Carolina Cookbook* (Columbia, 1954), p. 23. "Pour hot vinegar, bacon fat, salt and sugar over shredded lettuce. Garnish with slices of hard-cooked eggs."
8. Edna Eby Heller, *Dutch Cookbook* (Lancaster, Pa., 1958), II, 24. See also Violet M. Cummings, "Spring Tonic," *Woman's Day*, March, 1963, p. 114.
9. Isabel M. Weathersby, "Wild Greens for a Tonic," *Ford Times Magazine*, April, 1962.
10. Interview with Mrs. George D. McLeod, Campbell, April, 1963.
11. Interview with Miss Faye Ratten, Cooper, April, 1963.
12. Interviews with Mrs. Lula Hall, Dallas, and David Boothby, Commerce, April, 1963.
13. Interview with Mrs. E. M. Sherer, Commerce, April, 1963.
14. Interview with Miss Edna Frazer, Dallas, April, 1963.
15. Interview with W. E. Baker, Longview, April, 1963.
16. Letter from Mrs. C. M. Hauser, Route 1, Greenville, dated May 6, 1962.
17. Interview with Mrs. Theda Baker, Longview, April, 1963.
18. Interview with J. M. Alford, Sulphur Springs, April, 1963.
19. Interview with R. L. Hefley, Campbell, April, 1963.
20. "The Raid."

The Penny Dreadful as a Folksong
JAMES WARD LEE

ALL THE GREAT American folksong collections list large numbers of songs which are not true folksongs. These are songs whose authors are known or whose histories can be traced from some recent source. Many are popular songs written by professional songwriters in Tin Pan Alley, and many arose out of the minstrel and music hall shows of the last century.

These are the folksongs which no one says much about. They are usually inferior in quality and tend to be highly sentimental ballads or ludicrous attempts at humor. Folksong collectors do not like to get them, but most find that for every "real" folksong they collect, they get six or eight "dreadfuls." Scholars don't write about them because they find very little to be said, and even in the headnotes to many collections the editors take a defensive attitude about having included them.

But such songs cannot be ignored completely because the singers, who are our only sources of songs, love these weepers and see no difference between a song like the very mawkish "The Baggage Coach Ahead" and the old and lovely Child ballad "The Dewey Dens of Yarrow." One of the things highbrow collectors do not like to admit, but are forced to, is that their informants have almost no taste whatsoever. To them, folksongs are all equal, or as Big Bill Broonzy is supposed to have said, "I guess all songs is folksongs; I never heard no horse sing 'em."

These non-folk folksongs usually fall into the same general categories as the traditional ballads and songs—songs of love, childhood, and war; humorous songs; songs of murder and sudden death;

morals and mottoes; dance tunes with words added; and songs of protest. Perhaps the songs of defeated love, fallen women, and lost children—the songs of the most maudlin sentimentality—are those most often collected as folksongs today. It is these songs, and especially those composed in America in the latter half of the nineteenth century, that this paper will be concerned with. For no one can deny that they swept America in the nineteenth century. They show up in all the great folksong collections; for instance, of the 833 songs in Vance Randolph's *Ozark Folksongs*, certainly three hundred are popular sentimental songs. *North Carolina Folklore*, which has 972 songs and ballads, has several hundred "penny dreadfuls" right out of the sentimental songsters. It is the popularity of these songs that Mark Twain is parodying in his Emmeline Grangerford episode in *Huckleberry Finn*. In fact the original of Emmeline, Mrs. Julia A. Moore, "the Sweet Singer of Michigan," published in 1877, and reprinted in 1878, a book of these songs called *The Sentimental Song Book*.[1] Twain calls her "The Queen and Empress of the Hogwash Guild."

Certainly young girls of the period emulated Emmeline in composing poems, and singing and drawing; and they loved, as young people do today, the popular songs. And these "dreadfuls"—written and published in the large cities of America and sold on fly sheets for a penny or in songsters for a dime—became quite popular before the Civil War. Their popularity grew until the end of the century. And the gay nineties, if histories of popular music can be believed, were spent in a maudlin orgy of sentimental singing. However, in the new century the desire for the excessively sentimental waned and comedians and comic-song writers began to parody the "penny dreadful."

For fear of painting too dismal a picture of the history of popular music in this country, I should point out that at the same time hundreds and hundreds of war songs, minstrel songs, fake foreign songs—"Abdul Abulbul Amir," for instance—were also being written and sold. But nothing exceeded the "penny dreadful" in popularity. And the term "penny dreadful" not only applies to sentimental songs but also to the cheap pulp fiction, both western and eastern, which found its way onto the newsstands of America.

These works of fiction—even more dreadful in some respects than the songs—were at least as moralistic and maudlin as the songs. And if possible they had a more insidious influence on American minds.

The "penny dreadful" press came to America after having had a great vogue in England in the first part of the nineteenth century. The names of Jemmy Catnach, John Pitts, and Henry Such are familiar to all students of British broadsides of the 1820's and 1830's. These London publishers of songs, scandals, and faked convict confessions made fortunes with cheaply printed songs, traditional and current. Catnach, the best known of the publishers—he had a biography written about him[2]—made a fortune between 1813 and 1825, a fortune in pennies and ha'pennies. In *The Broadside Ballad* Leslie Shepard tells us Catnach accumulated so many coppers that he

> used to take them to the Bank of England in large bags in a hackney coach. His neighbors would not change them for silver, dreading infection from the filthy coins collected by his broadside sellers. Eventually Catnach used to boil up the coppers in strong vinegar and potash to make them look like new coins. But all his workers were obliged to take their wages in copper, and week-end would bring their wives or mothers to help them carry home anything from ten to forty shillings all in pennies and halfpennies.[3]

Of course, the publishing of songs in America started long before the Revolution, and thousands of songs were published in many forms before and during the Civil War; but it was after the war, when the republic began to expand in all directions, that song publishing became a large industry. A list of U.S. music publishers will show that before the war they were located in all the major cities and that after the war the song publishing center moved to New York, where it has remained.

Most of the Tin Pan Alley and minstrel songs which folklorists have collected in this century come from the post-Civil War period, with a rather large number written in the eighties and nineties. Sad and sentimental songs like "Put My Little Shoes Away," "The Fatal Wedding," "Little Annie Rooney," "The Baggage Coach

Ahead," and "Break the News to Mother" all come from the last years of the century.

After the new century began there were still songs which got into the oral tradition and were collected by folklorists, but the number lessened—or perhaps professional entertainers supplanted folksingers as America's entertainers. This is certainly true after the invention of the radio.

As said earlier, the most dreadful of these songs are those of thwarted lovers, fallen women, drunkard fathers, and lost, deserted, or orphaned children. Many of the songs with children in them show the Dickens influence on nineteenth-century sentimentality. In "The Baggage Coach Ahead," written by Gussie Davis in 1896, a father and his little girl are accompanying the corpse of the deceased wife and mother who is in a coffin in the baggage car ahead. Vance Randolph, who includes the song in *Ozark Folksongs,* quotes a letter from Thomas Bailey Aldrich, who saw a whole theater audience moved to tears upon "the singing of this rot." He further says that a photograph of a baggage car flashed upon the screen caused tears to come to the eyes of "all the burglars and murderers in the upper gallery."[4] Such was the power of the penny dreadful.

The question of whether prohibition was brought on by Carrie Nation, by plays like *The Drunkard,* or by all the sentimental temperance songs has never been answered, but there were hundreds of antidrink songs written in America both before and after the Civil War. A disproportionately large number of these songs got into oral tradition, and drinking folklorists always insist they helped bring on "the noble experiment." But after all, who *can* suppress his temperance feelings when he hears these words from "The Drunkard's Lone Child"?

> Out in the cold I wander alone,
> With no one to love me, no friends, no home.
> Dark is the night, and the storm rages wild,
> God pity Bessie, the drunkard's lone child.
> . . . .
> Is it too late, temperance men? Please try
> Or poor little Bessie must soon starve and die;

All day long I've been begging for bread.
Father's a drunkard and Mother is dead.

Another theme, that of the rejected lover or runaway mate, was as much in style with popular song writers and the folk as temperance and childhood songs. One example of this sort of song which includes all the elements of sorrowfulness except drink is "The Fatal Wedding," published in 1893 and ascribed to W. H. Windom and Gussie L. Davis. Vance Randolph reports that it was still available in sheet music form as late as 1950, but it got into the oral tradition early and has been reported by Pound, Hudson, Greenleaf, Neely, Belden, and Randolph.[5] The song tells of a wedding scene one cold night and of a woman who is passing by with her child and sees the lighted church. After begging the sexton to let her in—"for the child's sake," of course—she breaks up the wedding:

I must object, the woman cried, in a voice so meek and mild,
The bridegroom is my husband, and this our little child.
What proof have you? the preacher said. My baby, sir, she cried.
She raised the babe then knelt to pray—the little one had died.

Of course the parents of the bride, out of gratitude, take over care of the woman for the rest of her life. Naturally, too, the bridegroom kills himself "before the dawn of day." And the song ends with this verse and chorus:

No wedding feast was spread that night, two graves was made next day,
In one the little baby, in the other its father lay.
This story often has been told by firesides warm and bright,
Of bridegroom, bride, the outcast wife and a fatal wedding night.
While wedding bells was ringing, while the bride and groom was there
Marching up the aisle together as the organ pealed a air
Telling tales of fond affection, vowing never more to part,
Just another fatal wedding, just another broken heart.

One more typical theme that shows the power and poignancy of the "penny dreadful" is the virtue of a fair maid. The favorite sport of Samuel Richardson's Pamela, as everyone knows, was to have long conversations with Mrs. Jervis and Mr. B about her "vartue." Well, virtue comes in for its share of treatment by the authors of popular songs of bygone times. One of the best songs of this type was published in 1896 and was called by the longish title, "My Mother Was a Lady, or If Jack Were Only Here." It deals with a young waitress in a big city who is spoken to familiarly by a salesman, and who amid tears says,

> My mother was a lady, like yours, you will allow;
> And you may have a sister, who needs protection now.
> I've come to this great city to find a brother dear,
> And you wouldn't dare insult me, Sir, if Jack were only here.

When the salesman asks her name, we learn—to no one's surprise—that he has known her brother Jack for years. The drummer then says,

> He'll be so glad to see you, and if you'll only wed,
> I'll take you to him as my wife, for I love you since you said:
> My mother was a lady . . .

This song, the epitome of all virtuous-maiden songs, is reprinted in *Read 'Em and Weep* by Sigmund Spaeth, who tells that it was used, along with a handkerchief dampener called "Take Back Your Gold," in a revival of *East Lynne* in the twenties.[6] It got into the oral tradition in America, and while it is not in many of the collections, it was known in Texas years ago. Mrs. Virginia Owens, a student at North Texas State University, learned the song from her grandmother who lived in Trinity in East Texas.

Nowadays, of course, middle-class taste will not allow us to like the excessive sentimentality of the "penny dreadful," though mawkishness does survive in the country and western songs; and the pulp "penny dreadfuls" are still with us in the form of confession magazines and in books by lady authors with triple names. In fact, perhaps sentimentality is with us as much as it ever was, except that now we require that it be couched in *New Yorker* style as Salinger does it or be hidden behind a hairy chest and a Hemingway character.

1. Julia A. Moore, *The Sentimental Song Book* (Grand Rapids, 1877).
2. Charles Hindley, *The Life and Times of James Catnach (Late of Seven Dials) Ballad Monger* (London, 1878).
3. Leslie Shepard, *The Broadside Ballad* (London, 1962), p. 82.
4. Vance Randolph, *Ozark Folksongs* (Columbia, Mo., 1946-1950), IV, 163.
5. *Ibid.*, IV, 277.
6. Sigmund Spaeth, *Read 'Em and Weep* (New York, 1926), p. 170.

The Ballad of Bob Williams

JACK SOLOMON

ALABAMA WAS ONCE a part of the West. When the early settlers, including the forebears of Bob Williams, a prototype of the Alabamian-Texan-Westerner, came down from the Carolinas and settled along the way through what is now Georgia and Alabama, they were going west. As the frontier passed and left Alabama in the east, the Mississippi River presented a geographical but not a cultural barrier.

Folklorists are familiar with several areas of kinship between Alabama folk and Texas folk. We need only look at the Texan's superstitions, remedies, and folk sayings to verify this kinship. From the eastern seaboard the oral traditions followed the pioneers as they moved west and south and then farther west. The same traditions were brought by those who followed the mountain route to Tennessee, Arkansas, and Texas.

In Alabama, for instance, it was thought that chicken manure tea would break out the measles. Alabamians who went to Texas took this belief with them. Some who returned brought back the belief that buffalo chip tea was the thing to use.

Early frontier Alabamians gave to the Texas traveler the bawdy, wild, picaresque tale abundantly exemplified by the Simon Suggs stories of Alabama. But Alabamians returning from Texas brought back the grand lie. Everyone who came back had seen the biggest cow, the driest desert, and the horniest toad that ever lived. A natural pride began to find expression. The tall tale became truly tall.

Stay-at-home folk in Alabama saw all westerners as Texans.

Whether from Colorado, Dakota, Arizona, if he was western he was Texan. They also saw this figure as either a hero or a villain—there was no middle ground. Folklore, which has a great capacity for turning heroes into villains, villains into heroes, can also add colors to a character which he in real life never possessed. There may have existed a paradox but never any shading. Jesse James was an outlaw, but he had "a heart of gold." Robert Ford shot a criminal, but he was always a murderer.

Students in my folklore classes at Troy State College in Alabama turned up several stories of fictitious visits to Alabama farms by the James boys. And one even photographed their graves in a Pike County graveyard!

But native Alabama outlaws pale beside their western counterparts. This was brought to my attention by four of my students—Tom Canady, Oby Baker, Claude Tom Ammerman, and Tom Fields—who found a ballad in Pike County based on a local murder. Unlike the western hero, the three murderers—Hale, Rivers, and Johnson—lack daring. They prey on an almost helpless family. Their career is short, consisting of one crime. They put up little fight, make almost no attempt to escape, and the strongest character requests privacy at his hanging, with no spectacle and no final, grand gesture. The tune to which the ballad is sung is undistinguished and lifeless. These same collectors, however, did turn up a ballad with vitality and vigor, "The Ballad of Bob Williams." The ballad makes no pretense of presenting a factual biography in song, but creates a lusty, zestful, delightful folk character.

As did so many Alabamians, Bob Williams "went to Texas" over half a century ago, returned to Alabama, "went to Texas" again, and somewhere along the line became famous, wealthy, notorious, and successful. The road to Texas was open and much used. "Going to Texas" was so popular that for the sake of convenience certain post offices in Alabama, Georgia, and other points east had a stamp which simply stated—"Gone to Texas."

Robert Lee Williams was a native of Pike County and became the third governor of Oklahoma. His biographers and friends, Edward Everett Dale and James D. Morrison, describe him as a paradox, a man of many moods and characters. Information is hard to come by in his native county. Friends and foes alike are reluctant to speak of him in the presence of strangers. Yet the legend of Bob Williams continues to live.

Pike County politicians returning from Democratic party national conventions often reported to their friends that they had seen Bob at these conventions, as he was often a delegate. The response usually amounted to a polite, "Is that right?"

The ballad, as found by my students and sung by local folk who have forgotten whether it was made up by one man or many, parallels, in the loosest fashion, the life of Robert Lee Williams. While his biographers paint him as the many-faceted, complex individual he must have been, the ballad presents him as a man too bad for Alabama, Mississippi, Louisiana, and Texas but good enough to become governor of Oklahoma. He must have undergone some kind of transformation, but the ballad says nothing of it.

> Young Bob Williams, a Pike County boy,
> Got caught buying votes in the town of Troy.
> And that's not all, I've heard it said,
> He even got caught a-votin' the dead.

This first stanza ignores the fact that Williams returned and left a second time for Texas. The circumstances of his leaving are yet a mystery, though, and at least one informant simply smiled and said, "I know he left in a hurry," when I asked if he had been caught in illegal voting practices. Dale and Morrison say this on page 44 of *Pioneer Judge* (Cedar Rapids, c. 1958): "There is . . . a rumor in Troy that some local politicians, under investigation for alleged irregularities in an election, encouraged Bob Williams to make the trip to the West because they feared his testimony if he should be summoned as a witness. It has been found impossible to verify this rumor and its truth is doubtful."

The chorus exaggerates his leaving and takes a humorous poke at the condition of the county's property and the character of its citizens.

> Bob Williams, Bob Williams, oh, we miss you so.
> You left Pike County, out West you did go.

>   We ran you out upon a rail
>   'Cause there was no room in the Pike County jail.

The next three stanzas are a high-spirited recounting of the semifictitious saga of Bob Williams. Stanza two reflects clearly the old rivalry between Alabama and Mississippi:

>   He went to Mississippi and thought he would stay.
>   Within four days they'd run him away.
>   Leave us, Bob Williams, oh, leave us, you cad.
>   If Pike County won't have you, you must be bad.

In the third stanza Bob moves on to Louisiana, but cannot remain there either. What trouble he got into is not specified.

>   He left Mississippi and went next door
>   To Louisiana and trouble galore.
>   He had two choices from which he could choose.
>   Either leave Louisiana or his life he would lose.

In the fourth stanza the ballad begins to take on what we southeasterners consider an authentic western flavor. The train, which became a popular symbol of the West for the Alabamians, here enters the ballad.

>   He then went to Texas and hoped to remain,
>   But Bob had to leave on the very first train.
>   They tied him up and packed him in a crate,
>   And shipped him out on the five o'clock freight.

Where can a man go who is not wanted in any state? The answer is given in the final stanza. Bob Williams helps create a new state!

>   He went to the north and there became great,
>   As the very first governor of Oklahoma state.
>   A-holdin' this office he was a success.
>   Bob Williams was glad that he had gone West.

The balladeer makes Williams Oklahoma's first governor, whereas in reality he was the third. In the laconic conclusion there may lurk a kind of pride in Bob Williams, who was so bad that he was run out of four states but finally became governor of Oklahoma.

But "The Ballad of Bob Williams" is not the only monument to his memory. Like most Alabamians who went to Texas and who either returned or sent back money, Bob Williams provided in his will restoration funds for his home church in Pike County, which is now known as the Williams Memorial Church. This edifice still stands and is used regularly as a place of religious worship.

Buckwheat Cakes, 1898 Variety

ROGER P. McCUTCHEON

THE SUMMER of 1898 was a memorable one for me. A boy of nine, I spent the summer on my uncle's farm in Nicholas County, West Virginia. My grandfather had acquired the farm before the Civil War and built the farmhouse himself; it is standing today and is owned by one of his grandchildren, my cousin, Grace Waller.

Nicholas County was never a very prosperous county, nor is it today. It is in southern West Virginia, and industry and traffic alike have passed it by. I was a town boy, used to town services, such as mail, police, water, lights, doctors, and a variety of stores. On the farm, we got our mail from the village store at Keslers Cross Lanes, a mile or so away, three days a week. The mail was brought in by horseback, in saddlebags. The only machinery around the farm was powered by horses: a mowing machine for the hay, a hay rake, plows and harrows, a road wagon. There was a horse-drawn reaper which could be rented for cutting the wheat; the threshing machine also was horse-powered, requiring eight horses to run it. Steam threshing machines were in use in the Dakotas in the 1870's, but the first one I saw in our county was in 1901. No electric service was available, and there were no gasoline motors. The nearest railroad was and still is some twenty miles away, then a two-day trip by road wagon. There were no telephones in our section of the county then. Mail order catalogues and parcel post would come in only in 1912. All these matters made a vivid impression on me, but I do not claim a total recall of those early times.

About buckwheat and buckwheat cakes, however, my memories are happy and clear. The buckwheat was planted in midsummer. It is a quick-growing crop, does well on poor soil, and when it blooms has a spike of white blossoms with a very heavy fragrance. "Buckwheat honey" is dark in color, and somewhat strong in taste. This honey is much loved by the Russians, I have read, but we always preferred clover honey or, better still, sourwood honey, both of which are lighter in color and more delicate in flavor.

When the buckwheat bloom was over, the whiteness of course disappeared. The color of the ripe buckwheat was distinctly black, and the grains had triangular sides, not at all like grains of wheat. The buckwheat was harvested in mid-September.

The buckwheat was cut by cradles; essentially these were scythes with long finger-like guides to collect the stalks so that they could be laid evenly on the ground. But in contrast with the scythe handle, which had a handhold for each hand, the cradle handle had one for the right hand only. Also, the cradler had a different stance, and used a different, flatter motion, when he was cradling. The cutting blade of the cradle required frequent whetting with a pocket whetstone, plus once or twice a day a thorough sharpening on the big grindstone. Turning the grindstone was a boy's job, and in this chore I made a small contribution.

After the buckwheat was all cut, it was raked into small sheaves. Each sheaf was held together by a wisp of the buckwheat, cleverly knotted by the man who had raked it up. The sheaves were bundled together into shocks with the grain end up, and two or more sheaves were spread out as a sort of roof for the shock. When the buckwheat was thoroughly dried out, the shocks were dragged to the threshing pen on a wooden sledge or stoneboat, pulled by one of the horses.

The threshing pen was a square pen perhaps two feet high made of chestnut fence rails, of which there seemed to be an endless supply around the barnyard. To catch the buckwheat grains the wagon sheet was spread on the ground inside the pen. Then rails were laid across the pen, carefully spaced an inch or so apart.

There were one or two old flails in the shed. These had long handles, to which were attached, by leather strips, short pieces which did the actual flailing. The dictionaries state that this short bar is called the swingle. I cannot recall this term's being used on our farm.

This year of 1898 the old flails were thought inadequate. So we made an expedition to the woodlot and selected a few hickory saplings, perhaps two inches through at the butt. These were trimmed and cut to an overall length of about six feet. Then each pole was marked off about eighteen inches from the top. At this mark the pliant, tough hickory bark was slit three or four times longitudinally for about three inches, and the wood beneath was carefully removed. The result was a five-foot pole with a short "swingle" for which the original hickory bark served as hinge. With these flails we were ready to thresh out the buckwheat.

A few sheaves of the buckwheat were placed on the top rails and carefully opened and separated. Then the flailing began, each man striking at the buckwheat stalks nearest him. As the swingles hit, the ripened grains fell through the interstices between the rails, and most—or some—of the straw stayed on the rails. When a section of the straw was judged to be thoroughly threshed out, it was removed to the straw stack. This stack grew all too slowly, but finally the last sheaf had been threshed, and we could put up the flails.

The wagon sheet had caught some broken pieces of buckwheat straw, as well as the chaff and the grain. To separate the grain we used a hand-driven "windmill." We ended up with several grain bags full of fairly clean buckwheat.

The real payoff, of course, came with the return of the buckwheat flour from Uncle Henry's gristmill, a water mill on Peters Creek. The flour still had to be well sifted in the meal sieve before it could be used for pancakes. The batter for these was started the night before they were to be served. My cousin Grace advises me that the amount of batter you make depends on the number of people you are serving. Her directions are:

Take buckwheat flour, warm water, a little salt, and sugar; make a stiff batter and set in a warm place overnight. (In our house, the batter was always mixed in a stone crock.) Next morning, add salt and sugar to taste, soda and baking powder, and buttermilk. Add some white flour and beat well. Then fry and go to eating, with maple syrup, sorghum, or whatever you prefer. Save some of the batter in a jar or crock for a starter, and make again as at first.

My father thought that buckwheat cakes were an essential part of any wintertime breakfast. Wherever we were living, we always had them. They were cooked on a well-greased iron griddle which was long enough to cover two eyes of the stove. For a year or so, as a dietary "improvement," we used a soapstone griddle and no grease. But the cakes did not taste as good, and the soapstone griddle disappeared. The cakes should be eaten hot, right off the griddle; this is more easily managed, naturally, if the kitchen is large enough to accommodate a breakfast table.

Of course, various records were set for buckwheat consumption, but as the cakes came from the griddle unstandardized, in various sizes and weights, the records mean very little. Country sausage was a worthy companion for the cakes. As my brother and I learned, yesterday's turkey gravy heated up made an excellent top dressing for the first half-dozen or so cakes; after that, maple syrup. My brother is remembered to have eaten seventeen buckwheat cakes at one famous breakfast, a record I never approached.

The buckwheat cakes in restaurants today are made from a processed flour, to which one adds only water. The cakes from the prepared mixes are quite wholesome, I am content to believe, but otherwise are pallid substitutes, unworthy of comparison with the cakes of 1898. Only once in recent years have I eaten buckwheat cakes from a batter prepared the night before. Each fall there is, or was, in Preston County, West Virginia, a county-wide buckwheat cake festival. All the restaurants co-operate. The batter is set the night before, and the cakes do have the authentic, slightly sour taste. I hope this festival may continue, so that one of our frontier staples may still be enjoyed, even if the present population may have done little to deserve it.

It may be remembered that Dr. Johnson gave in his *Dictionary* (1775) one famous definition which annoyed the Scots: "Oats: a grain which in England is generally given to horses, but in Scotland supports the people." Actually, this definition was adapted from Pliny, but the Scots resented what they deemed a national slur. It has been suggested that the definition of "buckwheat" in the *Oxford English Dictionary* (Bra-Byzen, 1888) may be a partial revenge: "The seed is in Europe used as food for horses, cattle, and poultry; in N. America its meal is made into 'buckwheat cakes,' regarded as a dainty for the breakfast table." Anyhow, Sir James Murray, the first editor of the O.E.D., was a Scotsman.

Jung on Myth and the Mythic
WILSON M. HUDSON

JUNG'S THOUGHT ON MYTH developed as an integral part of his general psychological theory. Myth is a product of the collective unconscious expressed symbolically in archetypal images, and hence it is a universal natural phenomenon. The impulse toward the creation and expression of myth existed in ancient man, and it exists also in modern man even though he may try to ignore or stifle it. Refusal by the conscious mind to accept messages from the collective unconscious may cause a split in the psyche and attendant disorders. Modern man needs myth to achieve psychic wholeness and maintain a proper balance between the unconscious and the conscious.

In 1909 Jung had a dream which led him to the concept of the collective unconscious. He explored a house—his own somehow—starting with the upper story, which was furnished in a rococo, somewhat antiquated style. The ground floor was medieval, the cellar was Roman, and underneath was a cave with primitive remains. Jung related his dream to Freud, with whom he was traveling to America, and Freud attempted to discover hidden death-wishes in Jung to connect with two skulls in the cave. Jung's own interpretation was that the dream provided an image of his psyche, the upper floor representing his conscious and the ground floor, cellar, and cave representing successively deeper levels of his unconscious. On the lowest level, within Jung himself, was the world of primitive man, hardly accessible to the consciousness. This dream became a guiding image for him; it was his "first inkling of a collective a priori beneath the personal psyche."[1]

Jung's dream caused him to read widely in works on archeology and mythology. He found many correspondences between ancient mythology and the psychology of primitives, which he then pursued intensively. Upon happening to read about the case of a Miss Miller, he was struck by the mythological character of her fantasies. Here was the catalyst which acted upon his knowledge of myths to produce his first book, *Wandlungen und Symbole der Libido* (1912), initially translated under the title *Psychology of the Unconscious* (1916) but now called *Symbols of Transformation*.

In this book Jung did not use the term *collective unconscious*, but he insisted that the unconscious has a generic significance, men being "closely alike in their unconscious psychology" in spite of wide individual differences on the conscious level.[2] The source of these unconscious similarities he suggested in his comment on the death of Chiwantopel, Miss Miller's hero: "For the symbols employed, the serpent which killed the horse and the hero voluntarily sacrificing himself, are primitive figures of phantasies and religious myths streaming up from the unconscious."[3] Jung brought in so much mythological material that in the preface to the second edition (1924) he had to declare that it was not his purpose to propound a general theory of myths but to illuminate Miss Miller's case. The justification for including the mythological parallels is that the creative fantasy "draws upon the forgotten and long buried primitive mind with its host of images, which are to be found in the mythologies of all ages and all peoples."[4] All of these images, he went on to say, make up the collective unconscious, which is potentially present in everybody everywhere. "This is the reason why mythological images are able to arise spontaneously over and over again, and to agree with one another not only in all corners of the wide earth, but at all times."[5] This view asserts that myths originated in the human psyche or brain, which functions uniformly with only minor variations, and it consequently implies that inquiries into the historical and geographical dissemination of myths are more or less superfluous.

Jung was correct in anticipating that the publication of *Wandlungen* would mark the parting of the ways with Freud. He differed with Freud on the psychological meaning of incest, the transformation of the libido, and other matters. He knew that Freud would reject the religious and symbolic significance which he ascribed to incest on the basis of the mating of close relatives in many cosmogonies and myths. Jung denied that there was a natural impulse to commit incest; in his view the pharaohs and other ancient rulers who married sisters or daughters or mothers were imitating the gods and hence were activated by religion rather than natural inclination. The break with Freud was inevitable. Freud never did like Jung's term *collective unconscious,* but in dealing with supposed archaic vestiges in the mind of modern man he made use of a scarcely distinguishable concept. This he called *Massenpsyche* in *Totem and Taboo* (1912-13); in this mass or collective mind "mental processes occur just as they do in the mind of an individual."[6] Without the assumption of such a mind, he said, social psychology could not account for psychic continuity, but he would not commit himself on the question of how guilt feelings for the murder of the father of the primal horde could be transmitted to distant generations. The pressure of criticism forced Freud to face this question again at a later time, but he failed to provide his critics with a satisfactory answer.

Jung's hypothesis of a collective unconscious rests upon the multitude of resemblances between the fantasies and dreams of contemporary men and older myths and fairytales of which they could have had no knowledge. There is a personal unconscious derived from personal experience, but the collective unconscious is impersonal, having been formed during the prehistory of mankind. Jung analogized the development of the psyche to the development of the body, holding that Haeckel's principle of the recapitulation of racial evolution by the individual is true psychically as well as biologically. He frequently spoke of the "contents" of the collective unconscious, though he did not intend to indicate any kind of specific historical memories. His most refined definition is that the collective unconscious is "a certain psychic disposition shaped by the forces of heredity."[7] The unconscious is prior to the conscious, to which it gives rise, and is much more primitive. When modern man is in a state of diminished conscious intensity comparable to that of primitive man, the collective unconscious speaks to him in dreams, fantasies, and visions.

The contents of the collective unconscious Jung calls *archetypes*. He often refers to archetypes as if they were images, particularly in his early works, but more precisely he considers them to be determinants of form.[8] They are pre-existent, inherited forms which give definite shape to the materials of the collective unconscious. They are comparable to whatever in a liquid mineral causes it to assume a certain crystalline structure when it hardens. The actual image or representation is not inheritable, only the possibility of forming archetypal images. There is a very wide variation in the images belonging to a given archetype. The archetype, having its origin in the collective unconscious, is not fully representable and so must remain partly incomprehensible. The effect of the archetypes can nevertheless be observed.

Archetypes make their way into the conscious part of the mind seemingly from the outside and of their own accord. They are autonomous, sometimes forcing themselves in overpoweringly. They have a numinous quality; that is, they have an aura of divinity which is mysterious or terrifying. They are from the unknown. It may be that a white-bearded old man appears to give advice that promises salvation or seems to threaten destruction. The meaning of the archetype is difficult to interpret and is often ambiguous. Whatever archetypes may mean, they have great power to move or disturb. Since they cannot be brought over fully into the conscious mind, they must be expressed in mythological images or symbols.

Myths are conglomerates of archetypes held together psychologically. In moving toward the concept of the archetype Jung first used the term *primordial image*, which he borrowed from Burckhardt and continued to use after defining *archetype* in the Jungian sense. Other terms which he equated with *archetypes* are the *motifs* of comparative mythology, the *représentations collectives* of Lévy-Bruhl, and the *mythologems* of Kerényi. All of these are to myth as parts to the whole. Jung of course found in them a basic meaning in accord with his own interpretation. Traditional myths, which have possessed form for some time and have been transmitted historically, and modern myths have the same ultimate source, the archetypes of the collective unconscious.

Myths are first of all, insists Jung, psychic phenomena that reveal the nature of the soul. As psychic phenomena they require psychological interpretation. They are not created by primitive man to explain the processes of nature allegorically. The primitive's unconscious has an irresistible urge to assimilate outer sense experiences to inner psychic events, so that when he mythologizes natural processes such as the coming of spring he is symbolically expressing the unconscious drama of his psyche by means of projection. The consciousness of primitive man is much narrower in scope and lower in intensity than that of civilized man. The primitive is in a preconscious state; he does not think consciously, but thoughts come to him. "The primitive mentality does not *invent* myths, it *experiences* them," says Jung.[9] "Myths are original revelations of the preconscious psyche, involuntary statements about unconscious psychic happenings, and anything but allegories of physical processes."[10] Myths none the less have a vital meaning, for they constitute the psychic life of a primitive tribe, which begins to fall apart when it loses its mythological heritage.

There are two large classes of archetypes, one having to do with situations and the other with figures. Jung does not often deal with archetypal situations, probably because they are very numerous, being limited only by the number of typical situations possible in life. He concentrates on archetypal figures, of which he enumerates six principal ones: the shadow, the anima-animus, the mother, the child (including the child hero), the maiden, and the wise old man. These personified archetypes are bipolar; they have a positive and a negative aspect, and so are capable of either helping or hurting. They appear over and over again in myths as well as in dreams, fantasies, and visions. They have a way of interpenetrating each other and so are difficult to isolate. They cannot be reduced to a simple formula.

The shadow is made up largely of materials from the personal unconscious, but it may draw on the collective unconscious and manifest itself archetypally. Because of its connection with the personal unconscious it is the most readily accessible of the archetypes. It represents the repressed, primitive, inferior side of the psyche and is mostly negative, though not wholly bad.[11] The further removed from the consciousness, the more likely it is to break out in an unguarded moment. The conscious personality and the shadow must live together somehow or neurotic dissociation will develop. The contents of the unconscious and the conscious must be integrated for the sake of psychic wholeness. Coming to terms with the shadow is the first step in individuation, which has psychic wholeness for its goal.

The concept of the shadow plays a very important role in Jung's treatment of Christ, whom he considers "the still living myth of our culture."[12] Besides being our culture hero, Christ "embodies the myth of the divine Primordial Man, the mystic Adam."[13] Adam was made in God's image and Christ took upon himself man's image; in Jung's psychological language this means that Christ is an exemplification of the archetype of the self. Jung finds that Christ as a symbol of the self lacks wholeness from the psychological point of view because he does not include a dark side. This is owing to the separation of Christ and Lucifer into irreconcilable opponents, which occurred in the New Testament and was enforced by the interpretation of the Church Fathers. The "real devil" first appears as Christ's adversary.[14] There is evidence in the Old Testament that Lucifer was not originally separated from the God-image. This corresponds with Jung's psychological observation. "In the empirical self," he says, "light and shadow form a paradoxical unity."[15] After the work of the Fathers there was still a psychological need for a complement to the bright figure of Christ; this is shown by the development of the legend of the Antichrist, who is nothing else but Christ's shadow. Antichrist is complementary to Christ as the shadow is to the ego-consciousness.

Lucifer should be the fourth, which added to the three makes absolute totality, says Jung. It is not possible to distinguish empirically between a symbol of the self and a God-image. The symbols of the self which arise spontaneously from the unconscious take the form of circles or quaternities. The circle has wholeness because it is undivided; the quaternity because it is the smallest number of parts into which the circle is naturally divisible.[16] Psychologically three is a defective quaternity, an arrestation of a process leading to the formation of a quaternity. The concept of the Trinity (Father, Son, and Holy Ghost) is incomplete and to be made into an absolute totality requires the addition of Lucifer. So Jung argues in *A Psychological Approach to the Dogma of the Trinity*. The four figures would be joined in two pairs of related opposites with axes intersecting at right angles to make a *complexio oppositorum*, a fourfold image of wholeness in the form of a cross.

The difficulty of combining Lucifer or Satan (evil) and the Trinity (good) can be overcome only by means of symbols or myths. In the Book of Job Satan is identified as one of God's sons and the contradiction in God's nature is quite apparent.[17] When thought of as a combination of two contradictory elements, God is a *conjunctio oppositorum*, a conjunction of opposites. The story of Lucifer's fall from Heaven and his corruption of man in the Garden of Eden is therapeutic myth.[18] According to a certain Gnostic view the devil is Satanaël, God's first son, and Christ is His second. Clement of Rome held that God rules the world with Christ as His right hand and Satan as His left. These myths and symbols have healing value for the psyche in that they make possible a reconciliation of opposites which would otherwise cause dissociation and lead to neurosis. Opposites that cannot be united rationally can be united symbolically.[19] The shadow or the dark side of God and the self can be banned from the conscious but not from the unconscious mind, in which case it is likely to break out in disruptive fantasies or more serious disorders. "Myths . . . give expression to unconscious processes," says Jung, "and their retelling causes these processes to come alive again and be recollected, thereby re-establishing the connection between the conscious and the unconscious."[20]

The shadow has many manifestations. It is embodied in the primitive trickster figure met with in the mythology of the Winnebago Indians and is discernible on higher levels also.[21] This figure is God, man, and animal at once, a creator and a forerunner of the savior. Towards the end of the Winnebago cycle the dark aspects of the trickster seem to disappear, but they have only withdrawn into the unconscious so that the conscious mind can free itself from the fascination and compulsive quality of evil. The therapeutic effect of the myth consists in its preservation of the earlier low moral and intellectual stage in the mind of a more highly developed individual. The dark half of the Mercurius of the alchemists has an affinity with Lucifer. Set is the shadow of Osiris, Prometheus of Zeus, and Mephistopheles of Faust. Hitler was the shadow of the German people, the personification of all the inferiorities of the Germans, who were collectively possessed—that is, they were dominated by a powerful archetype from the unconscious, in this case overwhelmingly negative.[22] By the process of projection they were able to attribute their negative qualities to "enemies" inside and outside of Germany. This psychic split had world-shaking consequences.

The anima and the animus can be perceived after the integration of the shadow. The anima represents the feminine element in a man and always has a feminine image; the animus is the masculine element in a woman and has a masculine image. Since the anima belongs to the unconscious and a man is masculine in his consciousness, anyone who can recognize his anima consciously and harmoniously in her projected form has made a big step in the process of individuation; failure to recognize and face her indicates dissociation or lack of wholeness. The same is true of a woman and her animus. The compensatory nature of anima or animus with relation to the ego-consciousness is obvious. Jung likes to speak of the anima and animus as a syzygy, a union of opposites or a *conjunctio oppositorum,* though the two could not exist in the same person.[23] The anima is readily projected upon a real woman—often mother or wife—and she mingles with the archetype of mother or maiden. Jung correlates the anima with Eros. An anima figure sometimes appears in the company of the archetype of the wise old man, who is her complement. For projection of her animus a woman usually selects her father or husband. The animus correlates with Logos, and for this reason the chthonic mother is the complementary archetype.

Anima and animus, Jung says, have since ancient times formed the archetypal basis of all gods and goddesses, by which he does not mean that divine beings cannot be manifestations of other archetypes too.[24] Most men are afraid of their anima, and so she frequently appears as a witch or temptress. She can also be very pure or holy; in medieval times she was the Queen of Heaven and Mother Church. The marriage of Christ with the Church would then be a divine syzygy. In Gnostic tradition when the reincarnated Helen of Troy, after being rescued from a brothel, accompanies Simon Magus, anima and wise old man are companions. Jung once had a vision of a beautiful young blind girl and a white-bearded old man, who explained that they were Salome and Elijah.[25] She stood for the erotic and unconscious, he for intelligence and knowledge. Miss Miller's hero Chiwantopel was an animus fantasy. The anima may take on the appearance of Aphrodite, Persephone, or Hecate. Anima and animus have many forms and much power.

The wise old man is a kind of fatherly authority-figure, though he is not a father. He can assume the guise of a doctor, priest, magician, teacher, or seer. Among primitive people he is a medicine man. It is his function to give helpful guidance or counsel, and he often makes his appearance at a moment of bewilderment. He has a dark or chthonic manifestation as a dwarf or animal. He can be a practitioner of black magic, and sometimes he is intentionally misleading or even threatening. The best-known figures of the wise old man mentioned by Jung are Orpheus, Merlin, Hermes Trismegistus, and Nietzsche's Zarathustra. He might have also instanced Chiron, the centaur who instructed Asclepius, Achilles, and Jason. Jung discussed the wise old man at length as he shows himself in fairytales,[26] which draw on the collective unconscious as do myths but have a lower degree of numinosity. This archetype was especially interesting to Jung because first Elijah and then another wise old man, whom Jung saw vividly enough to paint and whom he named Philemon, appeared to him early (c. 1914) in his confrontation with his unconscious.[27] Jung's experience with Philemon contributed to the sharpening of his insight and the formation of his theory of archetypes.

Representations of the mother are very numerous and reflect her ambivalence as both loving and terrible.[28] The earth as the great mother, the producer and nourisher of all living things, is a symbol deriving from the mother archetype. There are many mother goddesses—Demeter, Cybele, and the Virgin, to name a few. The mother archetype can be attached to anything that gives, sustains, or protects life, including animals and inanimate objects, such as paradise, the sea, a ploughed field, a cave, a deep well, or a cow. On the negative side are the goddesses of fate—Moira, Graeae, and Norns; here too are deep water, the grave, and devouring, entwining animals such as large fish and serpents. The mother's bipolarity is sometimes expressed in one figure; according to a medieval allegory the Virgin is not only Christ's mother but also his cross. In India the paradoxical mother is Kali. Men are attracted to or repulsed by their mothers according to which of her aspects seems dominant. Women may identify themselves with or react against either aspect of the mother.

The mother image and the anima are not separate archetypes inasmuch as they invariably mingle in a man's psychological development. In a man there is also a mingling between his anima and the maiden or kore. Jung says that in a man the kore belongs to the anima type. A woman easily combines the mother archetype and the kore, so that for her this figure is alternately mother and maiden. The kore and the mother are counterparts; the two occur together in the Demeter-Persephone myth. Jung holds that the feminine influence was much stronger on this myth than the masculine because the role of Hades is only that of a seducer, an intrusive disturber. The Demeter cult reflects, he says, a matriarchal order of society.

The great maiden goddesses are kore figures; so are corybants, maenads, and nymphs. Women often see the kore as an unknown young girl, sometimes as an unmarried mother. Negatively, the mother or kore might take the form of a cat, snake, or bear. The helpless maiden may be exposed to dangers such as devourment by reptiles or ceremonial sacrifice. There may be bloody or obscene rites to which she is subjected. She might have to make a descent to the otherworld, as Persephone did to the terrible realm of Hades.

Jung wrote his commentary on the psychology of the child archetype to accompany Kerényi's essay on the primordial child, the child god.[29] Going over again much of the ground covered by Rank in *The Myth of the Birth of the Hero* (1922), Kerényi dealt with a wide range of child gods from Greek, Roman, Indian, and Finnish mythology—Kullervo, Narayana, Apollo, Zeus, Dionysus, and others. As a good Freudian, Rank had ended up with a composite scenario which reduced the myths of his heroes and gods (Christ included) to the Oedipal or familial drama. Jung of course discussed the child archetype in Jungian terms.

After warning that no archetype can be fully explained, Jung states, "The child motif represents the preconscious, childhood aspects of the collective psyche."[30] Repetition of myths about the child and ritual re-enactment of the mythological events place the image of man's childhood again before the eyes of the conscious mind and thus preserve a connection with the unconscious. This compensates for the one-sidedness and extravagance of the conscious mind. When a part of the psyche is split off from the consciousness it may take possession of the personality. "If, then," says Jung, "the childhood state of the collective psyche is repressed to the point of total exclusion, the unconscious content overwhelms the conscious aim and inhibits, falsifies, even destroys its realization."[31] The figure of the child and the myths about him are symbols with the power of uniting opposites.

Jung goes on to develop an interpretation of the child as potential consciousness striving to be born and grow stronger—that is, to separate itself from the unconscious. The child god may become a young hero and thus acquire a new symbolical significance. The god is wholly supernatural or divine and the hero is human but almost supernatural—hence semidivine. The god personifies the collective unconscious still not integrated and the hero represents a synthesis of the "divine" unconscious and human consciousness. The child-become-hero has made progress toward psychic wholeness. In this way Jung all but turns the myth of the child into an allegory of the Jungian individuation process.

The six archetypal figures discriminated and discussed by Jung do not exhaust the statistical regularities, he says. They are the ones which he most frequently encountered and constantly had to take account of in his long career.

Modern man needs myth for the attainment of psychic wholeness and balance. The problem of ancient man was to enlarge the sphere of his consciousness; the problem of modern man is not to lose contact with the collective unconscious. The penalty for this loss is dissociation and neurosis, not merely in the individual but in nations of men. The ego-consciousness now thinks it is the entire self. The great psychic split of our times, which is reflected in politics, can be healed only through symbols or myths, which can unite opposites that cannot be reconciled rationally. In spite of the fact that the unconscious shadow began early to split off from the image of God, which is indistinguishable from the image of the self, the Christian myth remained vital and effective for a thousand years before it began to weaken. This weakening reached a culmination in the twentieth century when the shadow, magnified by a process which Jung calls inflation, was collectively projected by Hitlerian Germany and produced an irruption of evil. Naked evil has apparently taken permanent form in Russia, says Jung. He characterizes the present condition of the world thus: "One half of humanity battens and grows strong on a doctrine fabricated by human ratiocination; the other half sickens from the lack of a myth commensurate with the situation."[32] In the absence of an adequate myth, the attempt to demythologize Christianity and thus make it more acceptable to modern man is altogether misguided.[33]

Christian myth has not developed so as to cope with our problems today, though it might have done so. Tendencies to guide the myth in the direction of wholeness were evident in Gioacchino da Fiore, Meister Eckhart, and Jacob Boehme, but they were ignored or stifled. Jung saw one good sign, however, in the official promulgation (1950) of the dogma of the Assumption of the Blessed Virgin Mary, which elevated her to a place in heaven beside the Trinity.[34] This gave recognition to the popular belief, a thousand years old, that the Mother of God dwelt in heaven and acted as mediatrix for mankind. Mary is the Christian version of the mother archetype, and when she entered heaven she did not leave behind the archetype's chthonic side; her entry symbolically represents a union of earth and heaven or of matter and spirit, despite the contrary assertion of dogma.[35] Mary added a feminine element to the masculine Trinity, and so here is a hierogamy, says Jung, with a personified "divine" woman appropriately replacing an organization in the marriage of Christ and the Lamb identified as the Church. Such a hierogamy promises the birth of the divine child who is to become man's savior. According to Jung's psychological interpretation, which differs from the theology of the papal promulgation, this would be a kind of revisionist myth. It should be noted that when Mary joins the Trinity she completes a quaternity, which Jung always sees as a symbol of wholeness.

Though he had to substitute a psychological for a theological interpretation, Jung at last found some slight authority for adding the dark element to the Trinity and thus producing the fourfold *complexio oppositorum* which he felt was required for the symbolical expression of absolute totality. The myth must put aside its dualism of God-devil and take monotheism seriously. When these opposites are symbolically united, Jung says, the ambivalence in a creator god causes no more difficulties. "On the contrary," he continues, "the myth of the necessary incarnation of God—the essence of the Christian message—can then be understood as man's creative confrontation with the opposites and their synthesis in the self, the wholeness of the personality."[36] It is now not God and man that are being synthesized but the opposites within the God-image. "That is the meaning of divine service," Jung concludes, "of the service which man can render to God, that light may emerge from darkness, that the Creator may become conscious of His creation, and man conscious of himself."[37] This is the epitome of Jung's *Weltanschauung*. It is, he states, an explanatory myth which developed within him over a period of many years.

Neither Jung's revised Christian myth nor the more personal myth which he constructed for himself is likely to gain any degree of popular credence or influence. Modern man has not found the myth that will repair the great psychic cleavage between an overdeveloped consciousness and a stifled unconscious which he would like to ignore. In our apocalyptic day, when the end of the world through atomic fission seems not only possible but probable, symbols of wholeness are appearing spontaneously from the collective unconscious in the form of unidentified flying objects in the skies.[38] UFOs are always round or spherical and so have the shape of the mandala, a universal symbol of wholeness. That UFOs are reported from all over the world is evidence of a general psychic disposition: man is fearful and wants to be saved. He does not know that UFOs are an unconscious compensation for his lack of psychic wholeness. Like other archetypal manifestations, they are numinous and ambiguous—have they come to earth to help or hurt mankind? Sometimes they seem to be operated by invaders from outer space bent on conquest; sometimes they land and little men of superior wisdom emerge to say that they have seen the plight of the world and have come to offer aid and advice. UFOs are symptoms of a general and profound psychic disturbance, says Jung; he does not anticipate that they should ever give rise to myth with psychotherapeutic value.

Myth is an indispensable component of Jungian psychology. Jung did not formulate his psychological theory and then discover that it was applicable to myth; myth was there almost from the first. Only as much of his theory as is primarily relevant to myth has been allowed to enter into this discussion, but myth is very close to the center of Jung's psychology. It is deeply involved in his view of psychic health and his concept of the individuation process, both of which have to do with large groups of men as well as with individuals and hence can be used to make characterizing statements about nationalities and historical periods. Jung can present the whole history of man as a struggle for individuation.

With the stipulation that the psyche is not altogether knowable or explicable, Jung attempts to account for the origin and ubiquity of myth in the collective unconscious, its affective power in its numinosity arising from its archetypal nature, and its functional significance in mediating between the conscious and the unconscious mind and in reconciling opposites. Myths often have a uniting, healing function, or by compensation they may indicate an excessive tension between opposites. Jung says that opposites are necessary for cognition and for the production of psychic energy, but they must be held together by myth-symbol so that they do not cause a split in the psyche. Jung's dialectic movement here is first to discriminate opposites and then to reconcile them through a symbol, which being on another level is a "supraordinate third."

In general it can be said that Jung is much attracted by syncretism and paradox.

What Jung had to contribute to the study of myth was psychological insight. He addressed himself to the basic questions that arise in mythological studies and produced a theory of myth stated in terms of his own variety of psychology. The validity of his theory depends on his hypothesis of the collective unconscious and its autonomous, numinous archetypes. If this is rejected, Jung cannot be said to have shed much light on myth. His six figures are then deprived of their theoretical source and power; their remaining value would be that they comprehend a multiplicity of mythical personages under a few large types. Such a unification is good, but the mythologist working with a wide range of materials finds it necessary also to make finer distinctions for purposes of identification and communication. Jung did not invent or revise a modus operandi for dealing with mythology. This has been provided by the inclusive classification of motifs and tale types begun by the Finnish school of mythologists and elaborated by Stith Thompson and his associates. Jung reached down for what he considered the deepest explanation of myth possible.

1. C. G. Jung, *Memories, Dreams, Reflections*, trans. Richard and Clara Winston (New York, 1963), p. 161.

2. *Psychology of the Unconscious*, trans. Beatrice M. Hinkle (New York, 1916), p. 198.

3. *Ibid.*, pp. 455-56. The patient's real name was not Miller.

4. The 1924 foreword repr. in *Symbols of Transformation*, in *The Collected Works of C. G. Jung*, trans. R. F. C. Hull (New York and London), V (1956), xxix. Here Jung says, "The sum of these images constitutes the collective unconscious, a heritage which is potentially present in every individual."

5. *Ibid.*

6. *Totem and Taboo*, trans. James Strachey (London, 1950), p. 157. See my article, "Freud's Myth of the Primal Horde," in *A Good Tale and a Bonnie Tune* (Dallas, 1964), pp. 72-100. ("Publications of the Texas Folklore Society," XXXII.)

7. "Psychology and Literature" (first pub. 1929), in *Modern Man in Search of a Soul*, trans. W. S. Dell and Cary F. Baynes (New York, 1950), p. 190. This article is scheduled to appear in vol. XV of *Collected Works*.

8. See esp. "The Concept of the Collective Unconscious" (first pub. 1936-37), *Collected Works*, vol. IX, pt. i (1959), pp. 42-43; "Psychological Aspects of the Mother Archetype" (first pub. 1954), *Collected Works*, vol. IX, pt. i, pp. 78-79.

9. "The Psychology of the Child Archetype" (first pub. 1940), *Collected Works*, vol. IX, pt. i, p. 154.

10. *Ibid.*

11. *Aion* (first pub. as book 1951), *Collected Works,* vol. IX, pt. ii (1959), pp. 8-10, 266-67. In his conclusion Jung says the shadow "does not consist only of morally reprehensible tendencies, but also displays a number of good qualities, such as normal instincts, appropriate reactions, realistic insights, creative impulses, etc."

12. *Ibid.,* p. 36.

13. *Ibid.*

14. *Ibid.,* pp. 41-42.

15. *Ibid.,* p. 42.

16. *Ibid.,* p. 224, n. 7. Why isn't the circle "naturally" divisible into two parts? All that is necessary is to draw a straight line through the center, which is always known or readily discoverable. This is true when the circle is drawn around equal axes bisecting at right angles, as in the ancient ceremony of laying out a city.

17. Jung devoted a whole book to this problem, *Answer to Job* (first pub. 1952), *Collected Works,* XI (1958), 355-470.

18. *A Psychological Approach to the Dogma of the Trinity* (first pub. 1942), *Collected Works,* XI (1958), 196.

19. *Aion,* p. 180. Because opposites do not unite on their own level, they must be united by a "supraordinate third," a symbol. The symbol operates thus: "And since the symbol derives as much from the conscious as from the unconscious, it is able to unite them both, reconciling their conceptual polarity through its form and their emotional polarity through its numinosity." Many iconographical symbols are pictured in vols. V, IX (pt. i), and XII of Jung's *Collected Works.* For a great abundance of symbols, modern as well as ancient, see *Man and His Symbols* (London and New York, 1964) by Jung, M. L. von Franz, Joseph L. Henderson, Jolande Jacobi, and Aniela Jaffé.

20. *Ibid.* I have omitted "and fairytales" in order to avoid having to distinguish between myths and fairytales at this point in my article. The archetypal figures are harder to recognize in fairytales because of their heavier disguises, and they have a lower degree of numinosity.

21. "On the Psychology of the Trickster Figure" (first pub. 1954), *Collected Works,* vol. IX, pt. i, pp. 255-72.

22. "The Fight with the Shadow" (first pub. 1946), *Collected Works,* X (1964), 218-26. Ten years earlier Jung argued that Wotan, the archetype of the Germans and a very complex god, was taking possession of the German people through Hitler; see "Wotan," *Collected Works,* X, 179-93.

23. A chapter in *Aion* is entitled "The Syzygy: Anima and Animus."

24. *Aion,* p. 268.

25. *Memories, Dreams, Reflections,* pp. 181-82.

26. "The Phenomenology of the Spirit in Fairytales" (first pub. 1948), *Collected Works,* vol. IX, pt. i, pp. 207-54.

27. *Memories, Dreams, Reflections,* pp. 183-85. "At times he seemed to me quite real, as if he were a living personality. I went walking up and down the garden with him, and to me he was what the Indians call a *guru.*"

28. Jung's principal discussion is to be found in "Psychological Aspects of the Mother Archetype," pp. 73-110.

29. "The Psychology of the Child Archetype," pp. 149-81.

30. *Ibid.,* p. 161.

31. *Ibid.*, p. 164.

32. *Memories, Dreams, Reflections*, p. 331; see the whole passage, pp. 327-39.

33. In "Psychological Aspects of the Mother Archetype" (p. 105) Jung states, "Theologians would do better to take account for once of these psychological facts than to go on 'demythologizing' them with rationalistic explanations that are a hundred years behind the times." In *Answer to Job* (p. 408) he asks, "What is the use of a religion without a mythos, since religion means, if anything at all, precisely that function which links us back to the eternal myth?"

34. Jung's fullest discussion of the Assumption of Mary is in *Answer to Job*, pp. 461-69.

35. "Psychological Aspects of the Mother Archetype," pp. 107-10.

36. *Memories, Dreams, Reflections*, p. 338.

37. *Ibid.*

38. *Flying Saucers: A Modern Myth of Things Seen in the Skies* (first pub. 1958), *Collected Works*, X (1964), 307-433.

Contributors

FRANCIS E. ABERNETHY teaches at Stephen F. Austin State College in Nacogdoches. He is currently collecting stories and lore from the Big Thicket.

ANDY ADAMS (1859-1935) was born in Indiana, worked cattle and horses in Texas, had some experience on the trail to Kansas, and lived most of the latter part of his life in Colorado Springs, devoting himself to writing. Author of *The Log of a Cowboy* (1903), the acknowledged masterpiece of literature having to do with the cattle country, he disliked the "picturesque" overdoing of western life in literature, and earned a reputation for faithful depiction in his novels and stories.

JOHN Q. ANDERSON, a productive scholar in the field of folklore, is a regular contributor to the TFS annual and editor of a 1966 anthology, *Tales of Frontier Texas, 1830-1860*. He is chairman of the English department at Texas A & M.

A. L. BENNETT, who took his last degree at the University of Texas, now teaches at Texas A & M. He grew up in Belton.

MODY C. BOATRIGHT of the University of Texas faculty published his first article in *Texas and Southwestern Lore*, which J. Frank Dobie edited for the TFS in 1927. He became TFS assistant editor in 1937 and chief editor in 1943, continuing as chief to 1964. The author of many books and articles on folklore, the latest book being *Folklore of the Oil Industry* (1963), he is now making a full-length study of the cowboy as a national figure.

JAMES T. BRATCHER is a teacher and graduate student in English at the University of Texas. His article, which grew out of a seminar with Mody Boatright, won first prize in the TFS contest for 1964.

JAN H. BRUNVAND received his training in folklore studies at the University of Indiana. He is now teaching English at Southern Illinois University in Edwardsville.

JAMES W. BYRD, originally from Alabama, teaches English at East Texas State University in Commerce. He was president of the TSF in 1965-66.

J. FRANK DOBIE (1888-1964) was secretary and editor for the TFS from 1923 to 1943. About 1920 he resolved to collect "the tales of my folk and my land" as Lomax had collected cowboy songs. In his article on Lomax he tells of the friendship that existed between them for many years. Many of Dobie's pronouncements on folklore, collected by William D. Wittliff in this book, were taken from prefaces to the volumes he edited for the TFS. Everyone knows that Dobie exerted a strong and salutary influence on literary activity in Texas and the Southwest.

EVERETT A. GILLIS is a student of western poetry in all of its forms—ballads, hymns, and popular songs. He is chairman of the English department at Texas Technological College in Lubbock.

WILSON M. HUDSON became secretary-editor for the TFS in 1964. A teacher at the University of Texas, he is studying myth as it exists and functions today. His biography of Andy Adams was published in 1964.

JAMES WARD LEE, a native of Alabama, teaches English at North Texas State University.

JOHN A. LOMAX (1867-1948) founded the TFS in 1909 along with Leonidas W. Payne, Jr. The next year he published *Cowboy Songs*. He did more, with the assistance of his son Alan, to collect and preserve folksongs than anyone else in the United States.

J. T. MC CULLEN, JR., came to Texas from North Carolina. He

teaches Shakespeare at Texas Technological College, and maintains a scholarly interest in folklore.

ROGER P. MC CUTCHEON, formerly dean of the graduate school at Tulane and in his later years special advisor to the graduate dean at the University of Texas, was a man of range and talent. In his many academic activities he never saw people as mere names on a roster of an application blank. This is his last article; ten days after completing it he died of a heart attack in New Orleans.

PAUL PATTERSON knows West Texas from having lived there all of his life. He teaches at Crane in the Pecos country. Currently he is president of the TFS.

EUGENE MANLOVE RHODES (1869-1934) was born in Nebraska but was taken to New Mexico at the age of twelve. In New Mexico he did everything from working cattle to teaching school. He attended college in San Jose, California, and returned to New Mexico. In his stories and novels he tried to correct the East's misconceptions of the West. His longish story, "Pasó por Aquí," is the classic defense of the West's code.

E. J. RISSMANN is a retired businessman living in Austin. He has a firsthand knowledge of the folkways of the Hill Country.

JACK SOLOMON teaches at Auburn University. He came to Houston in 1964 and read his paper at the annual meeting of the TFS.

JOHN O. WEST wrote a dissertation on the "good" outlaw tradition in the Southwest. He teaches at Texas Western in El Paso.

WILLIAM D. WITTLIFF, a graduate of the University of Texas, is sales manager for the University of Texas Press. A Dobie collector, he has a large file of Dobie's statements on a variety of subjects.

Index

Adams, Andy, 31; his hat-in-mud tale, 100-109
Adams, James Barton, 81
Adventures of a Ballad Hunter, 5-6, 7
Adventures with a Texas Naturalist, 10
Aldrich, Thomas Bailey, 167
Anderson, G. M., 51, 52, 53, 62
Archetypes, Jungian: traced to the collective unconscious and related to myths, 184-85; two large classes, 185; six principal archetypal figures, 185-91

Ballad about Bob Williams, 171-75
Battle, W. J., 10-11
Bear Creek, 151-56
Bedichek, Roy, 7, 10-11
Billy the Kid, 70-80
Boatright, Mody C., 3
Bonney, William H.; *see* Billy the Kid
Boone, Daniel, 51
Branding, 20
Broadsides, 166
Buckwheat: cultivation, 177; cutting, 177; grinding and sifting flour, 178; making cakes, 178-79; threshing, 177-78

Callaway, Morgan, Jr., 5
Casement, Roger, 7
Catnach, Jemmy, 166
Charcoal burning, 151-56
Cherokee Strip, 35, 36-37
Chittenden, Larry, 82
Clark, Charles Badger, 81, 82, 84
Collective unconscious, 182, 183-84, 192

202   INDEX

Corrals, 34-35
Cowboy: boots, 46-47; code, 27-31, 39-50; fiction about, 31-32, 33, 37; graces, 23; hat, 46; horse, 13-15; lingo, 12-25; movies about, 32, 51-69; play, 31; saddle, 15-16; songs, 4, 81-88; versatility, 35; work, 26-31, 33-38
Cowboy Songs and Other Frontier Ballads, 6

Dance calls, 23-25
Davis, Gussie L., 167, 168
Diction, cowboy, 12-25
Dobie, Bertha McKee, 10
Dobie, Elrich, 9
Dobie, J. Frank, 84; on folklore, 89-99, 116
Dobie, Red, 8
Doughty, Leonard, 7

Escapes, narrow, from death by bullets, 118-27

Fenley, Florence, 114-15, 116
Fletcher, Curley, 82
Folksongs, 3; Negro, 8-9; penny dreadfuls as, 164-70; *see also* Songs, Ballad
Food, folk; *see* Poke sallet
Fox hunting, 146-50
Freud, Sigmund, 181, 182-83

Gunplay, 31

Harvard University, 5-6
Hastings, Frank, 12
Henderson, Alice Corbin, 81, 85
Hero, Billy the Kid as, 70-80
Hogg, Will, 8
Honesty in the West, 49-50
Horse, cowboy's, 13-15
Hyatt, Bill, 12

Iron Head, 8

Johnson, Charlie, 84, 86-87
Jung, C. G., on myth, 181-97

Kerwin, Bishop, 7
Kittredge, George Lyman, 5, 6, 11
Knibbs, Henry Herbert, 81, 82

Lead Belly, 8
LeNoir, Phil, 81
Lincoln County War; *see* Billy the Kid
Log of a Cowboy, The, 100
Lomax, Alan, 8, 9
Lomax, Bess Brown, 4, 8
Lomax, John A., 3-11, 82, 83
Lomax, Ruby Terrill, 8, 9-10
Lomax, Shirley, 5
Longevity, relation of tobacco to, 128-35

McCauley, James Emmit, 3
Mix, Tom, 51
Moore, Julia A., 165
Motifs: F321.1, 116; F451.5.2.3, 116; K1847, 116; K1923.1, 116, 117
Movies, cowboys in, 32, 51-69; the Good Bad Man, 53-55; the Mounted Officer of the Law, 55-58; the Knight Without Armor, 58-60; the cowboy as non-hero, 60-62; patterns and conventions, 62-68
Mustangs and Cow Horses, 3, 4
Myth, Jung on, 181-97

Patterson, John, 39-40
Pattullo, George, 31
Penny dreadful as folksong, 164-70
Pitts, John, 166
Poke sallet, 157-63
Pollard, Fisher, 43-44
Prairie fire, 35-36

Ranch: SMS, 12-13; 7D's, 40-41, 48; 7f's, 42; Quién Sabe, 48
Randolph, Vance, 167
Ransom, Harry H., 3
Religious sect at Belton, 136-45
Roosevelt, Franklin D., 10-11
Roosevelt, Theodore, 6, 62
Roping, 20
Roundup, 36-37

Saddle, cowboy's, 15-16
Sallet, poke, 157-63
"Sanctified Sisters, the," 136-45
Schrier, Noah, 40
SMS ranch, 12-13
Songs: cowboy, 4, 81-88; publication of, 166; sentimental, 164-70; temperance, 167; *see also* Ballad, Folksong, Lomax, John A.

Songs of the Cowboys, 6-7, 81, 82
Spaeth, Sigmund, 169
Stephens, Harry, 52
Stories: baby-switching, 110-17; escapes from death by bullets, 118-27; fox hunting, 146-50; *see also* Tale, Tall tales
Such, Henry, 166
Symbols, 187, 192, 193, 194

Tale about the hat-in-mud, 100-109
Tall tales, 105
Temperance songs, 167
Texas, migration to, 171-72
Texas Folklore Society, 3, 4, 89
Thomason, John W., 7
Thorp, N. Howard (Jack), 6-7, 81, 82, 84-86, 87
Tin Pan Alley, 166
Tobacco and longevity, 128-35
Trail driving, 19-20
True Church Colony, 136-45
Twain, Mark, 117, 165

UFOs, their meaning according to Jung, 193-94

Virginian, The, 110, 116, 117

Waggener, Leslie, 5
Webb, Walter Prescott, 3
Wendell, Barrett, 5, 6
West Virginia, rural life there in the nineties, 176
Williams, Robert Lee, 171-75
Wilson, Tom, 40, 41
Windom, W. H., 168
Wister, Owen, 110-17

www.ingramcontent.com/pod-product-compliance
Lightning Source LLC
Chambersburg PA
CBHW030318080526
44584CB00012B/606